About Island Press

Since 1984, the nonprofit organization Island Press has been stimulating, shaping, and communicating ideas that are essential for solving environmental problems worldwide. With more than 1,000 titles in print and some 30 new releases each year, we are the nation's leading publisher on environmental issues. We identify innovative thinkers and emerging trends in the environmental field. We work with world-renowned experts and authors to develop cross-disciplinary solutions to environmental challenges.

Island Press designs and executes educational campaigns, in conjunction with our authors, to communicate their critical messages in print, in person, and online using the latest technologies, innovative programs, and the media. Our goal is to reach targeted audiences—scientists, policy makers, environmental advocates, urban planners, the media, and concerned citizens—with information that can be used to create the framework for long-term ecological health and human well-being.

Island Press gratefully acknowledges major support from The Bobolink Foundation, The Curtis and Edith Munson Foundation, The Forrest C. and Frances H. Lattner Foundation, The Freedom Together Foundation, The Kresge Foundation, The Summit Charitable Foundation, Inc., and many other generous organizations and individuals.

The opinions expressed in this book are those of the author(s) and do not necessarily reflect the views of our supporters.

Hot Takes

Hot Takes

EVERY JOURNALIST'S GUIDE TO COVERING CLIMATE CHANGE

Sadie Babits

ISLANDPRESS | Washington | Covelo

Design and Typesetting by 2K/DENMARK.

Sustainable Typesetting® ID: ST49535052-24-A01
The ID number certifies that this book fulfills the standards and recommendations of Sustainable Typesetting® providing reduced CO_2 emissions.

Library of Congress Control Number: 2024935680

All Island Press books are printed on environmentally responsible materials.

Manufactured in the United States of America
10 9 8 7 6 5 4 3 2 1

Keywords: bias; Climate Central; climate journalism; climate litigation; Covering Climate Now; disinformation; environmental justice reporting; environmental reporting; Freedom of Information Act (FOIA) request; global warming; Inside Climate News; Intergovernmental Panel on Climate Change (IPCC); misinformation; nature disaster reporting; NPR Climate Desk; objectivity; SciLine; self-care for journalists; Society of Environmental Journalists; solutions journalism; trauma-informed reporting; United Nations Framework Convention on Climate Change; UpRoot Project; Walter Cronkite School of Journalism and Mass Communication

For my Frank,
whose infinite love and support make
all dreams take flight.

To the journalists who read this book,
may these pages provide guidance, hope,
and courage in reporting on the most
important story of our time.

Contents

Foreword

If you're an environmental journalist, I hope you'll tell your reporter and editor friends who cover other topics to read this book.

Don't get me wrong—you should read it, too. Sadie Babits is one of the best environmental journalists in the business.

But one of the biggest things I've learned from ten years reporting on climate change and energy is that our industry needs to stop acting like global warming is solely an environmental story and start accepting that it's an everything story. We live in a world upended by deadlier heat waves, more extreme storms and droughts, bigger wildfires, and rising seas. Meanwhile, climate solutions—including cleaner energy, electric vehicles, and new forms of food production—are badly needed but disruptive in their own ways.

These shifts are only getting more dramatic. And they touch all facets of human life in the twenty-first century: cost of living, public health, geopolitics, food, technology, culture, even sports.

Environment reporters are doing our best to give people the information they need. But we can't do it alone. There's too much to cover. We need help.

As Sadie writes in this book, "Climate change is now an essential element in many of the stories journalists must report. I believe every reporter is now, to some degree, a climate reporter."

If you've never reported on global warming, that may sound daunting.

Fortunately, *Hot Takes* offers an excellent foundation to start telling these stories.

Don't feel well versed in climate science? Sadie gets you up to speed on the basics. Never written about climate policy or lawsuits against fossil fuel companies? Check out Chapters 3 and 8. Worried you might accidentally repeat misinformation? Chapter 4 teaches you how to spot scams and false claims, how to know when you should ignore them, and when you might take time to debunk them.

Hot Takes also details strategies for how journalists can give people hope—and stay hopeful themselves—while still painting a realistic picture of what's going wrong in the world. Sadie's chapters on solutions journalism, environmental justice, and the meaning of *objectivity* are crucial reading for reporters who want to be active participants in alleviating suffering through rigorous, fact-based, empathetic storytelling.

I nodded along with Sadie's observation that traditional journalism has created a blind spot in which reporters "can see what's wrong but can miss what's good."

"Suppose journalists report only on the problems brought on by a warming world," Sadie writes. "The collective story of human-caused climate change becomes one of existential doom—a fatalistic view that nothing can be done to stop global warming."

Fortunately, many environmental journalists are trying to do things differently.

When I started covering energy for *The Desert Sun* newspaper in Palm Springs, California, in 2014, the country's first big solar farms were just beginning to generate electricity in the desert about an hour east of the city. I wrote about the success stories of those solar farms: the state and federal policies that led to their construction, the technological innovations that had brought down the costs of renewable electricity, the potential to keep displacing planet-warming fossil fuels with clean energy.

At the same time, I didn't ignore the downsides. As Sadie advises in this book, I asked hard questions, exploring the potential for large-scale solar energy development to destroy wildlife habitat and disturb quiet lifestyles in rural communities. I also weighed those downsides against the urgent need to reduce heat-trapping pollution.

I've tried to bring that nuanced approach to all my reporting, and I'm confident that *Hot Takes* can help you do the same, even if you don't memorize every word, and even if climate change pops up in your reporting only once in a while.

Maybe you'll be writing about a major heat wave and realize you need to explain the connection to climate change and fossil fuel pollution. Maybe you'll be covering a wildfire, and a meteorologist will mention that intense drought played a role, and rather than just quoting them, you'll stop and ask whether climate change influenced the drought. Maybe you'll be walking in your neighborhood and see volunteers planting trees, and you'll discover their goal is to protect vulnerable residents against rising temperatures, and you'll get a great story out of it.

Could you do all that stuff now? Probably. But you'll do a better job after reading *Hot Takes*.

Lastly, let's say you're not a reporter; you're an editor overseeing breaking news, or politics, or sports. You should still read this book. You can use it as a source of ideas for your reporters and as a guide for them to bring climate into their stories.

The longer climate is siloed under environment desks, the harder it will be to solve this global crisis. And the greater a disservice newsrooms will be doing to our readers.

Those are my hot takes. Now let's get to Sadie's.

—Sammy Roth, climate columnist, *The Los Angeles Times*
November 2024

Introduction

"The more clearly we can focus our attention on the wonders and realities of the universe about us, the less taste we shall have for destruction."

—Rachel Carson, 1954

Waning sunlight filtered through the windows of the Cronkite Newsroom. Students had just returned for the fall semester at Arizona State University's Walter Cronkite School of Journalism and Mass Communication. They were braving 100-plus-degree days and adjusting to a semester-long course where they would learn to report, edit, and produce stories for TV, digital, audio, and social media in an actual newsroom. Warm light bounced off now-empty desks, backlighting one of my students. "Can I ask you a question?" she said. I pushed my chair back and invited her to join me. "What's up?"

I listened as Autriya shared her concerns about the semester. How could she get started building a beat on climate change? Did I have any resources that could help her get started? What stories might I, her editor, be interested in?

Each semester, I had a new group of students. They pitched me story ideas. We discussed. I said "no" to a lot, but some ideas I approved. I worked closely with my students on those ideas, which covered an array of topics: water, renewable energy, agriculture, extreme weather, climate science, and even sustainable fashion. Hardly any of my students came with a science background. A few were double majoring in journalism and meteorology. But most were like Autriya, interested in environmental issues like climate change and learning to develop the beat quickly.

Every semester, my students showed up brimming with questions, especially about human-driven climate change. Those studying to be meteorologists wanted to learn how to incorporate climate change into their broadcast weather segments. Others felt compelled to work on climate change but weren't sure whether journalism was the right path for them. Some just needed class credit to graduate, which meant getting a crash course from me on science, climate change, and environmental issues to pass.

Most of my students understood that Earth's climate had warmed. But they were less sure about why and about the science of climate change.

They asked probing questions: What happens if the Earth continues to warm? How confident are scientists that climate change is happening? What solutions exist to address climate change? Why is climate change so politically divisive? How could they develop a beat on climate change? Doesn't climate change mean some people are being hurt more than others?

They had questions about science, too: What exactly is the scientific method? How do you read and interpret studies? Where do you find and verify true science experts? How do you prepare for an interview with a scientist? My students' questions made me realize how complicated reporting on human-caused climate change can be, especially when someone is early in their journalism career. These conversations sparked the idea for the book you now hold in your hands.

I related to their questions and our discussions because early in my career I asked many of the same questions. I didn't get my degree in journalism. I studied political science and international relations. My job at Boise State Public Radio during college as a general assignment reporter opened the world of audio storytelling. That's where I gravitated toward environmental policy stories in Idaho's legislature, forest health, wildfires, public lands, and the debate over how to save endangered salmon.

I learned environmental reporting by doing. I wished I had a mentor or guide or an accessible guidebook for reporting on environmental issues, especially climate change. *Hot Takes: Every Journalist's Guide to Covering Climate Change* is meant to be that guidebook. It's born from my years of reporting on environmental issues, editing, leading public radio newsrooms, and working as NPR's senior supervising climate editor.

Covering human-driven climate change is becoming increasingly complex. I have learned through the years that it's a challenge not just for students and early career journalists but for veteran reporters, too. I have repeatedly seen reporters at every stage in their career challenged to adapt their skills and storytelling methods to this complicated topic.

Hot Takes is grounded in the recognition that climate change is now an essential element in many of the stories journalists must report. I believe every reporter is now, to some degree, a climate reporter. This book equips and prepares journalists at any stage in their career to recognize and make these climate connections, get the science and policy right, detect and debunk misinformation, avoid false equivalencies and doomist story framing, and incorporate rigorous reporting on solutions and responses that give audiences agency, all while practicing self-care for what can be a controversial and even dangerous beat.

To navigate the intersectionality of human-caused climate change, reporters need to understand and unpack what can be a complex narrative: There's historical context. Decades of delayed climate action. Immense issues of global inequality. The gravity of melting glaciers. Wildlife on the edge of extinction. Deforestation in the name of development and progress. Wildfires that force thousands to flee their homes every year. The growing human toll from climate-related catastrophes. The inundation of coastlines from rising waters. Inland flooding in the wake of cataclysmic storms.

Climate-driven calamities are happening alarmingly fast. Candid reporting on such realities is enough to elicit a sense of dread. This book describes ways that climate journalists can effectively report the truth about these harms without stoking doomism.

Another narrative has also emerged as more journalists report on our warming world: That is one of hope and possibility embedded in the harsh facts of science. The world has a solution: draw down planet-warming pollution rapidly. What we do today matters for future generations to come.

I see journalism's role as twofold in covering climate change: Inform and instill agency in people to see what's possible beyond the doom and gloom headlines and do what journalists do best—hold the powerful to account. The magnitude of this moment demands that journalists find the fortitude to break free from traditional storytelling methods and embrace new storytelling formats that help us all see the way forward.

The fast-paced nature of information sharing via social media and a crowded media landscape make climate reporting challenging. The myths generated by climate deniers, industry polluters, and some politicians litter the reporting journey with pitfalls everywhere. How can reporters best navigate these misinformation traps? How do journalists make the necessary climate connections in stories when there's so much noise and misinformation?

From my time teaching at Arizona State University to my role as a climate editor at NPR, I have had a front-row seat to the transformation of reporting on climate change. That transformation has rapidly evolved in recent years as more news organizations, including NPR, recognize the importance of covering our warming world. Newsroom leadership increasingly recognizes that stories about climate change can't be confined to a desk or beat. Rather, climate transcends any one beat in the newsroom.

Climate journalism is here to stay and rapidly evolving as newsrooms finally recognize the need to help inform people about the climate crisis. I write *finally* because it wasn't that long ago that being an environment reporter meant being mainly on your own in the newsroom. I remember those days. Now, journalists specialize in subsets within the climate beat: health, energy, social inequities, and the green energy transition. That's a signal that climate journalism isn't going anywhere. Newsrooms have dedicated teams and desks to cover the most important and pressing story of our time.

Hot Takes has taken place against this backdrop. The journalists, science communicators, and researchers I've interviewed for this book, combined with my own experience as a reporter and editor, have shaped the pages that follow. I have tried to write these chapters to withstand time and the changes ahead.

Policy developments, climate litigation, greenwashing, misinformation, and disinformation happen so consistently that any book struggles to remain relevant. Still, some things remain true. The majority of scientists agree unequivocally that climate change is happening, it is caused by humans, and it results primarily from the burning of fossil fuels. Research continues, though, to better understand the complexity of a warmer world, including the economic toll of climate change on people, the effects of wildfire smoke on people's health, and the influence of climate change on extreme weather. Geo-engineered projects continue to pop up, promising technological solutions to climate change. Misinformation and disinformation campaigns are just as prominent today as they were decades ago.

Hot Takes tackles all these aspects of reporting on our warming world. The book is divided into three sections. The first part explains how we have arrived at this moment with human-caused climate change. The second section examines how climate reporting narratives can be framed to engage people. The final section looks at emerging trends, including how journalists can report on extreme weather while taking care of themselves. Along the way, readers will find hot takes: key takeaways, facts, and reporting tips that make the reporting journey easier.

Journalism needs a new framework for how we report climate stories. Reporters must go beyond headlines that instill a sense of doom and dread and instead help us understand the implications of human-caused climate change and what's possible. We need moments of joy that come through reading about what communities, organizations, governments, and maybe even you are doing in your own life to respond to a warmer world.

Such a framework involves reimagining traditional reporting methods and asking what our role as journalists is in reporting on climate. It means abandoning a failed formula of reporting "both sides" and instead embarking on an equitable approach that allows for multiple perspectives and voices.

We must also practice the investigative ideals of journalism that have long given this profession its place as the fourth estate, a watchdog that holds the powerful accountable. We need this more than ever in an era of pervasive and crippling false information that threatens to erode the foundation of democratic nations.

Wherever this book finds you in your journalism journey, I hope its pages help you report on the most consequential story of our time. The future depends on climate journalism that informs and inspires communities globally to realize a climate future that is greener, brighter, and cleaner than what centuries of planet-warming pollution have created for us today.

CHAPTER 1

An Evolution in Climate Coverage

"The planet does not need more successful people. The planet desperately needs more peacemakers, healers, restorers, storytellers and lovers of all kinds."

—Dalai Lama

More than 170 cyclists roll off the start line at the 2024 Tour de France opening stage in Florence, Italy. They swarm through the city streets against a backdrop of stone buildings and cultural history, pedaling easily until they reach the city limits. Then the attacks start, one after the other, as teams position themselves for the hilly 128-mile race ahead.[1] It's nearly 100°F, and the pack of riders has strung out along the road—a blur of color streaking through the Italian countryside. The road pitches up for the day's first climb, and several riders break away from the main group.

But British cyclist Mark Cavendish isn't with them. He's one of the best sprinters in the world and completed the Tour de France sixteen times, winning thirty-four stages. The stage wins have happened on flat roads where he conserves his energy, supported by his team, only to strike like a cheetah in the final moments of a stage to secure the win. A thirty-fifth stage win would be historic. He'd break cycling legend Eddy Merckx's long-held record during this three-week race.[2] But he's struggling. The hilly course doesn't suit his skills, and it's hot.

A teammate squirts Cavendish's neck with water and puts ice down his jersey. He's dizzy. He stops along the road and throws up. He remounts his bike. Cavendish isn't going to give up on the first day of the Tour. But he's nearly last as he slowly grinds up the first climb, with 100 miles left to go.

Cavendish knows if he doesn't make it to the city of Rimini close enough to the winner, he'll be disqualified, his dream of breaking the stage-win record dashed.

He's not the only professional cyclist to struggle in the hot, humid temperatures. Riders chug water bottle after water bottle. They pour water on each other, anything to stay cool.

Cavendish will eventually make it to the finish line in time to start the next day's stage. After the race, Cavendish's herculean effort will make the sports headlines, but the cause of his suffering will not.

On a different stage, a fashion model steps confidently into a vast domed room at Espace Niemeyer in Paris. Her steps are in sync with synthesized beats as a booming voice calls out, "In fashion, mushrooms are the future." The woman moves deftly around the circular stage, expressionless, her near-floor-length gauzy green jacket billowing in her wake.

It's the spring 2022 ready-to-wear collection by designer Stella McCartney on display during Paris Fashion Week. Fifty different looks, all inspired by mushrooms, are on display, from bodysuits to cargo pants with the sides slit open. Some of the dresses are inspired by the underbelly of a portobello mushroom. The story headlines in fashion magazines and major media outlets played up the mushroom-inspired collection: "Stella McCartney Does Mushrooms in Paris," "Stella McCartney Channels Mushrooms in Trippy Paris Show," "Stella McCartney's Mushrooms Are the Future."[3]–[5] But there's also an untold story: Why mushrooms?

A continent away, shoppers peruse the vegetables and fruits at a neighborhood grocery store in Phoenix, Arizona. Some glance at the large avocados and then push their carts along. One avocado costs more than three dollars. Grocery bills continue to escalate for food staples, including bread, rice, and olive oil. Questions arise as to why grocery bills have climbed nearly 25 percent over three years when inflation has been dropping.[6] National and local news outlets regularly report the uptick in grocery prices. What's missing from those stories is what's driving food costs higher.

These are three hot takes on seemingly unrelated topics: sports, culture, and economy. Yet all three have something in common, an unreported story behind the headline: human-caused climate change. Mark Cavendish's horrible day on the bike at the start of the Tour de France spotlights increasingly warm conditions for the famous cycling race that finishes in Paris. Pro cyclists must learn new ways to manage excessive heat, from cooling vests and ice packs to race officials spraying water on roads to keep asphalt from melting ahead of the racers. That's a sports story *and* a climate story.

Stella McCartney's 2022 spring collection may have been inspired by mushrooms, but some items were made from a byproduct of cotton harvests and a semisynthetic material made from wood pulp. She also revealed a small crescent-shaped black handbag made from the root structure of mushrooms.[7] McCartney has long championed sustainability practices in an industry that's historically been the antithesis of that. *Vogue, The Guardian,* and a handful of other media outlets reported on the shift to sustainable sourcing, but most missed the climate connection.

As for skyrocketing grocery bills, that, too, is a story about our warming world. For example, olive trees have struggled in Italy amid hot temperatures and ongoing drought. Harvests are smaller, but demand is high. So prices increase.[8] Staples such as corn, wheat, rice, and potatoes are susceptible to extreme weather. If it's too hot, rice, for instance, can't self-pollinate, which leads to lower yields. Consumers pay more at the grocery store with less rice on the market. Changes in temperatures and rainfall patterns will directly affect the crops and fruits grown worldwide and ultimately get reflected in prices at the grocery store.[9]

Human-driven climate change is in every aspect of our lives, so it's in every beat in the newsroom. Making these climate connections is part of the job, whether someone is a general assignment reporter, a sports reporter, or a journalist who covers culture and arts or business. We are all climate journalists now.

The ability to recognize, report, and make the climate connection clearly in stories while also getting the science right can be an overwhelming challenge. That's why this book exists: to support journalists, no matter where they are in their careers, with best practices and advice for reporting on the most important story of our time.

To do that, we must first understand how climate change has become the global issue it is today and how the media's coverage of this monumental problem has evolved. Then, we delve into the foundational science every reporter must know to make accurate climate connections in stories. Part I concludes with the history and the evolution of international, national, and local efforts to address climate change.

Part II focuses on the forces influencing climate narratives and how to counter them. Journalists will learn to navigate the complicated world of misinformation, disinformation, and greenwashing by politicians and corporations that don't want carbon-emitting practices replaced by renewable energy. Climate reporting also raises questions about journalism's long-standing practice of remaining objective and what that means today in a crowded media landscape.

Climate change also intersects with social justice issues, and its impacts fall most often on those who have contributed the least to global warming. Part II explores those injustices and how to report on communities most affected. It ends with a practical guide for developing climate stories that empower people to see what's possible through responses and solutions to a warming world.

Part III examines emerging trends in climate coverage, including the expanding role of litigation to try and hold corporations and governments accountable for addressing climate change. The book finishes by acknowledging the formidable work ahead for journalists who report on a warming world. Interviewing survivors of climate disasters can be heart-wrenchingly difficult. Witnessing trauma and the suffering of others can last a lifetime. The continuous act of reporting on a warming planet—the pain felt from the loss of ecosystems and species and the migration of people away from rising seas—affects our well-being. The trauma from reporting on human-driven climate change is not to be underestimated. Part III concludes with advice and self-care practices to help journalists protect their hearts and minds.

This book was written during a period of acceleration among media organizations that recognized the urgent need for climate coverage in the United States and beyond. That acceleration has happened against a backdrop of increasing extremes brought on by human-caused climate change. An urgency exists, too, for journalists to capture emerging climate narratives to help inform people of the implications of and responses to global warming.

The Rise in Climate Reporting

Not long ago, being an environmental reporter—let alone a journalist who covered climate change—was a niche role in the newsroom. In my early years as a radio journalist in the West, I needed a well-focused, compelling story to pitch before an editor would say "yes." Some editors just didn't see environmental stories as a priority because they are hard stories to tell, and they often evolve over long periods of time. Daily story assignments usually relegated my environmental reporting to the back burner, but in between deadlines I focused on developing and reporting stories about protecting public lands, endangered species, and forest health.

Hot Take: *Human-driven climate change touches all aspects of life, including sports, business, culture, and policy. Journalists must make the climate connection clear for audiences regardless of the beat they cover.*

I started in journalism when climate change was garnering more attention. Fights brewed on Capitol Hill over whether global warming was real and whether humans were to blame. The media framed early stories about climate change as a battle between scientists and climate deniers. These debates typically divided sharply along party lines between liberals and conservatives. I saw this through my reporting early in my career, including the reintroduction of gray wolves in Idaho and Montana, efforts to protect endangered species such as salmon and spotted owls, and managing forest health and wildfires. I was a journalist on the cusp of climate change, as both a developing issue and a journalism beat. It was hard to find other journalists like me who cared about the natural world and our impact on it and who wanted to investigate and expose those impacts. I wasn't the only one who felt alone on the environmental beat.

Michael Kodas, a journalist, photographer, and author, remembers the pushback he would get from editors when he pitched a climate story. "I can remember mentioning that climate should be a beat and kind of being laughed out of a meeting," he recalled.[10] Kodas was met with similar reactions when he and colleagues at the *Hartford Current* would pitch a climate-related project and be "completely shot down." The newspaper, Kodas says, just wasn't interested.

Washington Post deputy climate and environment editor Juliet Eilperin remembered when only a small group of journalists covered climate stories. "It was seen as this niche, almost entirely scientific topic—as opposed to a global phenomenon with broad implications," Eilperin told *The Columbia Journalism Review* in an interview.[11] More than thirty years ago, climate reporting meant trying to tell a compelling story about something that would happen centuries from now. That's what long-time climate journalist Andrew Revkin called a "slow drip" issue: the changes were hardly noticeable decades ago, delaying the urgent need to respond.[12]

That changed in 1988, when climate change made the headlines. Wildfires lit up Yellowstone National Park that year.[13] Thick smoke blanketed massive swaths of the Amazon rainforest from human-lit fires, prompting *The New York Times* to publish "Vast Amazon Fires, Man-Made, Linked to Global Warming."[14] Much of the United States baked under excessive heat that would be remembered as the "great heat wave of 1988."[15]

That same year NASA climate scientist James Hansen testified before members of the US Senate Energy and Natural Resources Committee that his research showed that the planet was warming up. Global warming would generate extreme weather, such as heat waves, and he was 99 percent certain human activity was driving it. "In my opinion, that the greenhouse effect has been detected, and it is changing our climate now," Hansen said.[16] His testimony received widespread media coverage with alarming headlines including "Global Warming Has Begun, Expert Tells Senate."[17]

Also in 1988, the United Nations Environment Programme and the World Meteorological Organization established the Intergovernmental Panel on Climate Change (IPCC). The UN General Assembly endorsed the creation of the IPCC and tasked it with developing the world's first "comprehensive review and recommendations with respect to the state of knowledge of the science of climate change."[18]

The IPCC's formation and subsequent task merited barely a whisper in most media outlets. Early reporting on climate change was like that: intermittent and splashed across front pages when something significant occurred, like Hansen's testimony. Research finds that reporting done by the US prestige press, including *The New York Times* and *The Washington Post*, electrified a "denial discourse" in the late 1980s and early 2000s over climate change. The journalistic norm of maintaining balance generated a false narrative that pitted climate scientists against climate deniers.[19]

The George W. Bush administration, for example, held a three-day conference on global warming in December 2002. The meeting came after a year of "global warming scares" *The Washington Post* reported. Glaciers in the Bolivian Andres were rapidly melting that year, and an ice shelf in the Antarctic "shattered and collapsed into the sea." A *Washington Post* reporter noted in coverage of the conference that the administration acknowledged "that global warming poses serious problems." However, officials had "numerous uncertainties" about the causes and effects of a warming world. Then President Bush called for "a decade of research" before committing to "anything more than voluntary measures to stem carbon dioxide and other greenhouse gas emissions from industry and vehicles that have been closely tied to global warming."[20]

That statement illustrates the perpetual uncertainty about climate science that the media in the US perpetuated. Climate stories regularly pitted climate scientists against climate deniers, creating a "both-sides-ing" narrative that sparked debate over whether climate change was real and, if it was, what was driving it.[21] The echoes of that style of climate reporting reverberate to this day. However, a lot has changed since those early years of climate reporting, and now, not a day passes without climate change in the headlines. So what's changed?

Climate Journalism Arrives

Some clear shifts have led to growth in climate journalism, starting with the fact that the science of climate change and what's causing it is settled. That's a significant change from when James Hansen first testified before Congress in 1988. Scientists now unequivocally agree that human activities, largely the burning of fossil fuels, have caused global warming. Since 1970, the global surface temperature has increased faster than in any other fifty-year period in the last 2,000 years.[22] Planet-warming pollution—carbon dioxide, methane, and nitrous oxide—has steadily climbed. Most people around the world are experiencing the impacts of a warmer world.[23] Sea level rise. Disappearing glaciers. Heat waves. Drought. Flooding from torrential rainfall. Hurricanes. Wildfires. Historic temperature records are being broken. Global temperatures were the warmest on record in 2023, leaving some scientists shocked at the rate of acceleration.[24] "Sirens are blaring across all major indicators," says UN secretary-general António Guterres. "Some records aren't just chart-topping, they're chart-busting. And changes are speeding up."[25] Then 2024 toppled the previous year's record to become Earth's warmest recorded year. Sea ice coverage in Antarctica was the second-lowest on record, alongside 2024's record heat.[26]

National and international media have recognized that human-driven climate change is a significant and urgent story to cover. In recent years, media outlets have added reporters to cover our warming world from major organizations to regional and local outlets.

The Media and Climate Change Observatory at the University of Colorado Boulder, which began in 2007 at the University of Oxford, tracks global media coverage of climate change. Nearly twenty years ago, climate coverage showed up as a blip, but within the last decade coverage has increased, with more people focusing on it.[27]

The year 2021 broke the all-time record for climate stories reported globally. However, journalism job losses, combined with competition for headlines about political crises, contributed to a dip in global climate stories, with a decline of 14 percent in 2022 and another 4 percent in 2023.[28] Global coverage of climate change or global warming continued to fall in 2024, with a drop of 16 percent from 2023.[29]

Despite fluctuations in coverage, climate journalism is far more robust than it used to be. The days of being the lone environmental reporter in the newsroom are gone. Large teams are now dedicated to environmental and climate-related coverage at national and international news outlets such as *The Associated Press, The Washington Post, The New York Times*, NPR, and CNN. TV meteorologists increasingly help make the climate connection in their forecasts. Local news publications, public radio stations, and TV stations might have at least one reporter covering environmental and climate stories.

Michael Kodas, who once proposed climate change as a beat, is now a senior editor at *Inside Climate News*. Juliet Eilperin became the deputy climate and environment editor at *The Washington Post*. As for me, I'm the senior supervising climate editor for NPR's climate desk, which was formed in 2022. As part of my role, I oversee a public radio collaborative of climate reporters across the country and work with NPR climate desk reporters.

"It's been incredible to see, certainly based on my experience at the *Post*," explained Eilperin in a *Columbia Journalism Review* interview, "how journalists in recent years have connected the dots. Climate has become a story for the business section, the sports section, the national and metro desks, and everywhere else in the newsroom."[30]

Because climate change affects nearly everything, news organizations have been working to help journalists who aren't steeped in climate reporting understand the basics. At NPR, other desks, radio shows, and podcasts turn to the climate editors and journalists for help. I often answer questions and review scripts and digital stories before they are aired or published to check the climate context and ensure that the science is right. During extreme weather, such as a blistering heat wave or a developing hurricane, we send out newsroom guidance about how climate change broadly impacts such events. The goal is to give journalists and editors who don't regularly cover climate change easy-to-use language to drop into relevant stories.

Peter Prengaman, who leads the AP's global climate and environment team, says his team has held several climate-related training sessions for the entire organization, on topics such as evaluating scientific studies and spotting greenwashing. "Training has really helped make people more comfortable," he says.[31] Climate change coverage at *The Washington Post* also goes beyond the desk. "We're also constantly in communication with colleagues on other desks. There's no arm-twisting," explained Eilperin in an interview with *Columbia Journalism Review*. "The level of excitement and eagerness among our colleagues to participate in these kinds of stories (climate) is extraordinary."[32] It *is* extraordinary because it wasn't that long ago that climate coverage had a low profile in the daily news zeitgeist.

Climate is such a massive topic that, in recent years, newsrooms have added reporters who specialize in a specific aspect of climate coverage, such as the injustices brought on by climate change or the energy transition. *Inside Climate News*, for example, was launched in 2007 with two reporters to fill the gap in climate news in the United States. Now, the digital publication has more than twenty reporters, many focusing on particular areas, including climate activism and health and climate justice.[33]

For *Inside Climate News* senior editor Michael Kodas, climate journalism's transformation is a recognition of how important climate change is and "how neglected it has been for so long." The days have disappeared when reporters had to push to get their editors to say yes to a climate pitch, he says. The challenge is how to cover so much that falls under the climate umbrella. "We have to prioritize," Kodas says. "We have more climate stories coming from all of us than we have the bandwidth to report and get published."[34]

Climate journalist Amy Westervelt has been a part of this transformation. She remembers her first climate-related story around 2002. She was in the San Francisco Bay area reporting on clean technology such as electric vehicles and their batteries. Stories about how to green a home and climate politics, Westervelt says, were also showing up in the news. Back then, though, the idea of "anyone writing a personal essay about climate was totally ridiculous," Westervelt says. "Now I feel like there's almost every different flavor of story."[35]

Investigative climate and accountability journalism is happening far more than in those early climate reporting days. Westervelt points to 2015 as a watershed moment for investigative climate journalism. That year *Inside Climate News* published a nine-part groundbreaking investigation by reporters Neela Banerjee, Lisa Song, John Cushman Jr., and David Hasemyer called *Exxon: The Road Not Taken*.[36] Their reporting revealed that the oil giant knew about climate change in the 1970s and then covered it up. "Ever since the Exxon Knew stories, that really opened up a whole bunch of interest," recalls Westervelt.[37] That interest has only grown in recent years.

Two years later, in *New York Magazine*, David Wallace-Wells's essay *The Uninhabitable Earth* was published with the opening line, "It is, I promise, worse than you think."[38] Wallace-Wells detailed an apocalyptic reality of climate change left unabated—a world in economic collapse, scorched by the sun—a personal and grim take on the state of climate change the likes of which hadn't been seen.

Climate scientist Michael Mann responded with an opinion piece in *The Washington Post* noting the rise in climate doomism after the Trump administration withdrew the United States from the 2015 Paris Agreement. He pointed out that "doomist narratives" were showing up in respected news outlets. Wallace-Wells's essay was an example. Mann wrote that the risks of climate change left unchecked should not be understated, but "there is also a danger in overstatement that presents the problem as unsolvable and future outcomes as inevitable."[39] Climate change stories, from personal essays to accountability reporting, had entered the mainstream.

Who's Covering Climate

A shift is also under way in who is entering the climate reporting field: Today's climate journalists are more ethnically diverse, and they are transforming what has historically been a predominantly White male profession. I've seen this shift firsthand and made it my professional mission to help cultivate this transformation through roles I've held, including my tenure on the Society of Environmental Journalists (SEJ) board.

Journalists such as Halle Parker embody this transformation and give me hope about the future of reporting on the environment and climate change. Parker defines herself as a Black environment reporter who reports on climate change. She wanted to be a sports reporter and had a passion for social justice issues. Her first reporting job out of college was working as a county government reporter in Virginia. She covered the state's largest county—Pittsylvania County—where agriculture was big business. Parker reported a lot about farmers, and in 2018, Virginia had unpredictable weather—spans of torrential rain followed by spans of crippling drought. Farmers, she remembers, were confused. They were used to shifting with Mother Nature over the years, but this was different. "They were really struggling," Parker says.[40]

She knew about climate change but hadn't fully understood how weather extremes could affect people until she reported on what farmers were going through. Seeing those farmers struggling "made it [climate change] feel more real to me." Parker realized climate change was "clearly going to be one of the largest issues of my lifetime." She saw climate change as an area of coverage where she could build a career that combined her interests in social justice with the environment.[41]

Parker isn't the only one who has reached this realization. I saw this convergence of social justice and environmental and climate-related interests in several of my students while teaching at Arizona State University's Walter Cronkite School of Journalism and Mass Communication. They were studying at a time when protests over racial injustice and police brutality had swept across the country. They saw the White male patriarchal society that had defined journalism as oppressive, and many of the pillars of journalism, such as objectivity, didn't seem to work in a society where so much injustice needed to be addressed. My students asked questions. They were fired up. I see their impact today as they have gone on to jobs in digital, television, and radio news.

Journalism organizations, such as the Uproot Project, have formed to support and foster a new, much more diverse core of journalists, who are continuing to join the climate reporting ranks. Meanwhile, SEJ, which was created more than thirty years ago by a small group of White journalists, has worked to prioritize and embed diversity, equity, and inclusion into everything it does. That slow transformation is something I helped during my time as president of SEJ's board of directors. That long-overdue work means SEJ's membership is changing, too. The board is more representative of the members it serves, and diversity at SEJ's annual conference has increased through fellowships and outreach.

Support, resources, and mentorships have also increased as more climate journalists enter the profession. In recent years, new organizations have sprung up to help journalists cover climate change, such as Climate Central, SciLine, Covering Climate Now, the Uproot Project, and journalism collaboratives. The increase in support for climate journalism indicates that the need remains high.

What Audiences Want

Children born today will never know a world without climate change or extreme weather. In fact, children who were born in 2020 will live through a "two- to sevenfold increase in extreme events" especially heat waves. That's compared with people who were born in 1960.[42] Human-caused climate change has already altered the planet, and those impacts will only intensify in future years.[43] In the United States, research has found that most people think global warming is happening, and 58 percent understand it is human caused. Most Americans surveyed say climate change affects many environmental problems, including air pollution, drought, water shortages, rising sea levels, and even power outages. Although there is a general recognition of global warming and its impacts, 65 percent of Americans rarely discuss it with family and friends.[44]

Yet the American Psychiatric Association has found most people surveyed in the United States are "somewhat" or "extremely" anxious about how climate change is affecting the planet, and more than half share similar anxieties about how climate change affects their mental health.[45]

These insights come at a time when more journalists are reporting on climate change. However, more than half of the Americans surveyed don't see much climate news even though they want it.[46] What's going on if there's more reporting on climate than ever before?

Part of the answer is that news avoidance globally remains high, up 39 percent since 2017. Worldwide, the same percentage of people say they feel worn out by the relentless nature of news and tired of news outlets covering the same set of stories with only slight variations.[47] For over a decade, climate stories have focused primarily on the extreme impacts and the catastrophic aftermath, the doom-and-gloom headlines.

How people get their news has also changed dramatically over the decades. US newspapers as a news source have plummeted from 47 percent to 16 percent since 2013. TV as a source of news also dropped significantly during that period, from 72 percent to 51 percent. People are going online or to social media for their news.[48] While national media, including *The New York Times*, *The Washington Post*, and NPR, have built up reporting teams on climate change, other news outlets, especially television, have not prioritized this reporting.

How climate stories are framed matters. A recent survey by the Reuters Institute found people globally want positive climate news and climate developments and want to know what can be done.[49] When people in the United States were asked what questions they would pose to experts about global warming, they responded by wanting to ask what countries such as the United States can do to reduce global warming: "Is it too late to reduce emissions and stop global warming?" And "How do you know that global warming is caused mostly by human activities, not natural changes in the environment?"[50] Those questions offer insight into what areas of climate coverage will resonate with people the most.

From my experience as a climate editor, I often see another challenge in climate reporting: failing to help readers fully understand the connections to climate change. Stories about flooding, hurricanes, wildfires, and droughts that omit the influence of climate change and its causes do a disservice to readers. Climate change communicator Susan Hassol has seen this failure to connect the climate dots in stories. Extreme weather has the fingerprints of climate change, caused primarily by burning fossil fuels. There's nothing natural about global warming. "That entire thread is so important for people to get, and it's very rare to see it done," Hassol says.[51] In the following pages, journalists will learn how to make that climate connection confidently.

Understanding people's attitudes, beliefs, and questions about climate change can help journalists and editors develop stories where the science is accessible, and people might actually walk away feeling empowered to take action on the pressing challenges brought on by a warming planet.

Climate Reporting: "It's Complicated"

Mark Schleifstein has spent most of his decades-long reporting career covering environmental issues, including hurricanes and eroding coastlines. Many of the stories he's reported over the years have developed into complex stories. He pulls on a story idea like a thread in a sweater that unravels over time. Climate change stories especially have so many elements that Schleifstein says his editors know that "my favorite curse word is 'It's complicated.'"[52] As a reporter for *The Times-Picayune / The New Orleans Advocate*, Schleifstein knows hurricanes reveal where communities' climate vulnerabilities lie. It's not just a story about a hurricane rapidly spinning up in the increasingly hot waters of the Gulf of Mexico; it's about sea level rise, warming temperatures, eroding coastlines, and community preparedness, and all those connections must be made in his stories. Covering climate change is complicated; getting climate stories right can be surprisingly hard.

Climate journalism is challenging because the science can be intimidating and overwhelming for new journalists. Misinformation and disinformation campaigns aim to divert attention from industries such as oil and gas, creating confusion about the true state of the climate crisis. Climate change is a social justice issue that exposes the deep inequities faced by communities that bear the brunt of its impacts despite contributing the least to the problem. Litigation is increasingly significant as more governments, organizations, and communities take oil giants to court to seek compensation for climate-related damages. Understanding the history of global climate response efforts, including treaties and policies, is essential for grasping the current state of global warming. Furthermore, covering climate change can be emotionally taxing over time, as the sheer scale of the issue can lead to anxiety and a sense of doom. Being a journalist who wants to incorporate or focus entirely on climate change means getting comfortable with a vastly complex and intertwined coverage area.

What We Know About the Science

Journalists don't need a science degree to report on climate change. In fact, several reporters featured in this book do not have a science background or shied away from science. However, reporters do need to know the basics of climate science to avoid making mistakes in interpreting the science or misrepresenting it. What climate change means for the planet is actually straightforward. Susan Hassol, who has spent most of her career communicating about climate science, explains climate change this way: "It's real. It's us. It's bad. Experts agree. And there's hope."[53] These five essential phrases tell you everything you need to know about our warming planet.

It's Real

Climate scientists have known for decades that Earth's climate has been warming, and human activities, primarily the burning of fossil fuels, have driven rising temperatures globally.[54] The IPCC started to assess and gather climate change science in 1988.[55] The scientific consensus over whether people were responsible for rising temperatures grew with each assessment. The IPCC's Fourth Assessment in 2007 marked a turning point. That's when climate scientists agreed that human-caused climate change was "very likely" happening.[56] Their confidence has only increased over time, with the latest assessment stating that climate scientists now know that human activities are the "unequivocal" cause of climate change. "It is virtually certain," the report states, that human-induced increases in greenhouse gases have led to global warming.[57]

Since 1880, the average global temperature has increased by about 2°F, or 1.1°C. Most of that warming has occurred since 1975.[58] Global warming comes primarily from burning fossil fuels such as coal, oil, and gas. These fuels generate pollution—methane, carbon dioxide, and nitrous oxide—that traps heat in the atmosphere.[59]

Just as a blanket retains your body's warmth, Earth's atmosphere traps some of the sun's heat to keep the planet warm for life to thrive. However, if you add extra blankets, eventually you get too warm. Human activities, such as burning fossil fuels and deforestation, add "extra layers" to Earth's blanket by increasing the amount of greenhouse gases such as carbon dioxide. As a result, more heat gets trapped. Scientists say Earth is warming at a rate never seen before.[60]

It's Bad

Human-caused climate change has already had wide-reaching impacts around the globe.[61] "That's not because Earth was a perfect temperature before and now it's not," explains Hassol. "It's because we built and developed our society around the climate that we had. And any change from that is going to cause problems."[62]

Glaciers and ice sheets are disappearing. Plants and trees are blooming earlier in the year and animals are moving to new regions.[63] Extreme weather, from droughts to catastrophic flooding, causes billions of dollars in damages every year.[64] Sea levels have already risen 8 to 9 inches,[65] and "that rise has accelerated in recent years," says Hassol.[66] Warmer temperatures in the Arctic and Greenland have led to melting sea ice and warmer oceans.[67] What happens in the Arctic can be felt all the way in the Gulf of Mexico.[68] "The increase in sea level, the increase in extreme weather events are the ways that we see climate change in our lives," says Hassol.[69]

Human-caused climate change also affects animals and plants at different rates. Warmer temperatures and increased moisture are shifting animal migration patterns.[70] "Ecosystems don't shift as a whole; the animals and plants move at different rates," Hassol explains. Birds can shift fairly easily, but plants don't. "You have this tearing apart of ecosystems, which is one of the reasons we have so much loss of species that we're seeing related to climate change and why it's the greatest threat to species."[71]

Experts Agree

The science is clear: The warming of our world is caused by humans.[72] For years, however, the science remained contested. Conservative political leaders, think tanks, and oil and gas companies lit a firestorm of disinformation to muddy the validity of science. The "climate wars," as climate scientist Michael Mann calls them, lasted decades, and several scientists, including Mann, were subjected to vicious character attacks.[73] Mainstream media presented a false balance in climate coverage, often giving equal time and credence to climate deniers alongside scientists. Research finds that people in the United States today significantly underestimate the actual scientific consensus on the fundamental causes of climate change.[74]

Debates are far more nuanced as scientists actively investigate the implications of how Arctic warming will affect the jet streams or how atmospheric and oceanic circulation patterns are being affected by extreme weather.

"There's always aspects of the science that are still under active investigation," Hassol says, but "the basic science is very well settled."[75]

There's Hope

Humans are why global temperatures have warmed 1.1 to 1.2°C (1.98°F) globally. The world will probably reach a 1.5°C (2.7°F) increase in the near future. Because humans caused climate change, we also have the power to stop it. The future rests in our hands. "Once we eliminate the production of heat-trapping pollution, climate change will stop," Hassol says. "Very quickly, within a decade, temperatures will stabilize. They're not going back down."[76]

The Spiderweb of Misinformation

Climate journalist Amy Westervelt's story about oil companies knowing that carbon capture is not a solution to climate change is an example of the responsibility journalists have to expose misinformation, disinformation, and greenwashing that industries such as the oil and gas companies continue to push. As Westervelt writes, people have probably seen positive oil and gas company ads that tout carbon capture and storage (CCS) as a solution in national media outlets.[77] Fossil fuel companies' messaging suggests that by capturing and storing carbon dioxide emissions from power plants and other sources, CCS technology can keep these planet-warming gases from contributing to global warming.

However, Westervelt reports that industry whistleblowers have shared internal documents with *Drilled* and *Vox* that say otherwise. Those documents, coupled with a federal investigation, "reveal an industry that is decidedly more realistic about the emissions-reduction potential of carbon capture and storage technology, or CCS, than it presents publicly."[78]

This is a classic case of climate misinformation and disinformation. CCS might help reduce emissions in sectors such as steel or concrete manufacturing. However, the IPCC has pointed out that CCS could achieve only a modest reduction under the most perfect circumstances. How much? Just over 2 percent of global carbon emissions by 2030.[79] This stark contrast between the industry's portrayal and scientific assessments highlights the critical need for journalists to investigate and challenge these narratives.

The oil and gas industry's aggressive promotion of CCS can be seen as a form of greenwashing, where companies exaggerate or misrepresent the environmental benefits of their actions to maintain a favorable public image. By emphasizing CCS as a key solution, these companies distract from more effective measures, such as reducing fossil fuel use and investing in renewable energy sources. This not only misleads the public but also risks delaying the urgent actions needed to address climate change effectively.

Journalists play a crucial role in exposing such disinformation. By scrutinizing industries' claims, consulting independent experts, and relying on rigorous scientific data, journalists can help the public see through the greenwashing. Investigative and accountability reporting are essential to ensure that the public and policymakers are not swayed by misleading narratives and can make informed decisions based on the best available evidence. Misinformation, disinformation, and greenwashing have been prolific for decades. Journalists can find it challenging to address the myths. How do reporters hold industries to account? Chapter 4, on misinformation and disinformation, provides guidance on detecting and debunking misinformation from some of the country's leading researchers and journalists.

The Role of Climate Policy

Every year, world leaders, negotiators, scientists, and activists from nearly every country gather for a Conference of the Parties (COP), a global summit on climate change held under the United Nations Framework Convention on Climate Change. The scale of these gatherings is staggering. For example, COP27, held in Sharm El Sheikh, Egypt, brought over 45,000 people together, including journalists from around the world.[80] Naveena Sadasivam was among them. She describes covering COPs as "chaotic and stressful" but also fun, acknowledging, "this is why we're journalists and reporters, we want to be in the thick of things."[81]

The two-week-long summit requires stamina to report on as delegates work nearly around the clock to negotiate agreements that could shape Earth's future. One of the most critical international treaties on climate came out of COP21 in 2015. The Paris Agreement established a goal to limit global warming to well below 2°C (3.6°F), ideally keeping the average temperature increase to under 1.5°C (2.7°F).[82] The treaty was groundbreaking in shifting the global response to climate change by mandating that countries develop and submit national climate action plans, known as Nationally Determined Contributions.[83] The Nationally Determined Contributions outline how each nation will reduce emissions and adapt to climate impacts, with the understanding that the commitments will be updated every five years.

Sadasivam describes fourteen days of working twelve hours a day with hardly any breaks. Reporters at climate policy conferences must navigate a maze of side events, press conferences, and closed-door negotiations, often held simultaneously in different parts of a massive conference venue. Access to high-level meetings can be limited, which adds to the challenge of getting information. "It's like drinking out of a firehose. It's just pure insanity," Sadasivam recalls.[84]

Covering COPs and translating what happens to the public is part of reporting on climate change. Sadasivam and other journalists covering these international gatherings know they need a plan for approaching coverage. Understanding the history and agreements of the past also helps to inform future stories about global actions.

Journalists must also know what policies are in place nationally to address climate change. In the United States, the Biden administration implemented the country's first major climate policy, the Inflation Reduction Act, which established billions of dollars in incentives to electrify the United States and move away from fossil fuels. The Inflation Reduction Act is just one of many relevant policies, but there are other landmark laws to know. The Clean Air Act is among them. It regulates air quality in the United States. The Endangered Species Act protects wildlife on the brink of extinction and will continue to have a prominent role in biodiversity and conservation in a warming world. The National Environmental Policy Act is another US law that requires federal agencies to undertake a thorough review process before deciding whether to move forward with a major project such as a highway or a mine.

Chapter 3, on significant international and national policies and treaties, provides an essential overview of the most important elements of climate policy and how to incorporate them into stories.

Climate Change in the Courts

Litigation is an emerging aspect of climate coverage that further complicates what journalists need to know. I learned from my students at Arizona State University just how overwhelming reporting on environmental cases can be when you're covering your first court case. Who's suing whom? And over what? More journalists will need to become increasingly familiar with reporting on litigation.

Courtrooms are becoming an arena where rulings—or the lack thereof—can shape the direction of future climate action, from interpreting laws to influencing climate policy. That's happening as governments and corporations face growing pressure to act on climate change. *Juliana v. United*

States (2015) is recognized as one of the earliest cases to attempt to hold the government accountable for climate change.[85] Twenty-one youth plaintiffs argued that the federal government violated their constitutional rights by allowing planet-warming pollution to build up in the atmosphere. The Department of Justice has worked for years to delay and dismiss the case.[86] As of this writing, the *Juliana* case has not made it to trial, but it has inspired similar legal action by youth in other states, including Montana and Hawaii.[87]

However, youth-led climate cases aren't the only ones, although they generally get media coverage because their stories are compelling. A growing number of lawsuits aim to force fossil fuel companies to reduce greenhouse gas emissions, and others seek financial compensation for damages emitters have caused. The majority of climate-related cases, at least in the United States, concern regulations.

As more cases are filed globally, reporters must learn how the courts work, how to read cases, and how to interpret judicial opinions, along with following what happens after decisions are made. Covering climate litigation can expose corporations' financial and ethical responsibilities, reveal the human stories behind legal actions, and shed light on how the judicial system is being used to address one of the most pressing issues of our time. Chapter 8, on climate litigation, includes guidance on accessing court documents, understanding the elements of a lawsuit, and tracking developing cases.

The Skills Needed for Reporting on Climate

The intersectionality of climate change, spanning science, policy, and the extreme impacts of rising temperatures, creates a complex and challenging landscape for reporters. Understanding the intricate connections between climate change and many aspects of life is crucial, especially as the public comes to recognize the significant changes happening around the globe. Journalists will learn essential skills in the chapters that follow, from reading scientific studies to framing stories that make the climate connection clear. Those are tangible actions. What's less tangible are the natural instincts, such as curiosity, that make someone well suited to be a journalist, especially one who wants to report on our warming world.

Cultivate Curiosity

Ask any seasoned journalist what the most vital skill in their toolkit is, and the answer will almost always be curiosity. Freelance journalist and author Meera Subramanian, whose narrative nonfiction has graced the pages of

Nature and *The New York Times*, describes curiosity as the pivotal moment when something gives you pause and makes you wonder. This innate drive to ask questions, explore new angles, and burrow deeper into research is the foundation of distinctive and engaging climate reporting.

In a field as intricate and far-reaching as climate change, curiosity is not just a skill; it's a guiding compass. Subramanian puts it this way: "Appreciate that being a journalist means you get to take the time to go down those rabbit holes that other people might be curious (about), but they just don't have the time to do it." She says following the things you care most about translates to the audience regardless of the medium you work in. Curiosity is how journalists develop sources that lead to stories, which lead to even more. "Your knowledge base will just become deeper and deeper," explains Subramanian. "That will inform even better storytelling."[88]

Being curious means asking "why" a lot; that question serves journalists well. Journalists, especially reporters who are new, tend to overcomplicate questions. But part of being a climate reporter is translating science, for example, in a way that's accurate and accessible for people. That means not being afraid to ask the obvious or silly question. That "silly" or "stupid" question usually ends up being the right question for the audience.

Avoid Perfectionism

Climate change is an urgent story and is no longer a slow-drip tale, as it was decades ago. The impacts are being felt across Earth. It's multifaceted, requiring a newsroom-wide response to integrating climate into almost all stories. For Michael Kodas with *Inside Climate News*, it's about getting important reporting out to the world and not letting the perfect be the enemy of the good. That can happen as journalists try to perfect writing, get additional sources beyond the many they've already interviewed, or compulsively rewrite a story to get it absolutely flawless. I've helped numerous journalists—some of whom have been reporting for several years—who had become paralyzed by overthinking and overreporting. I confess I have done this with my own stories. In hindsight, those stories weren't improved by the additional stress or time that went into trying to get them perfect.

Yes, an additional interview or another day to write a story is what every journalist desires, and it's what every editor dreads. "One of the things that people fail to take into the equation of the significance of one piece of environmental journalism is the idea of urgency," says Kodas. The climate crisis is accelerating, so stories need to "hit fast and hard," he adds.[89] Journalists need to relinquish the idea of perfection in favor of publishing timely, important, and accurate information about the climate crisis.

Take Time

Although laboring over sentences can reach a point of diminishing returns, journalists will find tremendous value in taking time to develop relationships with the communities they cover. Ezra David Romero, a climate reporter for public media outlet KQED in San Francisco, knows this well. Some of his reporting on climate change intersects with communities that have historically been marginalized and are confronting past injustices.

Romero builds relationships with people in these communities over time, without an agenda. So when extreme weather strikes and floods a community, Romero has already developed relationships with people whom he can turn to for reporting. That's different from reporting on a community and then never returning once the story is done. Romero says community voices tend to get buried in stories, making sources feel unheard, disrespected, or tokenized. "What I try to do is spend a lot of time with them if I can," Romero says. That's not always possible for a pressing deadline, "but I do my best to really accurately honor their experience with nuance," he says.[90]

Find Joy

Covering climate change is a serious endeavor, but it's also a rewarding and fun career path. As I reflect on my journalism career, I see a life shaped by following my curiosity and pursuing stories that were challenging and, at times, heartbreakingly difficult. I've also had many moments of joy in the field, talking with people, listening to their stories, and asking questions. The people who've generously shared their stories and experiences with me still light me up with an immense sense of gratitude to this day.

I'm grateful to have found a profession that has allowed me to ask questions and to have an unofficial license to be a lifelong learner. My heartfelt advice is to trust that curiosity and find joy in doing something meaningful. Any journalist reporting on climate change will need that joy and hope to advance the narrative arc of our warming planet.

CHAPTER 2

Understanding the Science

"Greenhouse gas emissions keep growing. Global temperatures keep rising. And our planet is fast approaching tipping points that will make climate chaos irreversible. We are on a highway to climate hell with our foot on the accelerator."
—António Guterres, secretary-general of the United Nations

My editor's ears perked up one fall day when Stephanie, one of my graduate students, pitched me a story that involved Arizona's iconic saguaro cactus. She'd read in a study that saguaros in the Cactus Forest of Saguaro National Park were not thriving as they used to. Could saguaros, which can live between 150 and 200 years, survive in a warmer world? Were the state's iconic towering cactus already in decline? How could she tell this story?

We started with the study to see who the authors were and what they had found. The study looked at seventy-five years of observational data on saguaros in a section of Saguaro National Park near the Rincon Mountains outside Tucson. The researchers noted that new saguaros had taken root during a thirty-year period that was punctuated by drought conditions.[1] Yet present-day data told a different story, highlighting the complexity and nuance that can come through scientific inquiry.

Stephanie and I brainstormed potential interview subjects. She'd need to talk with people at Saguaro National Park, maybe a biologist. She'd need to bring the climate context into the story and talk with climate scientists about how climate change has affected the region. Stephanie would also need to talk with researchers who have been studying saguaros. Two study authors, Thomas Orum and Nancy Ferguson, caught our eye. They seemed dedicated to studying saguaros. We wondered whether they were sort of the caretakers of the saguaros—saguaro champions. What was their story? How did they start researching saguaros?

Stephanie reached out to the two researchers and discovered that Orum and Ferguson had spent a lifetime studying saguaros together. Even after they retired from the University of Arizona, the couple continued monitoring a section of saguaros they'd been studying for over forty years. Each year, they noted the number of arms on each cactus, height, and whether any damage was visible. Stephanie had found the main characters for a feature story that would be told through Orum and Ferguson's eyes while also getting at the larger question of what effect climate change has had on the saguaros.[2]

The couple's research focused on one part of the park. Evidence pointed to a decline in new saguaros, and we wondered whether this was happening elsewhere. That thinking led Stephanie to Saguaro National Park biologist Don Swann and other researchers who had discovered there were only seventy saguaros younger than fifteen years old among 10,000 saguaros surveyed in the park. Human-caused climate change and drought were suspected to be the reason why young saguaros were on the decline.[3]

How much had climate change warmed Arizona's national parks? Such a statistic would add a larger perspective to the story and show the impacts of human-caused climate change. Stephanie found that Saguaro National Park wasn't the only park experiencing changes from a warming world. A national study found climate change had caused national parks in the United States to warm twice as fast as the rest of the country. Sixteen of Arizona's twenty-two National Park Service sites had also witnessed a significant increase in temperatures due to climate change.[4]

What started as a small study that caught her curiosity eventually turned into Stephanie's enterprise project for that semester. She looked into the climate questions the study raised and discovered a narrative with Orum and Ferguson at the heart of the story, a compelling couple trying to watch over their beloved saguaros. Her feature checked all the boxes for a contextual climate-related story.

Stephanie's reporting journey with climate change is similar to what I saw with many of my students while teaching at Arizona State University's Walter Cronkite School of Journalism and Mass Communication. Like Stephanie, my students often asked me about the basics of climate change and the science. Many of them had been assigned to work with me on environmental issues in the school's professional program, Cronkite News. The semester they spent with me usually marked their first experience learning about all aspects of human-caused climate change. A few students were studying science or meteorology and understood the science basics but weren't sure how best to communicate about climate change. They all needed easy-to-understand references to get them started for a semester of being in a working newsroom.

Science remains the backbone of climate journalism, but it can be over-whelming and also intimidating, not only for early-career reporters but for veteran journalists as well.

Reporters must know how to read and interpret scientific studies. They need an essential understanding of how Earth's systems work and what warming temperatures do and do not cause. They need to understand the difference between weather and climate change. Generally, the fingerprints of climate change are on a lot of extreme weather such as hurricanes and torrential rainfall that causes massive flooding. But not all weather is related to climate change. Tricky. So journalists have to learn how to make the right climate connections in stories. Science moves at a glacial pace (pun intended), making it hard for scientists to say with certainty, in some cases, what's happening. So getting the attribution right matters. If a reporter misattributes, it can lead to rational skepticism of the larger truth of human-caused climate change, so it's important to get these dis-tinctions right.

Journalists don't need a science degree to report on climate change (although it can definitely help). But they do need to understand the sci-entific process, break down science jargon, and accurately make climate connections in their stories. It's no small task. This chapter provides a primer on the essential climate science basics, including context for stories. Then, the chapter explains how to communicate the science—the pitfalls to avoid, how to interview scientists, and how to read scientific studies. What follows is a practical guide to help unlock climate change science so reporters can more readily bring the necessary climate context into their stories.

Climate Science Basics

Reporters often assume that people understand the basics of how Earth's climate works. The reality is that people aren't paying nearly as much attention as a journalist might think. That's why reporters have to unpack the science for their audience. This applies to both science jargon and the actual science itself. What follows is an introduction to the essentials of how Earth's climate works: what the climate cycle is, how temperatures on the planet are regulated, how the climate has shifted, and how human activity is the cause. This is not meant to be a comprehensive guide because entire books have been written on these subjects, but this chapter provides the fundamentals for journalists to feel comfortable reporting on the basics of climate science.

How Earth's Climate Works

Earth's climate has constantly been changing through a series of natural processes, each a puzzle piece that, when locked together, have created a livable planet. That's important because climate stories are about *unnatural* climate change, created primarily by burning fossil fuels. Phrases such as "human-caused climate change" help convey that distinction and help make the climate connection for people. Understanding the current state of Earth's climate begins with knowing how climate should work.

Let's start with the atmosphere, which is composed of gases that wrap around the planet. The atmosphere is composed primarily of nitrogen (78 percent), oxygen (nearly 21 percent), and trace amounts of other gases such as carbon dioxide, methane, and water vapor.[5] This gaseous blanket absorbs and redistributes solar radiation, regulates temperature, and helps weather form.

The hydrosphere is another piece of the system, encompassing all the water on Earth, from oceans to rivers and groundwater to water vapor.[6] All this water—about 71 percent of Earth's surface—absorbs the sun's heat and moves it around the globe, releasing it back into the atmosphere.[7] That influences temperatures and weather patterns.

The cryosphere is all the frozen water on the planet, including ice sheets, glaciers, snow, and sea ice. Frozen water reflects solar radiation into space and influences ocean circulation and freshwater storage.

The land surface, or lithosphere, also influences climate because, like ice, land reflects solar radiation while also absorbing it. Continents, islands, and ocean floors store and release heat, affecting evaporation and the exchange of greenhouse gases (GHGs).

Finally, the last puzzle piece of the atmosphere is the biosphere. All living creatures, from plants and animals to microorganisms and ecosystems, make up this part of the system. The exchange of carbon dioxide and oxygen through the biosphere—between plants and animals and the atmosphere— includes organisms pulling in carbon and storing it. The destruction of massive swaths of forests, for example, reduces the natural storage of carbon dioxide.

How Earth Regulates Temperature

The greenhouse effect maintains habitable temperatures for life on Earth. Energy from the sun radiates down through Earth's atmosphere, where the surface absorbs it. Earth emits heat back into space, and some of that heat gets absorbed by GHGs in the atmosphere. Heat gets trapped naturally and then radiates back to Earth. When the system works, temperatures remain stable.[8] However, our climate system no longer works as it used to because the amounts of heat-trapping gases—mainly carbon dioxide, methane, and nitrous oxide—in the atmosphere are too high. The reasons are human caused, primarily fossil fuel burning, forest loss, agriculture, and other industrial activities. Carbon dioxide, methane, and nitrous oxide have sharply increased in the last century, trapping heat in the atmosphere, wrapping the planet in a blanket that amplifies the natural greenhouse effect.[9] This causes global temperatures to rise, which is known as global warming.

If global warming were a stone and that stone got dropped in the middle of a tranquil lake, the waves would ripple out for generations to come. That's the significance of human-caused climate change.

The Carbon Cycle and Why It Matters

Carbon is the "chemical backbone" of all living beings on the planet.[10] It occurs in molecules such as proteins and DNA in plants and animals. This chemical element is also found in our atmosphere, where it shows up as carbon dioxide. Carbon atoms continuously travel from the atmosphere to Earth and back again in the carbon cycle. However, the atmosphere has too much carbon dioxide—the most in 3.6 million years.[11] That gas traps heat from the sun, causing global warming.

The carbon cycle usually goes unmentioned in climate stories, yet it helps explain the urgent need to reduce emissions and protect natural carbon sinks such as oceans and forests. Understanding the carbon cycle helps people understand the significance of vast forest fires or clearing of land in the Amazon rainforest to make way for grazing, mining, or logging.

Photosynthesis, respiration and decay, oceanic uptake and release, and geologic processes all have a role in the carbon cycle. Plants and organisms, such as algae and phytoplankton, use the sun's energy to convert carbon dioxide from the air and water into a form of sugar. The byproduct is oxygen, which gets released into the atmosphere. This process, known as **photosynthesis**, leads to carbon being stored in trees and other plants. Plants, animals, humans, and even tiny critters release carbon dioxide into the atmosphere through **respiration**. Carbon returns to the soil or the atmosphere when organisms die and decompose. The oceans absorb carbon dioxide, which then reacts with water molecules to generate compounds that marine organisms can use or that sink deep into the ocean. Carbon dioxide gets released from the ocean when concentrations of carbon dioxide dissolved in the

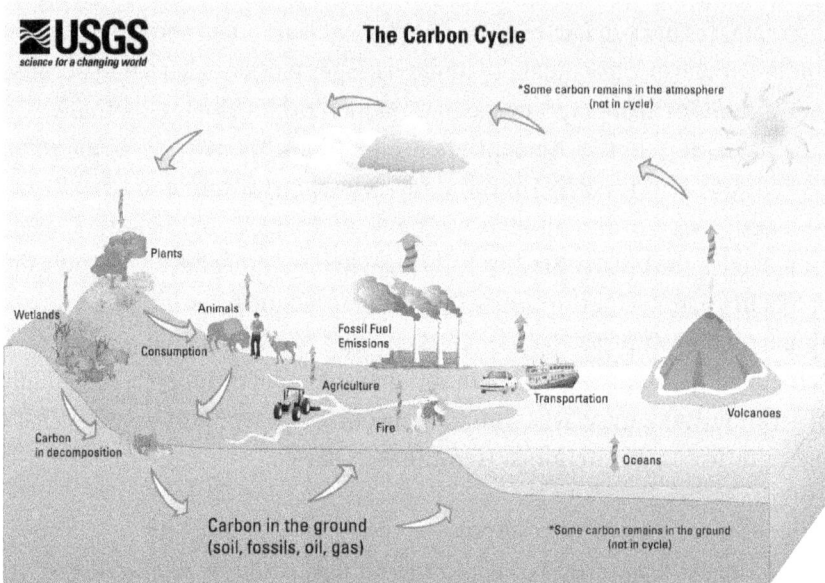

Figure 2-1. How the Carbon Cycle Works
The carbon cycle is a continuous loop that regulates the distribution of carbon on Earth and in the atmosphere. Journalists rarely reference this in reporting, but it's fundamental to understanding why greenhouse gas emissions must be dramatically reduced. Courtesy of USGS (https://www.usgs.gov/media/images/usgs-carbon-cycle).

water become too high. This exchange helps regulate Earth's climate. Since our planet and its atmosphere form a closed environment, the amount of carbon does not change, although carbon gets recycled repeatedly.

How People Altered the Climate

Our climate has warmed and cooled naturally throughout Earth's history. However, the Industrial Revolution forever altered the trajectory of weather, climate, and temperatures. Levels of carbon dioxide, methane, and nitrous oxide—what are known as GHGs—in the atmosphere began to rise in the mid-1700s. The advent of factories, industry, automobiles, and oil and gas drilling have all contributed to warmer temperatures. In the mid-1960s, this increase worsened, sharply rising in the 1980s and into the 2000s. Climate scientists unanimously agree that human activity has driven a significant increase in global temperatures, and the only way to limit or halt the warming is to reduce our use of fossil fuels dramatically. Human-caused climate change exists because industrialized countries such as China and the United States have emitted vast amounts of planet-warming gases.

Earth's climate has evolved over millions of years, influenced by volcanic eruptions, wildfires, and changes in the sun's energy. However, scientists agree that nothing can account for the rapid rise in temperatures in the last century other than the use of fossil fuels, which give off heat-trapping pollution.

Carbon dioxide, methane, and nitrous oxide are more prevalent in the atmosphere than at any time in the last 800,000 years. Such gases have increased the **greenhouse effect** and elevated surface temperatures on the planet.

How Much Has the World Warmed?

Human-driven climate change, from deadly extreme weather such as hurricanes that cause billions of dollars in damage to rising sea levels that will

ATMOSPHERIC CARBON DIOXIDE

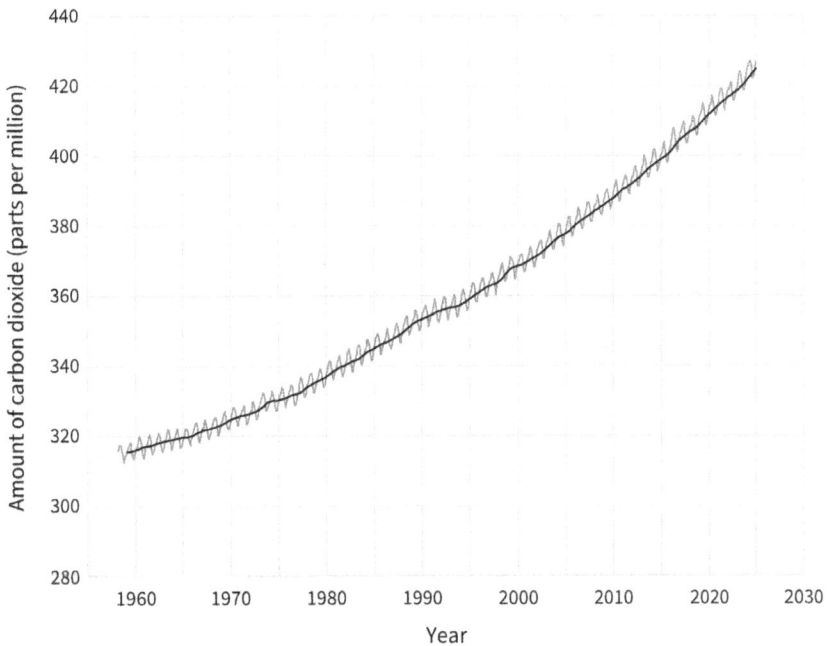

Figure 2-2. The Rise of Carbon Dioxide
In 1958, Mauna Loa Observatory in Hawaii began recording the amount of carbon dioxide in the atmosphere. This graph shows the station's monthly average carbon dioxide measurements since 1958 in parts per million. Seasonal increases in vegetation cause dips in CO2 in summer and upticks in winter when vegetation decays. However, human activities account for the long-term trend of rising carbon dioxide levels. Courtesy of NOAA Climate.gov (https://www.climate.gov/news-features/understanding-climate/climate-change-atmospheric-carbon-dioxide).

force people to relocate to higher ground, will be felt for generations to come. Climate scientists have "high confidence" that human activities, mainly through GHG emissions, have caused average global surface temperatures to rise 1.1°C (1.9°F) above preindustrial levels.[12] Globally, emissions have continued to climb with "unequal historical and ongoing contributions" from human activities such as burning fossil fuels for energy and cutting huge swaths of forests down.[13] Global warming is accelerating as emissions rise.

Since 1970, surface temperatures worldwide have increased faster than in any other fifty-year period over at least 2,000 years, according to an Intergovernmental Panel on Climate Change (IPCC) report.[14] Climate scientists have said the world needs to limit global warming to 1.5°C (2.7°F) to avoid the worst effects of climate change.[15] However, the world has not been on a path to meet that goal. The Arctic, for example, has already had average temperatures exceed 2°C above preindustrial levels (1850–1900).[16]

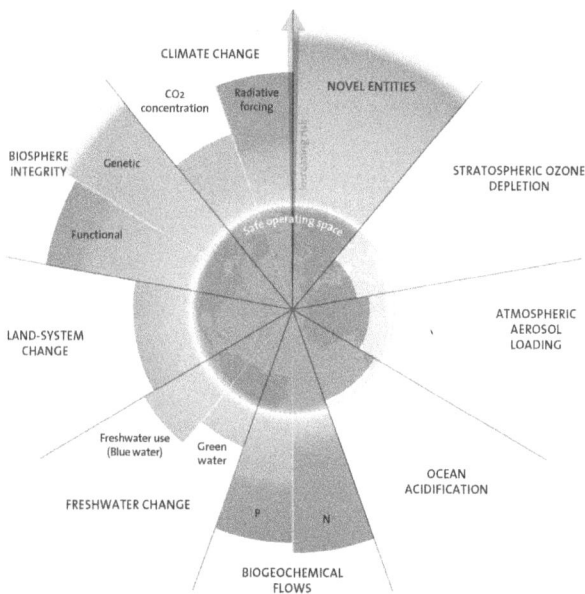

Figure 2-3. Crossing Planetary Boundaries
A team of scientists in 2023 quantified nine processes that regulate Earth's stability and resilience, including biosphere integrity, freshwater change, and climate change. The planetary boundaries represent the safe limits for pressuring Earth's systems. Six of the nine boundaries have already been crossed. The risk of irreversible environmental changes increases when boundaries are crossed. Courtesy of Azote for Stockholm Resilience Centre, based on analysis in Richardson et al. 2023 (https://www.stockholmresilience.org/research/planetary-boundaries.html#:~:text=The%20planetary%20boundaries%20concept%20presents,resilience%20of%20the%20Earth%20system).

The Paris Agreement, a climate change treaty, aims to limit global warming to well below 2°C (3.6°F) above preindustrial levels.[17] Efforts are focused on keeping global warming at 1.5°C (2.7°F), but the world is on track to significantly exceed that limit despite plans from each country to reduce emissions.[18]

Global warming at 2°C or above is considered a tipping point that, once crossed, could usher in dangerous simultaneous effects of climate change. More than a quarter of the world's population could face an additional month of severe heat stress every year; drought, along with hot temperatures, could heighten the risk of wildfire in places around the globe and intensify them in the already arid western United States.[19]

Why Global Warming Is Such a Problem

A 1°C (approximately 2°F) increase in global average surface temperature since the preindustrial era may seem like a tiny blip. But it takes a tremendous buildup of heat to shift global temperatures.[20] So even this small temperature increase is pushing regional and seasonal temperatures to extremes. The Arctic is the fastest-warming region on the planet; land areas are warming faster than the oceans. Warmer temperatures mean less snow cover and melting sea ice. Rainfall is heavier, which means more flooding, so more people are in harm's way. Habitats for plants and animals are also shifting, expanding for some species and disappearing for others. These effects build on each other in a vicious cycle.[21]

Scientists have "high confidence" that the increase in Earth's temperature has already led to massive impacts, harming people, plants, animals, and ecosystems. Developing countries—those that have contributed the least to planet-warming pollution—shoulder the disproportionate effects of human-caused climate change.[22] Tuvalu and the Marshall Islands, sub-Saharan Africa, and South Asian countries such as Bangladesh and Nepal, for example, have contributed little to emissions yet are already dealing with the consequences of climate change: rising sea levels inundating coastlines, drought, flooding and extreme rainfall, and melting glaciers.

What Science Says About the Path Forward

Global warming is accelerating—2023 shattered temperature records, becoming the hottest year ever recorded. That record was broken the next year, with 2024 becoming Earth's warmest year on record.[23] The planet is well on a path to exceed 1.5°C of warming (2.7°F).[24] The ongoing emission of climate-polluting gases will continue to cause global warming, and reaching 1.5°C will mean that "every increment of global warming will intensify multiple and concurrent hazards," according to the IPCC.[25] However, if communities can make "deep, rapid, and sustained reductions" in emissions, we can slow global warming in two decades. Scientists are highly confident that such a slowdown will mean "discernible changes in atmospheric composition within a few years."[26] The solution to climate change is to reduce the burning of fossil fuels drastically—a point that's largely missing in climate-related stories. However, that solution should be included in every climate story because the solutions exist, and all is not lost—a counternarrative to doom and gloom.

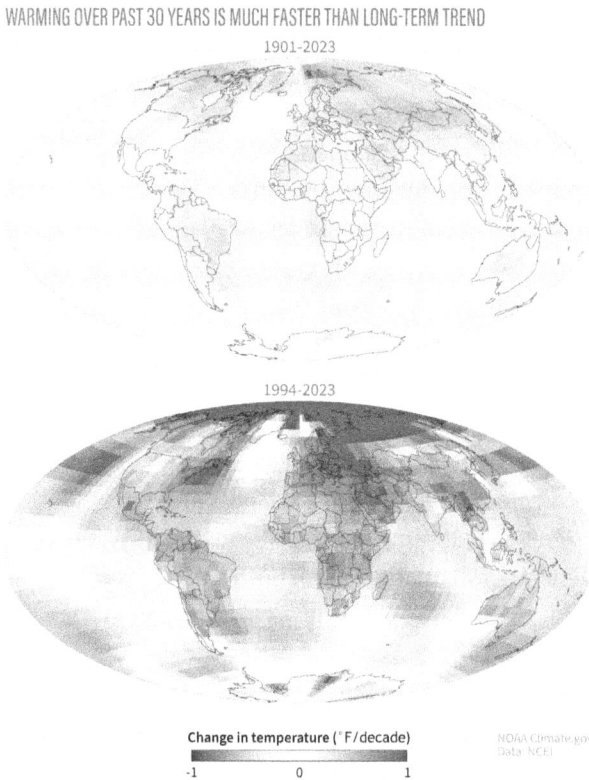

Figure 2-4. Warming Over the Past 30 Years Is Faster than the Long-Term Trend
Annual surface temperature trends from 1994 to 2023 (bottom) compared with the start of the twentieth century (top) show how rapidly Earth has warmed in recent decades. Some locations have already warmed by 1°F or more per decade. The Arctic shows the most dramatic differences because of the loss of reflective ice and snow, which amplifies the rate of warming. Courtesy of NOAA Climate.gov, based on data provided by NOAA National Centers for Environmental Information (https://www.climate.gov/media/15841).

Climate Change Quick Facts

- **1.1°C** (1.9°F): the average global temperature increase that has already occurred since the mid-1800s.
- **1.5°C** (2.7°F): the goal established in the Paris Agreement to limit warming to 1.5°C or less to avoid the worst impacts of human-caused climate change.
- **Scientists agree** the amount of global warming since the Industrial Revolution is without question caused by greenhouse gas emissions, primarily from the burning of fossil fuels. There are other factors, including deforestation and agriculture.
- **Climate change** makes droughts, heat waves, hurricanes, and flooding more intense and more frequent.
- **Social and economic inequalities** are amplified by climate change, with disasters hitting low-income people and communities of color the hardest.

Climate Change and Weather

Human-caused climate change is a global problem, but it's also hyperlocal. The effects show up in real ways: a period of extremely hot temperatures, record rainfall, changes in the optimal time to plant and harvest crops. So is climate change weather? It's a common question I was asked during my time teaching at Arizona State University. The short answer: *Weather* and *climate* are distinct terms.

Weather refers to the daily **short-term patterns** (e.g., a string of sunny days, the chance of rain showers, windy conditions, or the possibility of a foot of snowfall). The National Weather Service bases its daily forecasts for local communities on weather. The agency can then issue alerts for extreme weather such as epic snowfall that could make driving hazardous, a flash flood during monsoon season in the Southwest, or dangerously high temperatures.

Climate refers to **long-term weather patterns and trends** in a region over decades. As Earth's temperature rises, the frequency, length, and intensity of heat waves, hurricanes, and extreme rainfall increase. Climate change can also bring extreme weather to places that have historically not seen such weather, such as the epic flooding in Vermont in 2023 or increasing heat in New England.[27]

Weather and climate have historically been seen as separate. Andrew Pershing, who directs attribution, science, and climate fingerprinting at Climate Central, says that's changed as the science has become clearer. "We were really taught to keep climate and the weather separate," he says. That changed after the world's first attribution study, which looked at a heat wave in Europe that killed people. Researchers worked to quantify the extent to which climate change made that heat wave "more likely and more severe."[28]

The Scientific Method

Scientists often qualify their statements with phrases such as "more research needs to be done" or "additional study is needed." Reporters might find themselves frustrated by the inconclusive nature of such remarks. Why can't a scientist give a more definitive answer? The answer lies in how science gets done. The scientific method remains the pillar of scientific inquiry, the foundation on which scientific understanding evolves.

That process also generates uncertainty that, if not addressed in stories, can be used by some to deny that climate change is happening. Joan Meiners, a climate reporter at *The Arizona Republic*, says the role of "uncertainty and nuance in the scientific process" gets missed in climate journalism. Meiners, who has a PhD in interdisciplinary ecology from the University of Florida, switched to journalism after feeling frustrated by the slow pace of doing research and getting published. "I wanted to be part of getting the information to people in the moment when it's most relevant," explains Meiners.[29]

Now she sees the consequences of climate coverage that fails to fully explain the scientific method. The uncertainty in science, she says, "doesn't mean that our methods are flawed or our conclusions are wrong."[30] That distinction is critical for journalists to understand and include in climate stories. Knowing how scientists derive their conclusions helps inform the questions reporters ask and how they communicate the science accurately. All this is in service of informing the audience. Recall the steps of the scientific method:

1. **Observation:** Scientists notice something of interest in the natural world, and they begin to gather data. For instance, a climate scientist might look at past temperature data, examine cores drilled deep in ice, or find information on changes in sea level over time.
2. **Question:** Scientists generate questions to investigate the causes or patterns behind what they see. They might ask, "What factors are driving the increase in global temperatures?"

3. **Hypothesis:** This is a tentative explanation for what's being seen, which can be tested through research. In climate change research, a hypothesis might propose that an increase in carbon dioxide emissions translates to a spike in temperatures around the globe.

4. **Experimentation:** Scientists design and do experiments to test their hypotheses, aiming to control for variables and minimize biases. In climate science, this may involve analyzing historical climate data, running climate models, or doing laboratory experiments to study the greenhouse effect.

5. **Analysis:** Scientists analyze the data from experiments to determine whether the results support or refute the hypothesis. In the case of climate change, the overwhelming evidence supports the hypothesis that human activities, such as burning fossil fuels, are driving global warming.

6. **Peer review and replication:** Scientific findings are subject to peer review. Other experts in the field evaluate the research for its validity, methods, and conclusions. If independent researchers can replicate results, scientific consensus forms as evidence mounts to support the initial research.

The scientific method takes time—years, in fact—before scientists can confidently state that something is indeed happening and why. It took years of climate research before most scientists came to a consensus that primarily burning fossil fuels caused Earth's temperature to rise.

This is why interviewing scientists can be tricky: Reporters sometimes don't get clear answers to questions. The reason may have to do with the stage of current research. Reporters can ask scientists about what they will need to do before they can be highly confident in their findings.

The scientific method gives journalists a roadmap for evaluating the credibility of the research, helping distinguish between well-supported scientific conclusions and unsupported claims. The nuances of scientific findings can be shared in stories while addressing uncertainties that people need to understand.

Communicating Climate Science

We have focused so far on climate science, critical Earth processes, and the distinction between weather and climate—all foundational underpinnings to comprehending the science context of climate change. Such an understanding should give journalists more confidence in doing stories on climate change.

Another challenge in reporting on climate change is accurately distilling science so the audience understands it. Scientific terms are everywhere, and media outlets often adopt that jargon, assuming everyone knows what's meant. *Climate mitigation, greenhouse gases*, and *climate adaptation* are a few examples that surface in stories but are rarely explained. So, in addition to understanding the science behind climate change, journalists also need to know how to effectively communicate with scientists and convey science to their audiences.

In Science, Words Have Different Meanings

What a word means to a scientist can mean something entirely different to a nonscientist, such as a journalist. Take the word *theory*, for example. Most of us understand *theory* to mean an untested hunch. However, the word has quite the opposite meaning for a scientist.

In science, a theory is an explanation that's well researched and considers laws, hypotheses, and, of course, facts. The theory of gravity, for instance, explains why grapefruits fall off trees; the theory of evolution shows through fossils how species evolve. These theories are scientifically proven.

"The theory of global warming is like that (theory of gravity). We understand what's happening, it's very well established. We can use it to make predictions to the public," says Susan Hassol, who's spent more than thirty years as a climate change communicator.[31]

Climate deniers toss the word *theory* around like confetti to confuse people, sparking debate. They insinuate that climate change is a hunch, which is not true, but deniers use that lack of understanding to spread misinformation and delay climate action.

Those of us not trained in science generally think *theory* refers to what scientists call a hypothesis: an idea that needs to be tested. In science, the word *theory* really refers to something that has been thoroughly tested and proven.

Climate journalists must be able to translate scientific words in stories so people can understand them accurately. Hassol finds that journalists tend to pick up on scientists' lingo and use it in their reporting. "That's a problem," she says. "We want to educate them (the public) on what the terms mean. We don't want them to just come to adopt those terms and use them because that's not working for their audience."[32]

Lost in Translation

Translating science in stories starts with defining scientific terms *before* using them so people know what the words mean. For example, the term *greenhouse gas* often appears in stories without an explanation. An assumption is made that everyone understands the reference. But do they?

GHGs include carbon dioxide, methane, and nitrous oxide, gases that trap heat in the atmosphere and increase global temperatures. That's probably too much information to convey in a story, but alternatives exist. Phrases such as *heat-trapping gases* and *planet-warming pollution* explain what GHGs are. "Just by saying 'heat-trapping gases,' you're already helping your audience to understand the science," Hassol says.[33]

The phrase *climate change* can also be misleading because scientists use that term to define any change in Earth's climate. "This is why you hear the (climate) deniers constantly repeating 'climate has always changed,'" says Hassol. The climate has indeed always been changing, but the distinction is that "it's changing because of us."[34] Humans have caused temperatures to warm primarily by burning fossil fuels, and that's unnatural warming. By writing *human-caused climate change* instead of just *climate change* you help audiences make the climate connection.

Another common translation problem is how to reference temperature in stories. Scientists use the metric system, so temperatures are reported in Celsius, not Fahrenheit. Climate stories sometimes mention 1.5°C, which is a goal countries agreed to in the Paris Agreement to limit warming and stave off the worst repercussions of human-caused climate change. Europeans get the significance because they use the metric system, but that number sounds insignificant in the United States. Why should people care about a 1.5°C temperature increase? Convert that number to Fahrenheit and it represents a 2.7-degree temperature increase, which is significant for an American audience. My general guidance is that US-based journalists should reference Celsius first but *always* translate in parentheses what it means in Fahrenheit. Again, this is about helping audiences understand climate change.

Questions Matter

Generally, scientists agree human-caused climate change increases the intensity and frequency of certain types of extreme weather, such as dangerous heat waves. Ask a climate scientist about whether climate change caused a *specific* hurricane, for example, and the answer will probably be "no." That answer is not wrong, but it might be misleading because what

Converting Celsius to Fahrenheit

Most of the world uses the metric system, considered the international measurement standard. Science and international organizations, including the United Nations and the World Meteorological Organization, consistently use Celsius to communicate temperature-related data. Limiting warming, for example, to 1.5°C or less may sound insignificant to an American audience, but that translates to 2.7°F of warming. Journalists reporting for a US-based audience must include the degree of temperature change to help people understand the significance. It's easy to do the conversion.

1 degree Celsius of warming equals 1.8 degrees Fahrenheit. Here's the formula:

$$1 \times 1.8 = 1.8°F.$$

So when scientists say **1.1°C of warming has already happened globally**, the equivalent in Fahrenheit is

$$1.1 \times 1.8 = 1.98°F.$$

Note that **1.1°C is often rounded down to 1.9°F** when referring to the average global temperature increase that has already occurred since preindustrial times.

the scientist could mean is there has not been a study of that specific storm to look at the influence of climate change. Instead, reframe questions so that scientists can answer in a way that is precisely correct while helping the audience understand the broader context. For instance, "What role does human-caused climate change have in storms like this one? Are these extreme storms what people can expect as temperatures rise? How do you know that?"

Journalists have an important role in connecting extreme weather and climate change, says expert climate communicator Susan Hassol. Notice in the questions above that a climate scientist isn't being asked about the climate fingerprints of a specific storm. The questions get at the broader implications of climate change for extreme weather. Failing to make that connection is a failure of journalism to understand the scientific method.

Heavy rainstorms, hurricanes, wildfires, and droughts are all developing in an environment that's been fundamentally altered by human-caused climate change. Temperatures are warmer. There's more moisture in the atmosphere. "The oceans are warmer, [and] atmospheric circulation and oceanic circulation patterns are changing because of that. So how can you say that this is not to do with climate change?," questions Hassol.[35]

Journalists have a role in helping people understand that Earth's climate has changed in unprecedented ways because of human-driven climate change. Start by asking good questions of climate experts, which will then give reporters the needed context to help them make the connections about climate change.

Reporting on Weather and Climate

The weather is where climate journalists and TV meteorologists have an important role in helping people understand the influence of global warming. When a major storm strikes or summer heat ramps up, people pay attention. They need information, and they often turn to local TV meteorologists for answers. Journalists and meteorologists need to be ready for when that moment comes.

Extreme weather is often how people recognize and experience climate change, so the connection is essential. Nine out of ten adults in the United States have lived through at least one extreme weather event in the last five years.[36] That could be an extreme heat wave, drought, wildfire, epic winter storm, hurricane, or flooding. Among these same people, three quarters believe that climate change played a role.

Here's a common scenario: A hurricane gains power over warm waters in the Gulf of Mexico and barrels toward the Florida coastline; editors prepare their reporters to cover the developing storm and its aftermath. What climate context could a reporter or meteorologist add to their coverage of the storm? Simple language works. Scientists know that climate change makes hurricanes more powerful and intense.[37] Wind speeds are faster in a warmer world; rainfall is heavier too, which leads to increased flooding. Ocean temperatures in the Atlantic and the Gulf of Mexico have been abnormally high, which fuels tropical cyclones.

Wildfires are another instance where journalists can make the climate connection for audiences through straightforward language. Hot temperatures, less precipitation, and drought brought on by climate change make devastating wildfires more likely. They're not the only factors, though. Past forest management practices such as fire suppression have allowed vegetation to build up, generating fuel for wildfires. Development has encroached on natural lands, which means the threat of fire is real for homes in what's known as the wildland–urban interface. Fire seasons, especially in the arid parts of the western United States, have lengthened. Wildfires are happening earlier in the year and in places that haven't historically had fire, including the Arctic.[38]

In both scenarios, a study known as an attribution analysis will show how much a specific extreme weather event was influenced by climate change. These usually quick-turn studies are worth covering, but even before such an analysis is available, journalists should strive to include relevant climate change context.

Other resources can help reporters and audiences understand the influence of human-driven climate change, such as the Climate Shift Index from Climate Central. This index helps reporters explain daily temperature changes and how climate change affects temperature. It's based on a range from −5 to +5: The higher the positive value, the more likely it is that climate change affected a specific day. A Climate Shift Index level 5 indicates that a temperature occurred five times more frequently because of climate change. In other words, that high temperature or warm overnight low would be highly unlikely in a world without human-driven climate change.[39]

The index can help TV meteorologists make climate connections for audiences.[40] TV meteorologists are uniquely positioned to help the public understand climate change because they are seen, along with NASA, as some of the most trusted sources on climate.[41] Chris Gloninger, a long-time chief meteorologist and climate expert, says meteorologists need to connect the dots between extreme weather and climate change. Meteorologists are usually the people in the newsroom who have an advanced science degree. "If you feel comfortable enough to talk about a meteorite, the Northern Lights, a volcanic eruption, or an earthquake," Gloninger says, "then you damn well should be comfortable enough to talk about something that's part of our core curriculum."[42]

Becoming Your Newsroom's Climate Expert

Every journalist is at some point a climate journalist because human-caused climate change touches nearly every aspect of our lives, from the sports we play to the food we eat to the air we breathe. Major news organizations such as *The Washington Post*, NPR, and the Associated Press recognize this reality and have the resources to staff large teams to report on the many aspects of climate change. That's the exception. In most newsrooms, one reporter may be tasked with focusing on climate change. Independent or freelance journalists often have no one else to consult when pitching or reporting on climate stories. Journalists who develop the skills to cover climate change will probably become the champions for getting colleagues and the rest of the newsroom to understand how climate intersects with areas of coverage—beats or verticals—from sports to politics. These journalists become the climate experts in their newsrooms. That requires staying on top of the latest science and happenings in the climate space, reading what other journalists write, paying attention to studies, and developing sources. What follows are practical tips to reporting on climate change regardless of beat or media market size.

Get to Know the Research

The fundamental principles of climate science are well established, and there's overwhelming consensus among scientists that human activities are driving climate change. However, ongoing research continues to refine our understanding of complex systems, regional impacts, and potential tipping points. The influence of human-caused climate change on tornadoes in the United States, for example, remains an area of active research and discussion. So does research on the influence of warming temperatures on atmospheric rivers. These concentrated corridors of moisture sweep across large bodies of water, such as the Pacific Ocean. When atmospheric rivers smash into mountainous terrain such as the Sierra Nevadas or the Cascade Mountain Range, they dump intense rain on lower elevations and bring heavy snowfall to higher elevations. And understanding whether climate change affects turbulence in air travel remains another area of scientific exploration.

Journalists should immerse themselves in reading the latest research, studies, and developments in climate science to become familiar with new ideas. Hundreds of science journals exist, but be cautious, because some publications can appear reputable when in fact they aren't. A best practice for journalists is to choose journals that align with their areas of interest. Reporters interested in the intersection of health and climate can follow research from *The Journal of Climate Change and Health* or the medical journal *JAMA*. Reporters focused on the intersection of climate change and wildlife could consult the *Journal of Applied Ecology* and *Biodiversity and Conservation*. Reporters can also sign up for notifications from reputable science journals such as *Nature Climate Change, Advances in Climate Change Research*, the *Bulletin of the American Meteorological Society*, and *Atmospheric Chemistry and Physics*.

Sign Up for Newsletters and Press Releases

Newsletters that collect environment and climate reporting into a daily email can help journalists stay up on the latest stories and can spark ideas for reporting. The Society of Environmental Journalists weekday news digest rounds up environmental and climate reporting from across primarily the United States. Several major newspapers in the United States, such as *The LA Times, The New York Times*, and *The Washington Post*, also have blogs and newsletters exploring various climate-related topics. Some local public media outlets and local newspapers have environment- or climate-themed newsletters.

EurekAlert! and Science Direct send science-related press releases to a subscriber's email. These are two excellent sources of ideas that can lead to interesting reporting. Just remember that journalists should always be skeptical with press releases and use them only as a starting place for research.

Federal agencies such as the US Department of Energy, the Environmental Protection Agency, and the US Department of Interior have press releases that journalists can sign up for. Companies, political leaders, and environmental nonprofits such as the Center for Biological Diversity, the Sierra Club, and many others have media lists worth joining.

The *Federal Register* in the United States publishes notices about oil and gas permits and leases, endangered species listings, and renewable energy projects, among a wide array of potentially climate-related story ideas. This register is worth bookmarking, and reporters should get familiar with how the site works. The Government Accountability Office also releases reports and investigations that periodically focus on aspects of climate change, such as air quality monitoring and reviews of federal agencies such as the National Oceanic and Atmospheric Administration.

Reporters also should not underestimate the utility of an effectively composed Google alert. Interested in offshore wind development? Or how about carbon sequestration projects? Climate policy? Google alerts on those topics will ping directly to reporters' emails and can lead to potential ideas.

Follow Other Journalists

A great way to practice better climate journalism is to stay up on what other journalists are reporting, whether it's podcasts, YouTube videos, or traditional publications such as *The New York Times*. That also includes tracking journals such as *Nature* and *Science* and reading *The Guardian* and *The Washington Post*. *Inside Climate News* is a must-read, along with publications such as *E&E News* from *Politico* or trade publications. All will help reporters develop their beat.

Reading, listening, and watching climate stories can also help reporters think about their own stories and spark fresh story angles or follow-up coverage. A story about floating gardens in Bangladesh might make a reporter wonder whether something like that is happening in their country. For example, I remember reading a news article from an international paper about conflict over water rights in a remote part of Kenya near the base of Mount Kenya. I was living in Flagstaff, Arizona, in the early 2000s working for Arizona Public Radio (KNAU) and frequently covering water and drought issues. Drought was an ongoing concern in northern Arizona, and I was looking for new angles. I was intrigued by whether water conflict could erupt in the West. Could lessons be learned in Kenya to help Arizona and the West better prepare and respond to dwindling water supplies? Those questions ultimately took me to Kenya on a fellowship to report on water conflict and scarcity. The series I produced for KNAU's audience provided a different take on water.

Social media platforms can also be helpful. For example, I follow climate and environmental journalists on platforms such as Bluesky, X (formerly known as Twitter), and Instagram. *The Washington Post* climate account and Covering Climate Now are all examples of Instagram accounts worth following.

Talk with Experts and Scientists

A reporter will inevitably have questions after reading a study. If the journalist doesn't understand something, the reader won't either. Reporters should take time to talk with the study authors and experts. This calls for bravery. Reporters must ask the questions that seem "silly" or "dumb," because the answers to those questions will lead to the best insights for the audience. Asking study authors about why they pursued the research and what they hope will come from their work can also lead to personal revelations that humanize the research and the scientist.

Reporters will also need to interview other scientists who weren't involved in the research to give independent insights. Peer research provides validation and can potentially refute claims or bring a unique perspective. By talking with researchers who weren't involved in the study, reporters may learn that something valuable has been missed. As a general guide, it's good to talk with the lead study authors and two or three other researchers who can advance the study and help the audience understand the significance of the findings.

Such conversations will help reporters feel more comfortable with the science and findings. The reporter and the editor will ultimately decide whether a study warrants a story. But any story based on a study should include not just the significance of the findings but also how that research can be applied. Often that gets missed in "study stories," leaving the reader wondering why they should care.

Not every study deserves a story, though. Sometimes new research becomes another way to keep up with developments on the climate beat. Some studies can also provide valuable context for enterprise stories by helping to make climate connections for the audience. For example, a recent study from the journal *Nature Ecology & Evolution* found that extreme wildfires have doubled in the last twenty years in both scale and frequency.[43] Several national news outlets such as *The New York Times* did standalone stories about the findings—all perfectly appropriate. That's one way to handle such a study.

Another way is to fold such a study into a developing story or a feature that shows the relevance of the study in action. For instance, let's say a massive wildfire has been burning in the western part of the United States for a week; homes have been lost, and people have been evacuated. Immediate coverage centered on the threats and the firefighting response. Reporters have updated the story throughout the week, but now the editor wants something more in-depth that puts the wildfire into perspective—a step back from the daily news. Here's where a reporter can draw on climate science. Climate change coupled with decades of poor forest management has led to more intense and more frequent fires. How might those findings apply to where this particular fire is burning? Could this study on extreme wildfires be additional context? Absolutely. A reporter could talk with the study authors and others not associated with the research as part of the reporting. That story steps back from the breaking news to connect what's happening with the wildfire to relevant research. Ultimately such a story makes the climate connections for the audience.

Here's another example: The National Oceanic and Atmospheric Administration confirmed that since the beginning of 2023, many of the world's oceans have experienced massive coral bleaching, when the coral expel algae from their tissues as warm waters stress their systems.[44] Many news organizations covered that report. But journalists living near coral reefs could expand beyond the initial report. Efforts are under way to buy time by rescuing coral and breeding them in labs. How are such efforts going? What's needed to put the coral back in the water? Multiple angles exist that are nuanced and insightful, from raising coral in labs to cross-breeding. Talking with scientists who are involved in coral research can lead to several follow-up stories.

Hot Take: *Ask researchers how a study's findings can help the public understand an issue or how researchers intend to use the information in the future. That context can be valuable in reporting and helping people understand the significance of the study.*

Connect Science to People and Other Species

Human-caused climate change is not an abstract scientific concept; it has real-world implications for all of us, including changes in biodiversity. Reporters should be clear about the science in their stories, which requires interviewing scientists and experts. Reporters should also go beyond the experts and interview people who understand the impacts of climate change, from the injustices it causes to the solutions communities are pursuing. This requires seeing people as expert voices—farmers who've had to adjust their crops in response to warmer temperatures, homeowners who've had to rebuild after floods or wildfires, and those without housing who've lived through another heat wave. Lived experience is invaluable to understanding the complexity and reach of climate change. Worldwide, at least 85 percent of people have directly experienced the impacts of global warming, from crippling heat waves in Europe, Asia, and the Americas to devastating floods in Pakistan to brush fires in Australia to hurricanes smashing into Florida and other Gulf Coast states.[45] Climate change is personal. Therefore, stories should include personal experiences.

The devastation from extreme weather linked to climate change causes billions of dollars of damage every year. For many people, this means starting over; some are forced to relocate or accept buyouts for their homes. Others choose to remain and rebuild because family and cultural ties run deep and, in some cases, span generations. Reporters should humanize these stories by connecting the science of climate change to the experiences of people—and yes, wildlife and plant life, too—who are all bearing witness to a warming world and all its implications and opportunities.

Scientific Studies and Reports

As we just discussed, journalists need to regularly review studies and reports to stay up to date on the latest climate change science. Some of these studies will warrant stories because they mark a significant development or analysis. So let's discuss how to cover such research and incorporate it into your reporting.

National media outlets often cover a climate change–related study or report published in a major journal such as *Nature* or *Science*. Most journals allow reporters to review studies ahead of an embargo, with the understanding that the journalist will not publish a story until a specified date. Embargoes give reporters time to interview the study authors and talk with people who weren't involved in the study. Similarly, federal agencies such as the National Oceanic and Atmospheric Administration and NASA hold press calls ahead of a major study or announcement, offering an overview of the science and the opportunity to ask questions. In both cases, the story is written and edited in advance, so that when an embargo lifts, it can be published right away. I cannot stress enough how important it is to adhere to an embargo; breaking one undermines the credibility of both the reporter and the news outlet.

Not every study needs to stand alone as its own story; many can provide valuable context for a larger piece a reporter is working on. For example, imagine a story about the impacts of wildfire smoke on people. Instead of focusing solely on a study about the long-term effects of inhaling microscopic particles such as PM2.5, the reporter could weave such a study into a narrative about, say, a wildland firefighter diagnosed with asthma after years of working alongside a crew to put out wildfires. The study becomes an important layer of context that can help enrich the story without being its central focus.

That said, major studies or reports do merit reporting. For example, roughly every four years the National Climate Assessment (NCA) in the United States gets released. Hundreds of pages detail how climate change is affecting the country, current efforts to address climate change, what more needs to be done, and what the future could look like in a warming world.

This definitive climate assessment is what local governments lean on to write regulations from building codes to emission goals, and courts reference it to settle climate lawsuits. Reporters usually get a preview before the NCA is released, giving them time to digest key findings and prepare stories.

The assessment is a treasure trove of story ideas. A series of chapters broken up by region provides the latest science on everything from flooding and drought to hurricanes and heat waves. The NCA and other assessments, such as those from the IPCC, are not just significant reports to cover; they're resources to return to again and again, offering context and fresh story angles.

National journalists usually focus on the major takeaways from the NCA, but there are natural opportunities to localize it. How much have temperatures increased? How have rainfall patterns shifted? What's happening with the rise in sea level for those who live near an ocean? How is a region responding and adapting to climate change? These are all worthwhile questions to consider when reviewing the NCA and other reports.

By covering substantial assessments, journalists show they're following the climate beat, tracking key developments, and bringing vital information to the public so they can stay informed and engaged.

How to Read a Study

You don't have to be a scientist or a statistical wizard to read, comprehend, and report the findings of a scientific study. A good practice is to begin with assessing how legitimate the study is and deciding whether the findings are significant enough to warrant coverage. A reporter can start by reviewing what journal published the study. Does the study appear in a reputable journal such as *Nature*?

If it does, check whether it was peer reviewed, which is considered the gold standard in scientific research. Peer review means that independent experts—scientists not involved in the research—have evaluated the study's methods, data, and conclusions to ensure its validity and reliability. This process helps identify errors, biases, or flaws before the study is published. If a study has not been peer reviewed, a reporter should proceed cautiously. Peer-reviewed studies are more likely to stand up to scrutiny and serve as a solid foundation for reporting than ones that have not been reviewed.

Next, look at who the study authors are and what their credentials are. Researchers with a background in a particular field, such as climate science, and their affiliations with known institutions are more likely to produce reliable work. It's common to find researchers scattered around the globe and based at well-respected universities working together on a study. Googling or checking their LinkedIn profiles is one way to learn more about their work.

Scan the journal article to take in the title and then pivot to the abstract, which is a snapshot of the study and its primary findings. In a few paragraphs, the researchers synthesize the question or questions they wanted to answer, the methods they used, and their conclusion. From there, I recommend skipping to the conclusion to see how it stacks up with what's promised in the abstract and title. A reporter might then look at graphs and figures and read the study carefully, flagging questions that come up.

Reading a scientific study or report takes time and patience, especially for those who don't have a science background. There will be calculations and unfamiliar words that might require further research. It's also not uncommon to find yourself reading paragraphs over and over to fully grasp what's being said. Over time, you will develop your own approach to reviewing studies, and, with practice, it will feel less daunting.

Assess the Study Design

Various types of research exist, such as observational and experimental studies and review articles. Experimental studies, particularly randomized controlled trials, are considered the gold standard for establishing causation. Observational studies, on the other hand, can offer valuable insights into, say, trends, but they cannot prove cause and effect. Reporters should be cautious about drawing conclusions from a single study. Science develops with repeated research over time, which leads to stronger and more reliable evidence.

Look at the Sample Size and Diversity

A study with a large, diverse sample is more likely to produce reliable results than a small, homogeneous one. Journalists should be skeptical of studies with small sample sizes, because their findings may not be truly representative or relevant for a broader population.

Understand the Statistics

A basic understanding of statistical terms can help one interpret a study's results. A low P value (typically less than .05) indicates that the observed results are unlikely to have occurred by chance. However, a low P value doesn't automatically make a study valid, because other factors such as study design and sample size also play a crucial role.

Place the Study in Context

A reporter will want to consider the broader research on the topic before drawing any conclusions. Systematic reviews and meta-analyses can help synthesize multiple studies and provide a more comprehensive understanding of the research that's already been done.

Check for Conflicts of Interest

Potential conflicts of interest, such as funding sources or affiliations, can influence a study's findings. Reporters should be transparent about these factors in their reporting. In some cases the reporter and editor may decide a study is problematic because of who funded it or which organization it came from. Studies or reports from particular organizations, including environmental groups and think tanks, can be skewed to support an organization's cause or position.

Check References

Reporters should check to see what other studies and research papers are referenced. Do those references come from reputable researchers and institutions? References are like signposts along a trail because they point to other scientists and research that can be valuable for further sourcing and context that can shape the reporting.

Ask Questions

Scientific studies are often complicated, and even with this step-by-step guide, a reporter may not be 100 percent confident in the study's validity. That's why reporters need to interview the study authors and other experts. Reporters can also talk through their understanding with colleagues, which can help clarify the key takeaways.

Attribution Studies

Climate change will exacerbate droughts, floods, wildfires, hurricanes, and other extreme weather. We live in a time when the abnormal is the new normal. Science takes time, and the "new abnormal" leaves people wondering what drives such extremes. How much was wild weather caused by human-driven climate change? That's a question to answer in reporting on extreme weather. Attribution studies can help. These quick-turn studies identify how much an extreme weather event was influenced by human-caused climate change. Scientists examine current conditions and compare them with historical records that include time before fossil fuels to see the influence of climate change.

The World Weather Attribution (WWA) group brings scientists from around the world together to quickly assess extreme weather and find the signature of climate change. In the summer of 2023, heavy rains brought devastating flooding to Libya. In the city of Derna, nearly 4,000 people died, and thousands of people went missing after two dams burst. Researchers from the United States, Greece, the Netherlands, Germany, and the United Kingdom worked to figure out the extent to which human-driven climate change "altered the likelihood and intensity of the heavy rainfall that led to the flooding." They found that the torrential rainfall and flooding were so extreme in Libya that these events were up to "50 times more likely and up to 50% more intense compared to a 1.2°C cooler climate."[46]

Some attribution studies take more time, such as when scientists involved with the WWA looked at an intense drought that pushed 4 million people in southern Ethiopia, eastern Kenya, and southern Somalia to the brink of starvation. The drought started in 2020 and caused crop failure, water scarcity, and flash floods when intense storms came. Scientists in South Africa, Kenya, Mozambique, the United States, the United Kingdom, the Netherlands, and Germany discovered that if temperatures were 1.2°C cooler, a multiyear drought would not be possible. A conservative estimate found that climate change makes such droughts about 100 times more likely.[47]

Attribution studies help people understand how extreme weather is influenced by climate change. Reporters can interview study authors and talk with outside experts to understand how significant and relevant such research is, given that attribution studies typically aren't peer reviewed.

As with any study, remember that they can provide important updates, context, and understanding about aspects of human-caused climate change. Studies usually do not give solutions or offer ways communities can use the information in the future. That's where reporters can add nuance by asking sources how an attribution study can help people and regions prepare for future extreme weather brought on by human-driven climate change. The answer may lead to future stories to pursue. From my climate editor's perch, I don't think it's enough to put information out without helping people understand how the data can benefit communities, such as by helping them respond to and adapt to climate change.

Common Terms

As you read studies on climate change, some key terms will become familiar and eventually second nature. Just remember your audience probably isn't poring over these studies, so for many of them, these phrases still constitute jargon and require explanation. Such terms include the following:

Adaptation: This term, like *mitigation*, usually isn't explained in stories but should be. *Adaptation* refers to how societal systems can adjust to reduce the impacts of climate change and how to prepare for the long term.

Carbon footprint: The total amount of GHG emissions that can be directly or indirectly attributed to an individual, organization, or product. Some fossil fuel industries have used the term to try to deflect attention from their role in driving climate change by emphasizing individual responsibility. For example, in the early 2000s British Petroleum had a carbon footprint calculator for people to figure out their impact on the climate. The term *carbon footprint* remains popular, but it is rarely defined and can be misused.

Carbon sequestration: The process of capturing and storing carbon dioxide, either naturally through trees and soil, for example, or through technology that pulls carbon dioxide out of the atmosphere and stores it. Carbon capture and storage (CCS) is the technological approach to capturing and storing carbon.

Carbon sink: Any natural or artificial system that absorbs more carbon dioxide (CO_2) from the atmosphere than it releases. The IPCC considers sinks a way to reduce overall GHG concentrations. Forests and oceans, for example, capture tremendous amounts of carbon dioxide through processes such as photosynthesis and oceanic absorption. Artificial carbon sinks involve technologies like CCS, where CO_2 is captured from sources such as power plants and stored underground. Fossil fuel industries already market the ability to do this. But there are many questions about the viability of CCS that range from storage risks to the costs and whether it can be scaled to a size that could make a substantial impact in lowering emissions.

Climate justice: The equitable distribution of the benefits and burdens of human-caused climate change and climate policies. Writing about the implications of climate change for vulnerable communities and the concept of environmental justice is a must in climate reporting.

Climate models: Complex mathematical simulations of Earth's climate system, used to project future climate scenarios based on varying levels of GHG emissions and temperature scenarios. Models often get referenced, but rarely is there a brief explanation of how models work or their limitations.

Feedback loops: Processes that can amplify or dampen the effects of climate change. Positive feedback loops accelerate climate change, and negative feedback loops slow it down. This term is not used frequently, and when it is, there isn't an explanation of how feedback loops work or their role in climate.

Greenhouse gases (GHGs): Gases, including carbon dioxide, methane, and nitrous oxide, that trap heat in Earth's atmosphere and contribute to climate change.

Mitigation: Efforts to reduce planet-warming gases or enhance carbon sinks, such as the ocean. The term *mitigation* is often used in stories but is rarely defined. Be specific about such efforts before using the word *mitigation*.

Planet-warming gases or heat-trapping gases: Two alternative ways to refer to GHGs and their role in climate change.

Tipping points: Critical thresholds in Earth's climate system that, once crossed, could be irreversible and potentially lead to catastrophic changes. This popular phrase must be explained along with its implications.

Essential Reading and Resources

National Climate Assessment (NCA): The gold standard for the latest climate information in the United States is updated roughly every four years. It's the preeminent scientific source about the risks, impacts, and responses to climate change for every region in the country. The last assessment was published in 2023, with a specific focus on climate equity. https://nca2023.globalchange.gov/

SciLine: From the American Association for the Advancement of Science, this site connects journalists with experts in scientific fields, including climate change. SciLine's Quick Facts are an excellent resource for reporters on deadline, and they cover everything from heat and droughts to extreme rainfall and wildfires. It's easy-to-access information that helps reporters make climate connections in stories. https://www.sciline.org/resource-list/climate-communication/

IPCC's Sixth Assessment Synthesis Report: This report, released in 2023, summarizes climate change knowledge and the impacts and risks of climate change globally. It also covers adaptation to climate change and what can be done. https://www.ipcc.ch/report/ar6/syr/

World Weather Attribution Reporting Guide for Journalists: The guide includes the science behind attribution for an extreme event, how it's done, language reporters can use even when there is no study, and more. https://www.worldweatherattribution.org/wp-content/uploads/ENG_WWA-Reporting-extreme-weather-and-climate-change.pdf

What Journalists Need to Know When Covering Climate Change: NPR's climate team compiled the essentials for reporters on climate change and periodically updates it with the latest information. If you're on deadline, the guide is an excellent tool. https://training.npr.org/2024/07/23/what-journalists-need-to-know-when-covering-climate-change/

A Field Guide for Science Writers: The Official Guide of the National Association of Science Writers, edited by Deborah Blum, Mary Knudson, Robin Marantz Henig: This guide offers practical advice on writing clear, accurate, and engaging science journalism. For climate reporters, it provides essential tools for explaining complex scientific concepts (such as climate science) to the public. The guide also covers a wide range of writing skills, including doing investigations and writing features.

The Craft of Science Writing: Selections from the Open Notebook, by Siri Carpenter: Experienced science writers offer deep insights into science journalism in this essay collection. It includes practical tips on interviewing scientists, structuring stories, and translating technical language into accessible prose—all critical skills for climate reporters who need to effectively communicate the intricacies of climate science to broad audiences while maintaining scientific integrity.

All We Can Save: Truth, Courage, and Solutions for the Climate Crisis, edited by Ayana Elizabeth Johnson and Katharine Wilkinson: This anthology brings together essays, poems, and reflections by women climate leaders. It emphasizes diversity of voices and perspectives, which is crucial for journalists aiming to report on the broad, global impacts of climate change.

The Sixth Extinction: An Unnatural History, by Elizabeth Kolbert: Kolbert's Pulitzer Prize–winning book explores the ongoing mass extinction driven by human activity, especially climate change. It demonstrates how journalists can balance detailed scientific reporting with compelling storytelling.

CHAPTER 3

Essential Policy

> "Climate change is the single greatest threat to a sustainable future but, at the same time, addressing the climate challenge presents a golden opportunity to promote prosperity, security and a brighter future for all."
>
> —Ban Ki-Moon, former secretary-general of the UN

Nicholas Kusnetz, a reporter at *Inside Climate News*, started his story "Why the Paris Climate Agreement Might be Doomed to Fail" with a poker game of sorts. This game happened before countries agreed to the landmark international accord in 2015. Poker chips represented reductions in emissions. "The goal was to avoid 'catastrophe,' which players could achieve by contributing some of their chips to a collective pot," Kusnetz wrote.[1]

Players had to agree to a shared goal for the pot by pledging their contributions to cut emissions. If catastrophe was avoided, the players would get a substantial payout. The central question, Kusnetz reported, was to figure out whether the Paris Agreement's system of having countries review each other's pledges to reduce emissions would get countries to "make steeper emissions cuts."[2] Scott Barrett, an economist at Columbia University who researches international cooperation, designed the game to determine the likelihood of the agreement's success. Spoiler alert: The game revealed the system didn't work, hence the headline for Kusnetz's story.

Climate policy, like so much about reporting on the warming world, is complicated. It can be overwhelming to weave historical context into stories, let alone understand the timeline of significant international, national, and local agreements. I admit to being a total policy nerd and have often found myself reporting on environmental policies (public land regulations, forest policies, and climate) throughout my reporting career. As a climate editor, I've seen some reporters get excited about covering policy while others have wanted to cover anything but that. I get it. Environmental and climate policy is complex, but it's foundational to understanding how the world got to where it is when confronting human-driven climate change.

I'm highlighting Kusnetz's reporting on the Paris Agreement because it's an excellent example of how to cover climate policy—and the nuance of it—in a smart, approachable way. He could have started off explaining what the Paris Agreement aimed to do and whether that would be successful. Instead, he found an unexpected way into the story through an economist who was trying to understand the dynamics of international cooperation. Kusnetz didn't stop there, though. He asked the fundamental question: Were there examples of international treaties that have worked? He discovered there was one: the Montreal Protocol, an international treaty that got countries to reduce ozone-harming pollution in the 1980s.

That's where the story got more complex, says Kusnetz, because a chasm exists between the protocol and the Paris Agreement. The Montreal Protocol dealt with a class of chemicals that was "somewhat niche in the economy"—chlorofluorocarbons used in refrigeration and air conditioning—"whereas the Paris Agreement is about products that are like the absolute center of the economy," says Kusnetz. He addressed that "imperfect comparison" through expert interviews and analysis to make a nuanced policy story understandable. Starting the story with the game, he says, was "a way to try to get the reader into the story, because it got into the issues directly." It was more engaging "than just saying, 'This is the Paris Agreement and this is what's working or what's not working about it.'"[3]

Incredible stories lurk in the history of climate and environmental policy. I say *incredible* because stories such as Kusnetz's provide meaningful context, helping us see how we got to where we are and what could come. Yet adding this historical context takes time to research, a challenge for reporters who often face the pressure of looming deadlines. However, that history can inform questions to ask while also helping people understand how climate policy works in theory and in practice.

Journalists who recently started reporting on climate change are probably most familiar with the Paris Agreement. However, much earlier treaties and frameworks led to this collective action to reduce planet-warming pollution. This chapter gives an overview of that path, highlighting the foremost international treaties and national policies. This chapter also covers how states and cities are approaching climate policies, which is great for local reporters to know and follow over time. The journey begins with a brief history of what led to the world's first climate actions in the early 1960s and 1970s to the present day.

Climate policy continues to emerge across a multifaceted political landscape. Historic laws such as the Clean Air Act (CAA) and the Endangered Species Act (ESA) are being challenged even as global temperatures continue to rise. The federal agencies tasked with implementing these hallmark laws are also under pressure. The chapter examines evolving policy in the United States and landmark environmental policies that can serve as a reference guide in reporting.

A Brief History of Climate Policy

Mauna Loa rises from the Pacific Ocean, pushing 13,681 feet of rock skyward to form more than half of the Big Island of Hawaii. Long Mountain, as it's known, is among the most active volcanoes found on the planet. Mauna Loa has been a barometer of Earth's health for decades. The caldera summit houses the world's longest-running climate monitoring station, interrupted only once, in 2022, when an eruption rendered the site inoperable for several months.[4]

In 1958, Charles David Keeling with the Scripps Institution of Oceanography began collecting daily air samples at the observatory at Mauna Loa to understand Earth's atmosphere and how it could be changing. Keeling's work revealed something both awe inspiring and sobering: a consistent rise in the concentration of carbon dioxide in the atmosphere. His discovery became the bedrock of climate change science. The daily global atmospheric carbon dioxide concentration record is known as the Keeling Curve.[5]

Early indications of rising carbon dioxide levels from atop Mauna Loa warned of a dangerous path ahead. Concern among scientists grew in the late 1960s as carbon dioxide readings from the site steadily climbed. Early indications pointed to the burning of fossil fuels as the primary culprit, and Earth's climate was being altered.

During this time, a global effort to use space technology to better understand weather got under way. The UN General Assembly adopted Resolution 1721 in 1961, marking an early step in international cooperation on science. The measure was broadly about peacefully exploring and sharing outer space between countries, but it acknowledged the "marked progress for meteorological science and technology opened up by the advances in outer space." The assembly realized the global benefit of international cooperation in "weather research and analysis." The resolution called on countries, the World Meteorological Organization (WMO), and other agencies to conduct a comprehensive study to advance atmospheric science and technology. The goal? Understand the "basic physical forces affecting climate and the possibility of large-scale weather modification."[6]

Countries were asked to develop better weather monitoring systems. The resolution requested the WMO to work with other international agencies, including the UN Educational, Scientific and Cultural Organization, and non-governmental organizations, such as the International Council of Scientific Unions (ICSU), to submit a report to the UN detailing how to set up a global meteorological monitoring system.[7]

The WMO World Weather Watch and the WMO-ICSU Global Atmospheric Research Program were launched to enhance global cooperation in weather observation and to advance understanding of large-scale atmospheric dynamics. Although these programs were not specifically designed to study rising carbon dioxide levels, they contributed to the broader knowledge of atmospheric processes that would later aid in climate research.[8]

In 1974, the United Nations gathered for a special session of the General Assembly. A counter idea had emerged to global warming, showing Earth cooling and heading toward an Ice Age.[9] Winters in the Northern Hemisphere had been bitterly cold, and drought had beset the Sahel region from West Africa to Ethiopia.[10] Some scientists argued that natural climate variability could be the reason. Headlines stoked a narrative that cast doubts on whether global warming was happening, fueling early climate denialism.

The scientific debate caught the United Nations' attention again in the late 1970s. This time, the assembly asked the WMO to study climate change specifically.[11] Years later, the final report described global cooling as baseless, affirming the scientific consensus that greenhouse gases contribute to global warming.[12]

The 1974 UN gathering also pushed the WMO to convene a global conference on climate five years later. The World Climate Conference brought together hundreds of experts and scientists. Fifty-three countries and twenty-four international organizations, from the World Health Organization to the UN Environment Programme, met in Geneva, Switzerland. In the end, a group of 100 invited global experts issued a declaration to the world recognizing the "all-pervading influence of climate on human society."[13] They declared that "it is now urgently necessary for the nations of the world" and acknowledged three actions:

- To "take full advantage of man's present knowledge of climate";
- To "take steps to improve significantly that knowledge";
- To "foresee and prevent potential man-made changes in climate that might be adverse to the well-being of humanity."[14]

The 1974 meeting was one of many profound milestones along the international climate policy timeline, alongside the signing of agreements and formation of government entities. Another such important moment was the creation of the Intergovernmental Panel on Climate Change (IPCC) in 1988.[15] The IPCC began the same year that NASA scientist James Hansen testified before the US Senate, stating that human-caused climate change had begun.

The IPCC assesses the latest climate change science through its working groups, generating comprehensive assessments that form the backbone of international talks. The assessments have provided a window into the potential impacts of climate change, including the heightened risks of extreme weather and disasters.

The IPCC has published six massive science assessments between 1990 and 2023. The Sixth Assessment concluded with a synthesis report that underscored the urgency of the climate crisis, what the world can expect in the years to come, and what needs to be done.[16] These in-depth reports are a valuable reference tool in guiding climate change reporting. They are also pivotal for future global climate policy and action needed to rapidly lower planet-warming pollution in the years to come.

Equity in Climate Agreements

The global effort to lower planet-warming pollution has been littered with starts and stops, mired at times in intense political debate that has been front-page news. Over the years, countries have signed several substantial international agreements to meet the challenges of climate change, including agreeing to an international framework in 1992 known as the United Nations Framework Convention on Climate Change (UNFCCC). The convention has three primary aspirations: reduce emissions, adapt to climate change, and provide funding, or climate finance, for both efforts. However, global agreements can be hard. Some are legally binding, but without a single international court dedicated to addressing global issues, agreements are tough to enforce. Getting countries to unite to address climate change is a tricky and delicate business that relies on a foundation of holding each other accountable for meeting emission reduction targets.

Inequity introduces additional layers of difficulty to crafting effective climate policy. Developing countries have contributed the least to global warming yet are experiencing some of the worst impacts of human-caused climate change. Developed countries are the biggest polluters. So a fundamental question that undergirds much of the debate is whether developed countries have a financial responsibility to help other countries. Generally, through the UNFCCC, countries recognize the need for climate finance, and there has been progress in recent years.

Friction has historically existed because of the economic disparities between countries. Developed countries such as the United States, Canada, Australia, and many European nations have spent decades burning fossil fuels to industrialize and build their robust economies. By doing that, they have contributed the most to global warming.

Countries that are now striving to industrialize and build their economies are being asked to forgo the carbon-emitting practices that fueled the growth of today's economic giants; at the same time, they are experiencing the most dire impacts from climate change. South Sudan, for example, has been among the fastest-warming places in the world.[17] In the past thirty years, temperatures have increased by more than twice the global average. More than 60 percent of the population suffers from extreme hunger.[18] Climate change has brought devastating floods, while other regions face extreme drought.

Pakistan has contributed less than 1 percent of global greenhouse gas emissions, yet it is one of the countries most affected by climate change.[19] It's considered highly vulnerable to climate change and among the least prepared to handle it. In 2022, Pakistan experienced what UN secretary-general António Guterres called a monsoon "on steroids."[20] Colossal rainfall brought floods and landslides that affected 33 million people and sent food prices soaring.[21]

Climate disparities between countries will only intensify as temperatures warm, making it urgent for countries to keep their promises on plans to decrease emissions. Where does international responsibility lie? In recent years, acknowledgment of the inequities of climate change—long debated—has led to action. At the Conference of the Parties (COP) in 2022 in Egypt, countries established the "loss and damages" fund to help the most vulnerable countries deal with the effects of climate change.[22] Countries took another significant step in 2024 at global climate negotiations in Baku, Azerbaijan. At COP29, countries agreed to triple climate finance from $100 billion to $300 billion annually by 2035 "to help countries protect their people and economies against climate disasters, and share in the vast benefits of the clean energy boom."[23]

However, some delegates from developing countries at COP29 were upset by the outcome, arguing that $300 billion a year from industrialized countries pales in comparison to what vulnerable nations actually need to confront climate change.[24] It's important to clarify that the $300 billion goal includes both public and private dollars that would go through any fund or channel, whether development banks or climate funds. Debates over climate finance and the vast inequities among countries experiencing significant impacts from climate change will continue to be a major topic for journalists to understand and report on.

At the same time, global discussions of international climate policy will continue to evolve through the years, and the historical context of how climate policy has developed will be crucial for stories. That's why every reporter covering this issue needs to understand landmark international climate agreements, such as the Kyoto Protocol and the Paris Agreement. What follows is a breakdown of some of the most essential climate treaties, policies, and meetings that have set the stage for the global community's ongoing effort to reduce emissions.

United Nations Framework Convention on Climate Change

The UN General Assembly began in late 1990 to develop a negotiating framework for how countries could work together to address climate change. The assembly formed the Intergovernmental Negotiating Committee. Over five sessions, more than 150 countries discussed reducing emissions, from targets to timelines.[25] Countries also considered responsibilities that should be shouldered by developed countries and developing countries, along with ways to share technology.

Two years later, the international community approved a legally binding framework for global negotiations at the 1992 Earth Summit in Rio de Janeiro. A treaty established the United Nations Framework Convention on Climate Change (UNFCCC). Countries recognized climate change as a serious threat to life on the planet and agreed, in theory, to limit average global temperatures. Countries unanimously acknowledged that future agreements and policies would be needed to stabilize temperatures and that adaptation would be necessary to deal with the inevitable impacts of climate change.[26] The UNFCCC also recognized the need for climate financing to help developing countries.

The convention took effect in 1994, establishing a structure for international climate negotiations known as the COP. The 198 countries that signed the UNFCCC are known as the Parties, and they meet at least yearly to consider strategies to address climate change.[27] The COP reviews, prepares, negotiates, and implements policy through regular sessions, considering everything from emission reduction strategies to how much funding should be allocated to countries that shoulder the worst effects of warming.

The UNFCCC secretariat leads the global response to climate change. Around the world, 450 people work at UN Climate Change, which is led by an executive secretary.[28] In the early days the secretariat facilitated climate negotiations between countries. Today, the organization supports multiple entities that work to implement the UNFCCC, the Kyoto Protocol, and the Paris Agreement.

Support comes through technical expertise, analysis, and reviews of climate change information that Parties report. The secretariat is also tasked with keeping a registry of each country's plan to reduce emissions, known as Nationally Determined Contributions (NDCs), which was established as part of the Paris Agreement.[29]

Journalists are probably most familiar with UN Climate Change through the annual COPs. COPs are by far the largest and most prominent gatherings held by the secretariat. On average some 25,000 people attend COPs, including reporters.[30]

The Kyoto Protocol

The world's first international treaty to reduce greenhouse gas emissions was signed in 1997 at the Third COP in Kyoto, Japan. Heralded as a milestone in climate policy, delegates at the COP shook hands and hugged as the Kyoto Protocol was adopted.

The Kyoto Protocol required developed countries to reduce emissions to at least 5 percent below 1990 levels between 2008 and 2012.[31] It remains one of the few legally binding global emissions agreements, which eighty-three countries initially signed.[32] Even major emitters such as the United States and China signed. However, the United States ultimately refused to ratify the treaty, weakening its global impact.

The Kyoto Protocol officially took effect in 2005 and introduced the Clean Development Mechanism, a cap-and-trade system allowing developed countries to earn credits by investing in emission reduction projects in developing nations.[33] The Adaptation Fund was also established under the Kyoto Protocol in 2001 to support climate adaptation projects and programs in vulnerable developing countries.[34] Initially, money was mobilized through a percentage made on carbon credits through the Clean Development Mechanism, and millions of dollars have gone to adaptation projects over the years.[35] The fund is no longer part of the Protocol and is carried out through the Paris Agreement.[36]

The effectiveness of the Kyoto Protocol remains debated, with criticisms focusing on its limited scope and the failure of some signatory countries to meet their targets.

The Paris Agreement

The atmosphere in Paris at COP21 in December 2015 was electric as French foreign minister and president of COP21 Laurent Fabius gaveled a green hammer down to signal the adoption of the Paris Agreement and the end of two weeks of intense negotiations. Delegates erupted into applause; many embraced, and others cried.

The Paris Agreement signified a historic milestone in international diplomacy as 195 nations agreed to reduce greenhouse gas emissions to limit global warming. The legally binding agreement set the stage for unprecedented actions and investments toward a low-carbon, resilient, and sustainable future. "The Paris Agreement is a monumental triumph for people and our planet," exclaimed UN secretary-general Ban Ki-moon at COP21. "In the face of an unprecedented challenge, you have demonstrated unprecedented leadership," Ban Ki-moon said. "You have worked collaboratively to achieve something that no one nation could achieve alone. This is a resounding success for multilateralism."[37]

The Paris Agreement set a goal to limit global warming to 1.5°C above preindustrial levels and well below 2°C (3.6°F).[38] That goal is getting further out of reach; the planet's ten warmest years on record since 1850 have all happened in the last decade.[39] Countries also agreed to submit Nationally Determined Contributions (NDCs), detailed plans that set emission reduction targets to limit warming. NDCs are updated every five years.

The Paris Agreement also established the Global Stocktake as a mechanism to assess collective progress toward achieving the accord's long-term goals.[40] The Global Stocktake happens every five years, and 2023 marked the first comprehensive assessment of the world's progress in addressing climate change, adapting to its impacts, and providing the necessary financial support to developing countries. That initial report found that the world is not on track to meet the temperature goals outlined in the Paris Agreement, underscoring the urgent need to scale up efforts to reduce greenhouse gas emissions. Without significant changes, the report concluded that the world

LANDMARK CLIMATE MOMENTS

1988 — IPCC FORMED
The Intergovernmental Panel on Climate Change assesses scientific knowledge on climate change. The IPCC has completed six assessments examining all aspects of climate change including impacts and future risks.

1992 — UNFCCC CREATED
The United Nations Framework Convention on Climate Change laid the foundation for future international negotiations and agreements on climate change. It was adopted at the Earth Summit in Rio de Janeiro.

1997 — THE KYOTO PROTOCOL
This international treaty requires countries to establish targets to reduce greenhouse gas emissions. For industrialized countries, targets are binding.

2009 — COPENHAGEN ACCORD
This non-legally binding agreement, acknowledges the need to keep global temperature rise below 2°C above pre-industrial levels. Major developing countries including China committed to mitigation actions.

2015 — THE PARIS AGREEMENT
The Agreement aims to limit global warming to below 2°C, preferably to 1.5°C, compared to pre-industrial levels. Each country has a plan to lower emissions.

2020 — CLIMATE AMBITION SUMMIT
World leaders gathered virtually to mark the five year anniversary of the Paris Agreement by calling for ambitious updated policies, adaptation plans and stronger commitments in country-level plans to lower emissions.

2021 — THE GLASGOW COMPACT
Countries asked to commit to keeping global average temperature rise limited to 1.5 C. Developed countries agreed to give $100 billion yearly to developing nations. Countries asked to phase down coal power and fossil fuel subsidies.

2022 — LOSS AND DAMAGE FUND
Climate change means countries will suffer from droughts, floods, heatwaves and other climate disasters. Countries agreed at COP27 to a fund to help countries most vulnerable to climate change pay for losses and damages.

was on a path toward 2.5°C of warming by the end of the century, far above the target of 1.5°C.[41]

The assessment's outcomes were intended to inform and enhance future NDCs and ensure that global efforts are sufficient to meet the Paris Agreement's targets.

The Paris Agreement promised transformation and hope that went beyond recognizing present responsibilities to limit carbon emissions. Countries were called on to consider the long view and the impact decisions made at that time would have on future generations. "We have made history together," said Christiana Figueres, who was the executive secretary of UNFCCC at the time. "It is an agreement of conviction, of solidarity with the most vulnerable. It is an agreement of long-term vision, for we have to turn this agreement into an engine of safe growth."[42]

Mixed Progress and Challenges

The Paris Agreement persuaded nearly all countries, including major emitters such as the United States and

Figure 3-1. Timeline of Significant Global Climate Policies
The global response to climate change has been punctuated with critical policy moments and decisions, as outlined in this timeline, from the formation of the Intergovernmental Panel on Climate Change to the landmark Paris Agreement. Courtesy of the author.

China, to agree on individual emission targets. Although the agreement marked a significant milestone in global climate policy, its implementation has been inconsistent. Countries set their own targets, the NDCs, but the absence of legal consequences for failing to meet these targets has led to mixed results. Failing to provide an NDC or updating one can mean a country falls out of compliance, and they can be called out by the COP. Other countries could shame nations that fail to provide a plan to reduce emissions.

According to the United Nations Emissions Gap Report, global emissions have not declined quickly enough to stay within the agreed-upon temperature limits.[43] In fact, emissions are projected to increase, underscoring the challenges of achieving the Paris Agreement's goals.

In the United States, efforts to reduce emissions have been inconsistent, partly because of political shifts. The United States originally joined the Paris Agreement under President Barack Obama, a Democrat, who set ambitious targets to reduce greenhouse gas emissions by 50 to 52 percent below 2005 levels by 2030. The US plan included decarbonizing key sectors, such as electricity, buildings, industry, and transportation, to achieve 100 percent carbon-free electricity by 2035.[44] The plan also emphasized the role of agriculture, forestry, and land use in sequestering carbon.

However, the political landscape changed with the election in 2016 of President Donald Trump, a Republican and a climate change skeptic. He withdrew the United States from the Paris Agreement, rolling back environmental protections and stalling progress on climate action. The United States rejoined the agreement in 2021 under President Joe Biden, a Democrat, but such political flip-flopping can hinder the implementation of consistent climate policies.

Under the Biden administration, the US Congress in 2021 passed the Bipartisan Infrastructure Deal, which, among many other goals, promised to reduce greenhouse gas emissions by investing billions of dollars to develop the nation's electric vehicle infrastructure, improve public transit, and get more renewable energy flowing to the electric grid.[45]

The next year, Biden signed the Inflation Reduction Act (IRA) into law, the country's most significant climate legislation. This multi-billion-dollar package aimed to put US greenhouse gas emissions on a steady decline by providing financial incentives to transition away from fossil fuels. It signaled to the international community that the United States was committed to its climate responsibilities. However, the Climate Action Tracker, an independent scientific project that tracks government climate action, warns that the United States may fall short of its emission targets without additional policy action.[46]

The Bipartisan Infrastructure Deal and IRA spurred an economic transition from fossil fuels to clean energy. However, the reelection of President Trump in 2024 calls into question the future of these policies and climate investments. Journalists need to thoroughly follow and report on any changes to existing climate policies as new administrations take office and the political makeup of Congress shifts. Likewise, they will want to pay attention to new laws and regulations.

America's challenges are not unique. Australia, for example, also experienced political shifts that affected its climate policy. After a change in government in 2022, Australia updated its NDC to target a 43 percent reduction in emissions by 2030 compared with 2005 levels, improving its overall climate action rating from "highly insufficient" to "insufficient."[47] Like the United States, Australia would need additional policies to meet its targets, including reconsidering future planned fossil fuel projects.

Other major emitters have shown similarly mixed results. Russia, one of the world's top fossil fuel producers, committed to limiting greenhouse gas emissions by 2030 to 70 percent of 1990 levels.[48] However, since its invasion of Ukraine, Russia's progress has been rated as "highly insufficient" by the Climate Action Tracker, with emission reductions projected to fall far short of its targets.[49]

Saudi Arabia, another top global oil producer, updated its Paris Agreement commitment in 2021 to achieve net-zero emissions by 2060. Despite this pledge, the country continues to expand oil production, and meaningful climate action remains limited. Saudi Arabia's emissions peaked in 2015 but have not significantly declined since, and the country's commitment includes a "get-out clause" if international climate policies reduce its oil exports.[50]

India faces the dual challenge of lifting millions out of poverty while addressing climate change. The country has significantly increased its renewable energy capacity, particularly in solar power, and aims for net-zero emissions by 2070.[51] However, its expanded use of coal power plants raises concerns about its ability to meet this target.

Despite the challenges, the Paris Agreement has had successes. The European Union has implemented policies that could allow it to meet and even exceed its NDC target of reducing emissions by 55 percent by 2030.[52] The EU's "Fit for 55" package obligates member states to achieve these goals, although continued investment in liquefied natural gas and the lack of an updated NDC reflecting new targets remain issues.[53]

Each country's NDCs have indicated that they are insufficient to close the emission gap. At the writing of this book the world has remained on a path to exceed 1.5°C of global warming. To limit warming to 1.5°C, countries must cut greenhouse gas emissions by 42 percent by 2030 and by 57 percent by 2035.[54] If countries fail to do this, the world will be on track for a temperature increase of 2.6 to 3.1°C (~ 4.6 to 5.5°F). Transformation across all facets of life, from transportation and agriculture to financial systems, will need to happen to even come within striking distance of limiting global warming.[55]

Making Climate Policy Effective

The Paris Agreement has no real incentives for achieving success other than collective benefits if all parties work together to keep warming well below 2°C. There are also no penalties if countries don't meet their promises, although other countries could shame nations that fail to follow their NDC. But carrots and sticks have worked in the past.

The Montreal Protocol is one example of an international treaty that motivated countries through both incentives and penalties to respond to a growing hole in the ozone. Chemicals known as chlorofluorocarbons (CFCs)—the stuff used in refrigerators, air conditioning units, and even hair spray—contributed to a hole in the ozone. In 1987, countries adopted a plan to phase out CFCs by committing to hard limits. The plan banned the trading of CFCs. The market shrank as more countries committed to the Montreal Protocol.

The treaty offered incentives: a new market to replace CFCs. Technological innovation gave chemical companies certainty that they wouldn't lose business. More importantly, the protocol established a path for developed countries to pay the costs for less developed countries to meet the agreement. Pairing carrots and sticks "pressed countries not only to join but to comply: In the jargon of international diplomacy, the protocol was self-enforcing."[56]

However, Montreal and Paris addressed fundamentally different problems: Montreal focused on a particular issue that had a technological solution, whereas countries signed on to Paris to address an entire global industrial system. The success of the Paris Agreement rests on countries pushing each other to reduce their emissions and the feedback loop created by the NDCs and the GAP report. Countries ultimately must hold each other accountable if they fail to meet emission reduction goals.

The Glasgow Climate Compact

COP26 concluded in Glasgow, Scotland, in 2021 with a new package of requests for countries to build resilience to climate change, reduce greenhouse gas emissions, and provide funds to do so. The Glasgow Climate Compact also asked countries to phase down coal power and end government subsidies for fossil fuels.[57]

In theory that appeared to work, but in practice it was a different story. For example, in 2022, subsidies for global fossil fuel use more than doubled compared with 2021.[58] Oil and gas remained expensive and volatile because of a sharp decline in gas from Russia to Europe brought on by Russia's invasion of Ukraine.

As 2022 proved, international conflict can upend climate policy compacts. That's problematic when the success of the compact relies on countries meeting their promises. International climate policy may seem wonky and complex, yet it offers an array of ideas for stories that are often left untold. By knowing the key foundational agreements and history, journalists can unlock new story ideas and lines of questioning that can help illuminate future stories.

National Climate Policy

Most countries signed the Paris Agreement, which set the global framework for collective climate action. Each country was required to build a roadmap for lowering climate-warming pollution by a designated year.

These plans, the NDCs, vary widely in commitments and approaches. As mentioned, they are updated and reviewed every five years to see how the global emissions gap is closing. However, we have seen that NDCs are not enough to limit global warming to 1.5°C, let alone 2°C.[59] Yet they inform how countries approach climate policy and take climate action.

What follows is an overview to help journalists understand the complexity and scope of climate policies and approaches in different countries. Reporters can compare various nations' approaches to climate change, which can turn into distinctive stories. As a climate editor and a journalist, I have long appreciated stories that put national strategies, and even local developments, in an international context.

How climate policy looks in the United States differs from how China approaches reducing emissions or how African countries set policies. Economics, politics, and societal and cultural values make each plan unique. It's important to keep in mind that such national strategies will change over time, but the general idea remains: These policies are meant to reduce planet-warming pollution. Still, questions about the effectiveness of a national climate policy or its unintended consequences can lead to stories that are, at their core, about accountability.

For journalists, knowing what climate policies already exist and how they have worked—or failed—provides context while informing new story angles. Following developments on such strategies can lead to truly impactful accountability journalism.

National Climate Policy Strategies

Governments have multiple tools to lower planet-warming pollution and limit global warming, from divesting public funds away from fossil fuel companies to improving public transportation. Below, we'll review some of the most common strategies: carbon pricing, renewable energy mandates and incentives (including subsidies and tax breaks), fuel emission standards, and policies to protect forests and reforest land where trees have already been stripped away.[60]

Carbon Pricing

Sweden has the world's oldest and highest carbon tax, which was introduced in 1991 alongside an existing energy tax. Polluters pay for what they emit. The tax gradually increased over time as Sweden's greenhouse gas emissions steadily declined. The carbon tax remains a cornerstone of the country's climate policies and generates considerable revenue for the country's general budget. By following a polluter-pays principle, Sweden's tax has led to new clean technologies, improved energy efficiency, and increased renewable energy.[61]

Emissions trading systems and cap-and-trade are another form of carbon pricing—terms that are often used interchangeably. Countries establish the upper limit of a pollutant such as carbon dioxide. Companies can get permits (also called allowances) to emit a certain amount of carbon dioxide that can't exceed the limit.

Depending on the country, permits are sometimes free or obtained through an auction. Companies that emit less than their allotted amount can sell their remaining allowance to a company that plans to exceed its permit. The collective goal is to not exceed the cap, which can be adjusted downward, leading to fewer emissions.

The European Union has the world's most extensive emissions trading system, which started in 2005. The system covers some 12,000 power stations and industrial plants in thirty-one countries.[62] South Korea started an emissions trading system in 2015 by capping emissions from major sectors, with modest success.[63]

Carbon pricing aims to reduce total emissions, generate revenue for countries, invest in developing clean technologies, or help compensate communities that fossil fuels have long impacted.

Renewable Energy Mandates and Incentives

Many countries have worked to lower greenhouse gas emissions by requiring or incentivizing a shift to renewable energy sources such as wind and solar. Feed-in tariffs are a common national approach to remove anxiety for companies entering the renewable energy market by guaranteeing a fixed price for solar and wind fed to the grid.

China used feed-in tariffs for more than a decade to subsidize new solar and wind projects.[64] It worked so well that in 2021 the country halted the program because it was too far in arrears to pay subsidies.[65] China has become a world leader in developing renewable energy, a significant shift from a country that had long relied on fossil fuels as its main source of electricity.[66] Although emissions have continued to rise in China because of its reliance on coal, the country plans to get about 25 percent of its energy from renewables by 2030 and estimates its emissions will also peak that same year.[67]

India has taken a similar approach to China's, infusing renewable energy incentives into the country to encourage a renewable energy transition. The country wants 50 percent of its energy to come from non–fossil fuel sources by 2030—an updated goal in its 2021 NDC document.[68] India's government has offered tax breaks, subsidized loans, and cheaper land for renewable projects. Such incentives work. Solar installations have steadily increased and emissions have started to decline. India has seen a 33 percent reduction in emissions over the fourteen-year period from 2005 to 2019.[69]

Germany instituted a feed-in tariff system in 2000, guaranteeing fixed payments to renewable energy producers for every kilowatt-hour of energy fed into the grid. The price was high enough to guarantee a profit, compelling individuals and businesses to install solar panels, wind turbines, and other renewable energy systems.[70] The policy has been amended over the years, but it remains an example of how a country empowers people to invest in renewable energies. Unsurprisingly, greenhouse gas emissions have declined in Germany as solar and wind have come online.[71]

Fuel Emission Standards

Transportation remains a leading contributor to planet-warming pollution. In the United States, for example, the transportation sector accounts for 29 percent of the country's total greenhouse gas emissions.[72] That may not sound big, but according to the Environmental Protection Agency (EPA), transportation is the largest contributor to greenhouse gas emissions in the country.

Countries set fuel emission standards to limit carbon dioxide and nitrous oxide emissions from tailpipes. Fuel emission standards are often coupled with fuel efficiency standards, meaning a vehicle must achieve a certain number of miles per gallon of fuel.

The US Congress enacted Corporate Average Fuel Economy standards in 1975 to make cars and light trucks go further using less fuel.[73] We can look back now and say, "Hey, that's climate policy." But back then, the standards were meant to reduce the energy needed to power vehicles while also keeping costs at the pump low; lowering greenhouse gas emissions was not at the forefront of policymakers' minds.

The standards have become stricter over time, pushing automakers to make more fuel-efficient cars, which has sparked innovation. Roughly a dozen countries, including China, India, Japan, South Korea, and Mexico, have fuel emission standards. The European Union, which represents dozens of European countries, also has these standards.[74]

Policies to Protect Forests

The Amazon rainforest, often called the lungs of the Earth, covers nearly eight countries. Nearly 20 percent of the world's largest rainforest has been destroyed, sometimes illegally, to make way for cattle ranching, mining, agriculture, and development. Most of the destruction has happened in Brazil.

Scientists predict that if 20 to 25 percent of the Amazon is lost to deforestation, the consequences will be immeasurable to biodiversity and the release of carbon.[75] The rainforest's hydrological cycle relies on the transpiration of tree leaves and evaporation from the surface. Most of the moisture returns to the air when it rains. This cycle happens multiple times when it rains. The Amazon Basin provides 20 percent of the world's freshwater.

The Amazon rainforest, which absorbs and stores carbon dioxide, faces a tipping point. Wildfires and deforestation ebb and flow, depending on who's in political power.[76] Massive reforestation efforts, scientists say, could tip the balance back, especially in Brazil, where 20 percent of the forest has been lost—an area roughly the size of Germany. Forests provide natural ways—carbon sinks—to absorb carbon dioxide.[77] When trees are cleared, carbon dioxide gets released, contributing to global warming. Deforestation, agriculture, and other land uses are responsible for about a quarter of global greenhouse gas emissions.

In 2022, Brazil began the Amazon Protected Areas Program to address deforestation. Early efforts focused on improving environmental laws to protect the Amazon and establishing conservation efforts on large swaths of public land in the rainforest. Protected areas are meant to conserve biodiversity and sustainable uses, and other areas are designated as Indigenous lands and Quilombola territories—sanctuaries for Indigenous communities and traditional populations.[78] The protected areas act as a barrier against deforestation and have helped prevent illegal logging and land grabs. However, both still happen, depending on who leads the country.

Consolidated conservation is a key tool Brazil uses to meet its emission reduction goals established in the Paris Agreement. Other countries also use policy to protect forests.

Indonesia's rainforest—one of the largest in the world—has lost most of its original forests to illegal logging and palm oil plantations. In 2011, the country instituted a moratorium on new licenses needed to clear peatlands and forests. The ban was for land not already allocated for development.[79] In 2019, the country's president made the moratorium permanent.[80]

Sometimes other countries will offer countries financial incentives to reduce emissions, with limited success. In Indonesia's case, Norway promised to pay the country $1 billion if the country could slow emissions generated by deforestation and other land changes in the rainforest. However, Norway never paid the total amount, which led Indonesia to end the arrangement in 2021.[81]

However, the forest clearing moratorium protected forests that came under this designation far better than areas that were left out. The effort reduced only a small amount of climate-warming pollution—about 4 percent.[82] More than half of Indonesia's emissions come from forest areas, and the country plans to reduce emissions by 29 percent by 2030 to meet its commitments under the Paris Agreement.[83]

Reforesting Land

Policy efforts to reforest land—known as afforestation—are another way countries can lower greenhouse gas emissions. Several countries, including

India, Ethiopia, and China, have some form of afforestation policies, which are meant to help sequester carbon dioxide.

Ethiopia, home to some 120 million people, remains one of the world's most vulnerable places to climate change. Poverty, hunger, drought, and natural disasters put the country in a precarious position. Ethiopia has also lost most of its forests over the last fifty years, but there's hope through the country's Green Legacy Initiative.[84] Millions of residents have planted trees. The initiative, which started in 2019, represents an afforestation plan. In just one day in 2019, Ethiopia reported planting 350 million trees.[85] Millions of seedlings for high-value crops such as avocados, mangos, and papayas offer food security and economic value. New trees will help reduce carbon dioxide levels while also helping confront poverty and food security.

China also has a robust afforestation effort under way. The country lost much of its forests to timber harvests. In the late 1970s and 1980s, China launched several initiatives to replant forests, including what's known as the Three-North Shelter Forests program or the Great Green Wall project.[86] People have planted millions of trees to create a windbreak, which also helps to hold back the encroaching Gobi Desert. Another afforestation program targets croplands and encourages farmers to return cropland to forests.

State and Local Climate Policy

Journalists who want to see climate policy in action need only look to their town, city, or state to see how international and national climate policy plays out at home. Cities and states have taken the lead in countries where national climate policy has lagged or been nonexistent.[87] In the United States, for example, President Trump formally began to withdraw the United States from the Paris Agreement in 2019. New York and California governors responded by launching the US Climate Alliance. The message? States were still committed to the Paris goals.

States and cities have historically responded to national political fluctuations with climate policy by acting independently. Some states have focused on storing energy, setting low fuel standards, and building efficiency standards; others have established emissions trading initiatives. Reporters should familiarize themselves with what's happening in their communities to lower greenhouse gas emissions, and that usually starts with an internet search or an artificial intelligence query.

For instance, some cities and states have taken proactive measures to reduce emissions: installing or expanding bicycle infrastructure, as in

Paris and Amsterdam, greening buildings, and planting trees. In 2024, President Biden approved California's plan that new vehicles sold in the state be zero-emission starting in 2035, effectively banning the sale of new gas vehicles. The state has had a special waiver from the EPA to establish tough emissions regulations for decades, and other states have followed California's lead.[88] Such developments lead to excellent stories that help show what's possible as communities transition away from fossil fuels.

Hot Take: *Want to see climate policy in action? Journalists need only look to their town, city, or state to see how international and national climate policy plays out at home. Start by finding out whether your community has a climate action plan.*

One of the best ways for reporters to get started is to focus on a state's legislative session. Every year, state lawmakers consider a wide array of bills, some of which deal with aspects of climate change. Reporters can discover what legislation will be proposed or discussed in an upcoming session and then track what happens in the months to come. Some bills will aim to stop climate action and others will push it forward. Stories that explain the details of a particular climate-related bill before a session starts are invaluable for audiences. Reporters can write updates when there are significant developments and then follow up on the long-term implications of legislative action.

Besides state legislatures, cities and states have multiple tools to implement local climate policy. What follows are some of the common approaches that are used. Understanding these general practices can help reporters spot unique stories to pursue including reporting on lessons from other communities that could help their own.

Climate Action Plans

People continue to flock to the Sonoran Desert—home to Phoenix, Arizona, which is the fifth largest city in the United States—despite brutally hot summers. That's not new for Phoenix, but human-caused climate change has intensified heat waves there. Temperatures have warmed up more than 4°F since the 1970s.

Phoenix city leaders began generating a roadmap in 2015 to make Phoenix sustainable for millions of people by cutting emissions. They created what's known as a climate action plan (CAP), a detailed plan for how a city, state, or region can achieve net-zero emissions.

In 2021, Phoenix passed its 213-page CAP with established benchmarks, including to become a carbon-neutral city by 2050. The CAP pushes the city to use local and utility-scale solar power to make city operations carbon neutral by 2030. The city also has a plan to prepare for thousands of electric vehicles. Other goals include ensuring a 100-year water supply in a region grappling with dwindling water supplies and becoming more resilient to heat.[89]

CAPs aren't new. Since the early 1990s, some US cities have been at the forefront of trying to reduce greenhouse gas emissions. More than 600 city governments have CAPs that include regularly taking inventory of greenhouse gas emissions and setting targets to lower emissions.[90] Instead of top-down federal action, cities and states lead bottom-up efforts that, collectively, can add up to big changes.

CAPs generally establish goals, strategies, and monitoring efforts. The plans include an inventory of emissions from transportation, residential, industry, and government offices. Communities then have a baseline against which to measure future inventories to see how much progress has been made while also predicting where future emissions might go.

Specific targets aim to reduce greenhouse gases by a certain year, usually 2030, and decades-long goals to become net-zero. Strategies for achieving such benchmarks involve switching to renewable energy sources, improving public transportation, making buildings more efficient, and finding ways to make agriculture more sustainable.

In the United States, more than thirty states—California, Oregon, Minnesota, Iowa, and Pennsylvania, to name a few—have CAPs that outline resiliency strategies, economic and social goals, and renewable energy targets.[91] Most plans detail efforts to increase the efficiency of buildings and construction, which are responsible for a large percentage of emissions globally. Insulation, energy-efficient appliances, and use of renewable energy are common ways to increase building efficiency.[92]

Incentivizing a switch to electric vehicles is another common CAP strategy. Plans include creating electric vehicle charging networks and converting municipal vehicle fleets into electric ones, which is what the city of Philadelphia, for example, has been working to do.[93]

Organic waste generates methane and carbon dioxide as it decomposes. Many CAPs establish sustainable waste goals, including reducing food waste. San Francisco, for example, has a robust effort to keep the majority of waste out of landfills through recycling and composting.[94]

Houston, Texas, identified public transportation as a primary focus in its CAP. The city wants to reduce total vehicle miles traveled by 20 percent by 2050 by providing multiple options to access public transportation.[95] Most CAPs have some objective related to transportation because it is one of the leading contributors to global warming.

Renewable energy sources—wind, solar, hydropower, biomass—are hallmarks of CAP plans. Denver, Colorado, for example, plans to decarbonize its electric grid in part through wind and solar and transition to all-electric buildings. Internationally, renewable energy goals are often a centerpiece of policies.[96]

Do Climate Action Plans Work?

CAPs typically do not have any legally binding power to make actions stick. Of the 100 most populated cities in the United States, only forty-five have assessed emissions and set targets to reduce them. The goals generally establish an 80 percent reduction in emissions by 2050, which aligns with IPCC findings. However, goals fall short of plans to limit global warming to 1.5°C.

Reporting on Climate Action Plans

Journalists have an accountability role in finding out whether their city or state has a CAP. If one exists, reporters can look at when the CAP was adopted and whether it's been updated. Some plans also identify how they've reduced emissions. In some instances, CAPs are needed to access federal grants and incentives. Stories that update progress, or the lack of it, are worth doing over time.

CAPs should have timelines to meet goals, resources to implement the plan, and ways to monitor progress. Look at the objectives and find out who is involved. Ask what the city or state has done to meet its CAP goals. Are emissions decreasing? Where are the pressure points? If the city or state doesn't have a plan, ask why. Often, underreported stories lurk in these plans, and this can lead to a line of reporting over time.

Renewable Portfolio Standards

States can also lower planet-warming gases by requiring electric utilities to sell a certain percentage of power from renewable sources such as solar and wind. Renewable portfolio standards (RPSs) help reduce emissions and generate new economic opportunities. Such standards drive the multi-billion-dollar renewable energy market in the United States.

Clean energy standards are also common. Similar to an RPS, the distinction lies in how states define renewables and clean energy. Not all clean energy sources are renewable. For instance, nuclear energy does not emit carbon dioxide, but it's not considered renewable.[97]

California's clean energy standard requires utilities to have 100 percent clean electricity by 2045. The state also has an RPS that establishes that 60 percent of energy will come from renewable sources by 2030.[98] Clean energy can meet the rest of that standard.

RPSs vary by state, but most say that 40 percent of electricity should be generated by solar, wind, and other renewable energy. Renewable energy may be defined differently between states. In addition to wind and solar, Colorado's definition includes biomass, geothermal, and hydroelectric.[99] Hawaii's RPS includes the usual renewable sources and energy from ocean waves and currents.[100]

As always, an internet search is an excellent place to begin determining whether a state has an RPS. The state energy office is usually the place to go for information about the standard.

For example, typing "Oregon's renewable portfolio standard" into an internet search would direct a reporter to the state's Department of Energy and a standard that requires 50 percent of electricity to be from renewable sources by 2040.[101]

Next, look for the timeline. When was the standard set, and has it been changed? In Oregon's case, the RPS was established in 2007, and at that time only 2 percent of the state's power was generated by renewables. Nine years later, the legislature agreed to increase the percentage of renewables to 50 percent by 2040.[102] Such history becomes the practical context in stories.

Reporters can also delve into what qualifies as a renewable source of energy. In Oregon, the list includes wind, solar, wave, landfill gas and biomass, small hydropower, and thermal energy.[103] As I look at that breakdown, my journalist's brain wants to know what thermal energy looks like in Oregon and whether the state is capturing power from waves. Spoiler alert: Research is under way, but so far generating electricity from waves off the Pacific Coast has not happened. In other words, I would want to determine which renewable sources have the largest impact on the renewable energy portfolio.

That's a snapshot of Oregon's RPS, but another question is how the state tracks and certifies renewable sources. Oregon's energy office website makes it easy: The compliance reports are public and worth exploring to see how energy sources are actually doing.

A reporter can follow these same steps in their own state by contacting their state energy office through the media department. They can check out which utilities are involved in the state's RPS, too. Most will be large publicly traded energy companies, but there will also be stakeholders with smaller energy operations. Reporters can also reach out to environmental nonprofits because they usually have different views on how things are going.

Public utility commissions (PUCs) are state agencies that regulate services for electricity, gas, and water. PUCs hold regular public meetings, and their members consider electric rate increases, wielding tremendous power. Reporters who really want to know what's going on with America's energy transition should attend PUC meetings. PUCs often go underreported, and it's here that some of the most fascinating stories are playing out.

Pricing Carbon

Most states in the United States have RPSs, and a handful of states have gone beyond to attach a price on carbon. California, for example, has an aggressive plan to reduce greenhouse gas emissions, and a cap-and-trade program is a significant part of that plan. Like countries that have established such regulations, California set a limit on major global warming pollutants, which decreases over time. Economic incentives exist to develop clean energy sources. Allowances are given that equal the total amounts of pollution allowed, and every year there are fewer allowances, creating a competitive carbon price.[104] Companies that pollute more can buy offsets, usually at auctions.

Twelve states in the eastern United States, including Connecticut, Maine, Massachusetts, New York, and Pennsylvania, joined in creating a regional initiative to limit carbon dioxide emissions from the power industry in each state. Over time, the cap, as in California, lowers regional greenhouse gas emissions. The Regional Greenhouse Gas Initiative allows power plants and other companies to purchase allowances at regular auctions.[105]

Reporters need to educate themselves on how cap-and-trade programs work, how they began, and what's happened since they started. It's a complicated and often politically fraught topic, especially when state legislatures consider implementing such a system. However, stories about efforts to curb carbon dioxide emissions help audiences understand what is being done or could be done to address climate change. So reporters need to follow those legislative debates, pay attention to the auctions, and determine how a state monitors cap-and-trade programs.

Landmark US Environmental Policies

Most of America's environmental statutes came of age in the early 1970s. Rivers in some parts of the country were so polluted they caught fire. Air pollution blanketed some cities. Oversight of large-scale projects that could irreversibly harm ecosystems barely existed. The National Environmental Policy Act (NEPA), the Clean Air Act, and the Endangered Species Act, some of the country's earliest environmental laws, were enacted during that time to clean up waterways, reduce pollution, and protect species on the brink of extinction. Journalists should familiarize themselves with these foundational laws to understand the ways environmental issues such as climate change are addressed. The words *climate change* don't usually appear in the text, but federal agencies and courts use the laws to interpret actions that relate to climate change.

When I taught students about environmental reporting at Arizona State University, we often had conversations about the importance of the ESA or how projects on public lands such as mines must go through an approval process. Unless a journalist takes a law class or studies environmental policy, these issues are not typically covered in a university journalism curriculum. What follows is a reference guide of critical environmental policies—bedrock laws—that every journalist who covers climate change needs to understand. As new administrations come into power, new challenges to these regulations arise. Even though these policies have been in place for decades, they, too, are evolving and being challenged in the face of a warming world.

The National Environmental Policy Act

NEPA was a landmark law signed by President Nixon in 1970, and it requires federal agencies to consider the environmental impacts of any proposed federal actions such as permits for an oil and gas operation or construction on federal lands. Each proposed action includes a detailed and lengthy environmental impact statement, showing potential effects on natural resources and ecosystems.[106]

NEPA mandates that federal agencies consider, analyze, and propose alternatives with less environmental impact, which then get considered after a public comment period. Environmental impact statements must also identify the risks of a proposed project and provide solutions. For example, a mining company must show how it will clean up the operation once it ends.

For journalists, public comments can be a treasure trove of ideas and potential sources about a particular effort. Federal agencies usually host a series of public hearings to explain the project and to hear from stakehold-ers. The public testimony at such hearings can help journalists connect with sources and understand what's at stake. The *Federal Register* regularly pub-lishes hearing schedules and when public comment periods begin and end.

Human-caused climate change is a significant environmental issue that must be evaluated in the NEPA process.[107] Projects on federal lands must consider measures to limit greenhouse gas emissions.[108] For example, emis-sions must be considered in a proposal to drill for oil and gas. NEPA is also used to evaluate and permit clean energy projects, such as wind farms, solar installations, and hydropower facilities.

Federal agencies can be challenged in court over whether compliance with NEPA was adequately met.[109] Environmental groups and individuals have filed lawsuits arguing that an agency didn't follow NEPA. Judges sometimes rule that an agency hasn't followed NEPA and will require the agency to fix the issue.

The largest number of climate-related cases in the United States have to do with NEPA and state equivalents of the policy, mainly in California. "Those are typically suits saying that the environmental review of a particular project, or particular action, did not adequately look at the climate impacts," climate law expert Michael Gerrard says. Journalists will find NEPA and potential lawsuits related to it an excellent area for reporting on over time.

The Council on Environmental Quality administers NEPA and is part of the Executive Office of the President. However, numerous federal agencies are responsible for implementing NEPA, including the US Interior Department, the EPA, and the Department of Transportation.

The Clean Air Act

The Clean Air Act (CAA), passed in 1970, established national air quality standards to protect the public. Six major air pollutants are addressed: ground-level ozone, particulate matter, carbon monoxide, sulfur dioxide, nitrogen oxides, and lead.[110]

In the early years of the CAA, states were required to develop and imple-ment strategies to meet and maintain air quality standards. The EPA enforces the CAA and reviews standards.

The CAA tasks the EPA with setting emission standards for pollution sources, including industries, cars and trucks, and power plants, to reduce harmful pollutants released into the atmosphere and promote cleaner technologies.

Though not originally a climate policy, the CAA has real implications for climate policy today. Under the CAA, the EPA regulates greenhouse gases as air pollutants under certain circumstances, which has led to established regulations on emissions from major sources such as power plants and vehicles.

The EPA also sets fuel efficiency standards for vehicles and promotes cleaner and more fuel-efficient technologies, which can help reduce greenhouse gas emissions. The CAA's emphasis on reducing emissions and promoting sustainable practices aligns with broader climate policy goals to lower emissions.

In 2007, the US Supreme Court gave the EPA the authority to regulate greenhouse gases under the CAA when it ruled on *Massachusetts v. EPA*. Under the Trump administration that authority was revoked, then it was restored under the Biden administration—an example of how changes in administration have real impacts. "The Supreme Court has issued a whole series of rulings that make it more difficult for EPA to regulate," explains Michael Gerrard, who directs Columbia University's Sabin Center for Climate Change Law.

In 2022 the US Supreme Court ruled the EPA does not have the authority to establish caps on carbon emissions at the state level. The original act gave this power to the EPA, which encouraged states to seek energy sources that use less carbon than coal. The court ruled that only Congress has that authority.[111]

In 2024, the US Supreme Court temporarily blocked what's known as the EPA's "Good Neighbor" rule, which requires states upwind to draw down air pollution affecting states downwind. That same year, the court decided to leave a rule by the EPA in place that aims to reduce the emissions coming from power plants.

The Clean Water Act

The Clean Water Act (CWA), which became law in 1972, created limits on pollutants that can be discharged into waters (lakes, rivers, streams, coastal areas) of the United States. It's designed to safeguard water quality and promote sustainable water management practices.

The policy, which is enforced by the EPA, regulates and reduces pollution from point sources, such as industrial facilities and sewage treatment plants, and nonpoint sources, such as agricultural runoff.

Water quality in some parts of the United States at the time the CWA passed was terrible. Certain rivers, such as in Pennsylvania, were known to catch fire because the water was so heavily polluted. The statute aimed to clean up waterways and make them safe.

The framework of the CWA for managing and protecting water resources can help communities adapt and build resilience as sea levels rise and extreme weather continues. Proper water management can help with the impacts from floods, droughts, and other extreme weather.

CWA helps maintain aquatic ecosystems, which help store carbon dioxide, by regulating and reducing pollutants in the water.

In 2023, however, the US Supreme Court limited the EPA's ability to protect wetlands under the CWA, further restricting the agency's power. The move has raised concerns over how to protect wetlands, which store carbon.[112]

That's the not the only ruling the high court has made to restrict the power federal agencies have historically had. In 2024, the court overturned what's been known as the Chevron doctrine, which further limits the power of federal agencies.

In 1984, the Supreme Court ruled in *Chevron v. Natural Resources Defense Council* that if Congress didn't expressly answer a question at the heart of a legal dispute, then a court would need to uphold a federal agency's statute, such as the CWA or the CAA, as long as that decision was reasonable. This gave agencies such as the EPA latitude to make decisions by using technical and scientific expertise. Over the decades, the Chevron doctrine has been cited in cases thousands of times.[113]

The decision to overturn Chevron leaves it to Congress to decide environmental policy, and this could have real implications in confronting climate change. Cara Horowitz, an environmental law expert at the University of California, Los Angeles, told NPR that removing the long-standing doctrine marks an "obvious trend of hostility toward environmental regulations and the administrative state more generally that I think is making it really hard to tackle new and emerging threats like climate change."[114] In the years ahead, journalists will want to follow cases that challenge the Supreme Court's upending of Chevron.

The Endangered Species Act

In 1973, Congress passed the ESA, which created a pathway to identify and protect animals and plants on the brink of extinction.[115] The law passed at a time when climate change was barely a discussion point. Decades later, global warming threatens more than 10,000 species.[116]

Animals have already gone extinct from human-caused climate change. The brownish-red rodent known as the Bramble Cay melomys was considered among the first. The mouse-sized creature lost its habitat because of rising sea levels on a tiny stretch of land off Papua New Guinea's coast.[117]

The ESA provides a process for listing species as endangered or threatened and designates critical habitats needed for their recovery and survival. The ESA also prohibits the taking of listed species, which includes actions that harm, harass, or kill protected animals or plants without proper authorization.

The US Fish and Wildlife Service and the National Marine Fisheries Service establish and implement recovery plans for listed species, which include restoring populations and habitats.

Designating a species as threatened or endangered can take years and can lead to litigation that can delay the process. Environmental organizations such as the Center for Biological Diversity have filed lawsuits in the past for a variety of reasons, such as recovery plans being inadequate, or argued for why a species should be listed when it's been denied. For example, two species of Joshua trees found in California and Arizona were proposed to be listed because of climate change. However, the US Fish and Wildlife Service denied requests to designate the succulents despite legal action, saying that by the agency's count, the plants are plentiful.[118]

Species that fully recover population numbers can be considered for delisting. The once endangered bald eagle is an example of this.

The ESA intersects with climate policy in several significant ways. Climate change alters habitats, affects food sources, and causes more frequent extreme weather that threatens ecosystems and biodiversity. The focus of the ESA to protect critical habitats and promote species recovery aligns with adaptation and preservation efforts. By safeguarding habitats, the ESA can help wildlife cope with changing environmental conditions.

Protecting endangered species and their habitats can contribute to climate change mitigation efforts, too. Healthy ecosystems can sequester carbon and increase biodiversity, supporting resilience against climate impacts.

Federal agencies are required to consider the impacts projects can have on endangered species and their habitats. Because climate policy may involve infrastructure and energy projects, the ESA ensures such efforts are evaluated for their potential effects on at-risk species.

Federal Land Policy Management Act

The Bureau of Land Management (BLM) oversees 245 million acres of public land in the United States and roughly 30 percent of the country's minerals.[119]

The Federal Land Policy and Management Act (FLPMA) is the US federal law enacted in 1976 that gives the BLM the right to manage, use, and conserve public lands.[120]

FLPMA requires the BLM to balance multiple competing uses of public lands. Solar and wind development, oil and gas, coal, livestock grazing, hard rock mining, timber harvests, and outdoor recreation are all types of uses on BLM lands.

Geographic regions under FLPMA must have what are referred to as resource management plans that detail the long-term management strategies and objectives for public lands under the BLM's jurisdiction.

FLPMA addresses rights-of-way across public lands, such as for transportation and energy transmission infrastructure. The law also allows for land exchanges or sales to consolidate land ownership, facilitate public access, or achieve other public objectives.

The BLM manages lands for multiple uses, which are often at odds, especially as the impacts of climate change intensify. For example, oil and gas development on public lands can clash with conservation goals, particularly as these activities contribute to greenhouse gas emissions, which exacerbate climate change. For the first time in 2021, the BLM announced it would analyze the cumulative greenhouse gas emissions and the social cost of carbon for proposed lease sales, a shift driven by policy changes under the Biden administration.[121]

The BLM has a significant role in permitting and managing renewable energy projects on public lands. In fact, the agency has identified 19 million acres of public land well suited for solar development in several southwestern states and 20 million acres of public land in eleven western states that have the potential for wind energy.[122] FLPMA's multiple-use mandate requires the agency to consider climate-related factors when assessing applications for solar, wind, and geothermal energy development.

FLPMA also influences the management of federal lands for fossil fuel extraction, including oil, gas, and coal. Decisions related to leasing and development must consider environmental impacts, including greenhouse gas emissions.

FLPMA can also help preserve habitats that act as carbon sinks, sequestering carbon dioxide and mitigating climate change, given the BLM's conservation mandate. The agency identifies and protects areas with special environmental, cultural, or scientific value. Wilderness Study Areas, Areas of Critical Environmental Concern, and National Monuments all fall under the conservation category.

Journalists can track proposals and auctions for leases as part of their watchdog role and ask the questions about why something's being proposed. Remember, FLPMA means the BLM must gather public comment and hold public hearings. Journalists are allowed to attend and ask questions.

In 2024, the BLM finalized a sweeping new public lands rule that weighs conservation and land restoration with mining and energy development. "To support ecosystem health and resilience, the rule provides that the BLM will protect intact landscapes, restore degraded habitat, and make informed management decisions based on science and data," the rule states. "To support these activities, the rule applies land health standards to all BLM-managed public lands and uses, codifies conservation tools to be used within FLPMA's multiple-use framework, and revises existing regulations to better meet FLPMA's requirement that the BLM prioritize designating and protecting areas of critical environmental concern (ACECs)."[123]

The rule marks a huge shift in management under FLPMA. Conservation leases would be granted for restoring the land or offsetting impacts on other sections of land, along with leases for oil and gas.

Mineral Leasing Act

The Mineral Leasing Act (MLA) of 1920 governs the leasing of public lands to private companies to mine specific minerals, including oil and gas and coal. However, the MLA does not cover metallic minerals such as gold and silver, which are governed by the General Mining Law of 1872. The MLA outlines the procedures for acquiring leases, which usually involve competitive bidding. Lease terms, including their length, rental fees, royalty rates, and the rights and responsibilities of lessees, are also established.

The MLA mandates that mineral extraction on public lands follow environmental laws, including NEPA. It also specifies how revenue from leases, including royalties, gets distributed; a percentage goes to the federal government and the states where the extraction occurs.

The MLA reveals the complex relationship between federal policies, energy production, environmental protections, and climate goals. Reporters can use the MLA to investigate how energy policies might conflict with or support efforts to reduce greenhouse gas emissions. For instance, the leasing of federal lands for oil and gas extraction under the MLA often sparks debates about its contribution to planet-warming pollution, creating a rich field for exploring economic, environmental, and social dimensions. Journalists can also use the MLA to examine how energy production under its provisions aligns—or fails to align—with climate targets, as well as its impact on local communities, ecosystems, and national energy policies. What's the impact of leasing public lands for oil and gas operations on planet-warming pollution? How are the emissions caused by extracting gas regulated?

Environmental assessments are required for leasing public lands to extract minerals. Reporters will find environmental assessments indicating that national efforts to reduce planet-warming pollution don't align with the decisions made. That's a story. For example, the Willow Creek Project in Alaska is being developed by BP Oil because of long-held leases. That's despite legal challenges and a national effort to shift away from fossil fuels.[124] As the United States shifts from fossil fuels to renewable energy, the MLA will continue to be a source of much policy debate, which will lead to stories about those tensions.

Mineral Leasing Act for Acquired Lands

The Mineral Leasing Act for Acquired Lands of 1947 extends the original MLA to lease lands acquired by the government from private owners. As with other public lands, leasing and mineral extraction must comply with regulations such as NEPA and the CAA. Understanding this policy provides context for discussing fossil fuel extraction, environmental regulation, economic policies, and community impacts. Its relevance stretches from legal and economic dimensions to social and environmental considerations.

Outer Continental Shelf Lands Act

The Outer Continental Shelf Lands Act (OCSLA), enacted in 1953, governs the exploration and development of oil, natural gas, and other offshore minerals. OCSLA applies to lands submerged off America's coastlines within US jurisdiction. OCSLA sets the framework for leasing underwater lands for mineral extraction and offshore wind energy development. Its relevance to climate change reporting lies in its regulation of fossil fuel extraction and its potential role in renewable energy development.

Federal agencies, specifically the Bureau of Ocean Energy Management, must comply with environmental regulations such as NEPA before leasing offshore lands for mineral extraction. NEPA allows for the auctioning of leases, including for renewable energy projects such as offshore wind. Revenue from these leases goes to the federal government, adjacent states, and specific funds such as the Land and Water Conservation Fund.[125]

Oil and gas and offshore wind auctions are worth watching, especially for journalists covering the US energy transition. Although a single project may not have a significant climate footprint, they can collectively. Reporters can also investigate how offshore energy activities affect the marine and coastal environment, a topic that swirls with misinformation and disinformation as communities and groups that oppose offshore wind development try to stall projects.

Another rich area to pay attention to under OCSLA is the balance between energy development, economic interests, and environmental protection. Reporters can talk with trade groups, industry experts, and federal agencies about leasing policies, revenue distribution, and the broader implications for national energy and climate policies.

Climate and environmental policy may still feel daunting or overwhelming after you read this chapter, which spans international, national, and local policy. There's a lot to consider given that it's a topic that continues to develop with twists and turns, especially as political power shifts in countries. For reporters interested in going deeper on environmental policy, there are plenty of books and academic resources dedicated to this critical topic. I call policy critical because it's essential knowledge and history that reporters need to have at their fingertips. That historical and modern-day policy context provides clarity in stories as journalists report on climate action globally, nationally, or in their home communities.

Essential Reading and Resources

This Changes Everything: Capitalism vs. the Climate, by Naomi Klein: Klein explores the connection between global capitalism and the climate crisis, arguing that meaningful climate action requires a fundamental transformation of economic systems. This book is crucial for understanding the political and economic dimensions of climate change policy.

Values in Climate Policy, by David Morrow: This book explores the ethical and moral dimensions that influence decisions in climate policy. Morrow argues that values such as justice, equity, and responsibility are crucial for shaping policies that address climate change effectively while ensuring fairness across global communities.

Short Circuiting Policy: Interest Groups and the Battle over Clean Energy and Climate Policy in the American States, by Leah Stokes: This book examines how interest groups, particularly in the fossil fuel industry, have influenced and obstructed clean energy and climate policies at the state level in the United States. Stokes highlights the role of political and economic power in undermining progress on climate change while exploring how some states have managed to advance renewable energy initiatives despite these challenges.

Federal Public Land and Resources Law, by George Coggins, Charles Wilkinson, et al.: This law book is on my desk for a reason: I reference it all the time for context and fact-checking. Anyone interested in environmental laws and policies will find this text highly useful.

The Ministry for the Future, by Kim Stanley Robinson: Yes, this is a science fiction novel, but I highly recommend its detailed exploration of possible climate futures and the global policies needed to mitigate climate disaster. It's useful for journalists thinking creatively about long-term climate policy solutions.

CHAPTER 4

Debunking Misinformation and Disinformation

"A lie can travel halfway around the world while the truth is still putting on its shoes."

—Ancient saying

In mid-February 2021, the entire state of Texas was engulfed in a winter storm that brought frigid temperatures not seen since the winter of 1989. Roads turned icy. Snow fell. The state's electric grid couldn't keep up with demand. Millions of Texans were plunged into darkness, unable to heat their homes. Hundreds of people died. As the hours stretched into days, people without power wanted answers. When would the power come back on? During the freeze, the state's governor went on *Fox News*, blaming wind and solar for not being reliable in an urgent time of need.[1] But it wasn't true.

In a social media post on Next Door titled "Culver City Banning Gas Stoves?," a man named Wilson Truong warned neighbors about a proposal by city leaders to discourage natural gas in new homes and business construction. He called the plan "bogus," adding that he'd had an electric stove but switched back to gas "because it cooked better." In a nearly literal example of gaslighting, Truong wasn't actually a neighbor. Instead, he worked for a PR firm opposing the initiative.[2]

Oil giant ExxonMobil inked a carbon capture and storage agreement with CF Industries, a Mississippi industrial company that makes nitrogen products used in things such as fertilizer. Exxon said it would capture carbon dioxide from CF Industries' complex in Yazoo City, Mississippi, and transport and store those emissions. CF Industries would halve its planet-warming pollution, and Exxon would store more than 5 million metric tons total—the equivalent of taking 2 million gas-powered cars off the road and replacing them with electric vehicles. It was an unbelievable story, literally. No carbon has yet been captured.[3]

Climate scientist Michael Mann is renowned for a data graph that resembles a hockey stick. The data showed steady temperatures for decades (the hockey stick shaft). Then, the numbers suddenly spiked up (the blade). The graph dramatically depicted the timing and magnitude of human-caused global warming and shifted public understanding of the threat. Climate deniers fought back. Two conservative publications, *The National Review* and the antiregulation think tank Competitive Enterprise Institute, published commentaries attacking Mann and suggesting connections between Mann and a sex abuse scandal involving a football coach at Pennsylvania State University, where Mann taught at the time. In a subsequent defamation suit, Mann proved there was no factual basis for the personal attacks.[4]

Four different stories. Four different claims. All of them are false. Each represents an attempt by powerful interest groups to reframe the conversation about human-caused global warming. Misinformation and disinformation are rampant in the climate change space. Reporters today need the skills to detect and debunk false climate narratives and also to inform those who may unwittingly share misinformation about the goals and motives of those who perpetuate false stories.

In 2022, the World Economic Forum called misinformation a global risk and one in which efforts to thwart it have fallen short.[5] Misinformation and disinformation matter because such myths undermine efforts to decarbonize the electric grid, to transition to cleaner energy sources, and to implement policies that can put us on a path to slow the effects of a warming world.

This chapter helps journalists develop the ability to detect and debunk climate misinformation, whether it is spread directly by bad actors or shared unwittingly through social media. They'll discover why misleading information persists and is so prevalent and the best ways to correct these false narratives. They'll learn when a climate myth rises to a level that warrants debunking and how to avoid unintentionally amplifying fallacies. By the end of the chapter, journalists will better understand how to navigate a minefield of climate and renewable energy myths. That understanding begins with knowing the difference between misinformation and disinformation.

Getting Clear on Definitions

Misinformation and *disinformation* are terms commonly used to describe falsehoods and lies, but they are not the same. Disinformation is intentional, created by people deliberately seeking to deceive. Misinformation is wrong or misleading, but the people who share it don't necessarily realize it's wrong. False memes on social media are an example of both. A meme creator intends to spread a falsehood, but those who share the meme may not know they are amplifying a lie.

Claire Wardle has spent years studying misinformation and disinformation. She co-founded the nonprofit First Draft and now teaches at Cornell University. She calls disinformation "deliberate hoaxing, deliberately trying to cause harm," whereas misinformation is "unfortunately, what we're all being seduced into sharing just because we don't realize."[6]

Wardle thinks about her mother resharing something on Facebook as an innocent example of misinformation. "She would be horrified that she was doing anything wrong. She's doing it because she wants to help her community and her friends."[7]

Disinformation campaigns can be hard to detect. They are often organized and elaborate. A textbook example is the decades-long effort by tobacco companies to deny and deflect responsibility for the cancer-causing effects of smoking cigarettes.

More recently, extreme summer heat and blackout worries in 2022 prompted some state Republican lawmakers to claim that the public would not have enough power to run air conditioners because Democrats had pushed for renewable energy.[8] A similar false narrative came during the deep freeze and subsequent power outages in Texas. Conservative leaders in that state pointed fingers at wind and solar even though reporting revealed that natural gas distribution issues were the primary culprit.[9] Then there are the bots and trolls who frequent social media platforms. They pose as everyday people, but, in reality, they traffic in intentional, deceptive messaging campaigns.

Journalists covering climate face significant challenges because of the sophistication and sheer volume of myths and misinformation. I have had numerous conversations with reporters grappling with how to effectively dispel false climate narratives without amplifying falsehoods. As an editor, I sometimes feel like I'm playing a game of whack-a-mole, where every effort to dispel one piece of misinformation is quickly followed by another.

The steady influx of misleading information underscores the need for persistent vigilance and a strategic approach to confront the spread of climate-related falsehoods. It begins by understanding how today's complicated landscape of misinformation and disinformation evolved.

How Did We Get Here?

Researchers believe the rise in climate misinformation began in earnest in 1988. That's the year NASA climate scientist James Hansen told Congress that global warming was happening and the burning of fossil fuels was primarily to blame.

That same year, the International Panel on Climate Change was formed. The fossil fuel industry, conservative businesses, and lobbyists responded by creating the Global Climate Coalition. Its purpose? To generate skepticism over whether humans were indeed to blame for climate change.[10] From 1994 to 1997, the coalition spent $1 million every year to deemphasize climate change through members such as the National Coal Association and the American Petroleum Institute.[11] The coalition funded a $13 million ad campaign in 1997 that opposed the Kyoto Protocol, which became the world's first international treaty to require countries to limit and reduce greenhouse gas emissions.[12]

In 2002, the coalition fell apart as the scientific evidence for human-caused climate change mounted.[13] Some industries left the coalition, acknowledging climate change was, in fact, happening.

That didn't stop conservative think tanks from renewing efforts to manufacture doubt. New think tanks emerged, including the Competitive Enterprise Institute and the Heartland Institute. Both became prodigious sources of climate skepticism. These organizations mastered strategies to get their message in front of the media. They leaned heavily on authors of successful books about climate denial, lending an air of legitimacy to their message.

Environmental sociologist Riley Dunlap wrote about this phenomenon, saying these authors were viewed as experts on climate "regardless of their academic backgrounds or scientific credentials, and despite the fact that their books are seldom peer reviewed."[14]

So-called climate experts and conservative think tanks capitalized on journalism's traditional storytelling model of balancing both sides of a story. That gave false balance in climate stories.[15]

Early research by Max Boykoff and others found that national media, including *The New York Times*, *The Washington Post*, *The Los Angeles Times*, and *The Wall Street Journal*, contributed significantly to climate denial, starting in the late 1980s and continuing through the early 2000s.[16] Reporting stoked and legitimized the debate over whether temperatures were indeed increasing and whether humans were responsible.

"These press outlets have done this by adhering to the journalistic norm of balanced reporting, offering a countervailing 'denial discourse,'" which generates questions about the seriousness of climate change and the overall scientific evidence of climate change, said Boykoff.[17]

Media Disruption

Disruptions to the information ecosystem furthered the conditions for a rise of climate myths and misinformation. The growth of the internet and social media weakened traditional media outlets, reducing profitability, audience size, and credibility as publishing became more democratized. Journalists competed with anyone who had a cellphone. Anyone could claim to be a news source.

Filter bubbles have also weakened the information ecosystem. When we like or share content on social media, our feeds fill with similar stories, fed by algorithms. We develop confirmation bias through what comes into our social media feeds. As a result, the information we see becomes siloed and self-reinforcing.

Also gone are the days when people gathered to watch the evening news on one of three major networks: NBC, CBS, and ABC. Nightly news anchors such as CBS anchorman Walter Cronkite were household names who beamed into America's living rooms for nearly two decades, ending each broadcast with a declarative "and that's the way it is." No one today would say this. Cable news and a twenty-four-hour news cycle reshaped the format of televised news, making way for conservative and liberal-leaning talk programming—an early precursor to the information silos that exist today.

The demise of local and national newspapers also factors into the spread of misinformation and disinformation. Many newspapers, long seen as the news source of record, can't financially compete in a digital advertising world dominated by large digital platform companies such as Google and Facebook.

Increasingly, rural communities across the United States have little or no access to credible news and information. News deserts exist in 200 counties across the United States, according to research by University of North Carolina's Hussman School of Journalism and Media. Texas, one of the largest states in the country, has twenty-one counties without a daily or weekly newspaper. In a state with 28 million people, nearly 200 papers closed from 2004 to 2019.[18]

Social media fills the void. Roughly 48 percent of adults in the United States "often" or "sometimes" get their news from social media.[19] The volume of content on platforms such as TikTok, X (formerly Twitter), and Instagram is enormous. So is the amount of misinformation. Research finds social media creates echo chambers where algorithms recommend content that reinforces a user's worldview while suppressing contrary information.[20] Topics such as climate change or vaccines, for example, can quickly become polarized in this space, making it easy for misinformation and disinformation to spread.

Given these dramatic disruptions to how and where people get their information, it's no surprise that skillfully constructed, well-funded climate misinformation and disinformation campaigns have permeated mainstream media.

False balance stories in the media persisted through the early 2000s, according to an analysis of climate coverage from 1988 to 2002.[21] Nearly all scientists were convinced humans were causing global warming. Yet a few who dissented continued to receive equal time in mainstream media stories, which further spread misinformation.

"They (conservative think tanks) had a very robust voice, and the default for the mainstream media was to just do a both sides treatment, which gave a false balance approach that's improved over time," says John Cook, a postdoctoral research fellow at Monash University in Australia.[22] Cook runs the Climate Change Communication Research Hub at Monash and studies how to prevent manipulation.

Cook has spent years researching climate misinformation and how to confront it. His research showed that people's understanding of climate change diminishes when science is explained through a debate.[23] But the both-sides framing often used in journalism inherently presents climate stories as two competing viewpoints. The intent might be a goal of fairness and balance, but this approach fanned false narratives about climate change. Climate deniers received prominent attention in stories alongside scientists, bolstering misinformation and disinformation about global warming and our role in it.

Science and Journalism at Odds

Frustration brewed between scientists and journalists during this time, partly because of a lack of understanding about how each profession worked. Both worried about the lack of public engagement on climate change.

In 2003, prominent climate scientists and journalists in the United States began a series of workshops to learn from each other and find common ground.[24] Journalists learned about how science is done and the rigor behind the research. Scientists learned why journalists need story pegs and why they need clear ways to break climate science down for audiences to understand.

Reporters also shared how challenging it was to cover climate change because it "oozes, but doesn't break," explained then–*New York Times* journalist Andrew Revkin at one of the workshops.[25] Reporting stories that span geologic time requires a different approach from traditional "if it bleeds, it leads" narratives.

Respective challenges in science and journalism culminated in a 2008 report that forged a fresh path on communicating climate science and how journalists could accurately represent the science and frame scientific debates.[26] In the years since, climate deniers have mostly vanished from mainstream news climate stories, yet myths about climate change, solutions, and policy continue to thrive.

That shift aligns with Cook's recent research. He took two decades of climate misinformation and used machine learning to examine all types of myths. He discovered the science myths he had been debunking were the *least* common form of climate misinformation. The most common attacks now are aimed at scientists and climate science; for example, scientists are biased, scientists are in it for the money, and climate models can't be trusted.[27]

"It's about eroding public trust in climate science and scientists themselves," Cook says. Debunking those myths can be difficult because they require explaining how science works. He also discovered in the research that "there's a gradual transition towards solutions misinformation.... The future of climate misinformation will be about solutions."[28]

Common Misinformation About Climate Science

Climate change falsehoods run the gamut from outright denial to the techno-optimistic belief that humans can simply engineer their way out of the crisis of warming. John Cook has cataloged hundreds of climate science myths espoused by global warming skeptics.[29] I've highlighted some common ones in the list below that journalists might encounter. To be clear, all of these are wrong and easily refuted by science.

- Climate change isn't happening, or humans are not at fault.
- Scientists don't all agree that climate change is happening.

- It's a political ploy.
- Natural climate variability, not people, causes warming temperatures.
- Climate change won't have huge impacts on people, wildlife, or plants.
- Climate change can be addressed through simple and inexpensive technology.
- Curbing emissions will hurt the global economy.
- Extreme weather isn't becoming more frequent or extreme because of climate change.

This list is just the start. Cook's website *Skeptical Science* catalogs many more false climate narratives.[30]

Common Disinformation Tactics

Whereas misinformation is unintentional, disinformation is quite the opposite. All kinds of powerful interests, from oil companies to politically motivated activists to nongovernmental organizations, spread misleading and false information to generate doubt and denial in the public's mind. Past disinformation campaigns have successfully derailed or stalled work on climate action for decades by questioning climate science or falsely suggesting that scientists were divided over humans' role in causing climate change.

In recent years, the tactics have shifted from denial toward strategies that delay the green energy transition: shifting blame and responsibility for emission reductions from industries to individuals, casting doubt on the viability of renewables, and distracting attention from proven responses by shifting the focus to unproven, speculative technological solutions.

Oil giant Exxon, for instance, led legitimate climate research for decades. The company's scientists told corporate leaders that strong evidence pointed to fossil fuels contributing to global temperature rise.[31] In a total reversal, the company's top executives later used that information to launch an all-out campaign to raise doubt and questions about the science.[32]

Disinformation campaigns now exist to slow progress on renewable energy projects and climate solutions.[33] Solar and wind projects in local communities across the United States are the latest battleground in this effort.[34] They often use the tactic of cherry-picking facts to sow doubt and resistance to building these renewable projects in communities.

Here are some of the most commonly used disinformation tactics:[35]

- Data and evidence that are made up or distorted to support false climate narratives;
- Fake experts or fabricated scientific studies to support unfounded claims;
- Cherry-picking specific data points or events and falsely presenting them as evidence of wider truths;
- Misrepresenting positions of reputable scientists and scientific organizations;
- Character attacks on prominent climate scientists;
- Using conspiracy theories to undermine credible climate science;
- Amplifying lies or misleading information about climate change through social media and other online platforms.

Journalists need to know the most commonly used disinformation tactics so they can spot climate deceptions. Detecting these distortions is the essential first step toward debunking them. But climate disinformation campaigns continue to evolve their tactics, which makes it hard for reporters to keep up.

From Denial to Delay, Deflection, and Distraction

Historically, denial was the primary tactic of climate disinformation campaigns. But denial is no longer a viable strategy in the face of the overwhelming evidence of our warming world.

Michael Mann details the history of this evolving battle and how misinformation campaigns have changed in his 2021 book *The New Climate Wars*. He identifies powerful "forces of denial and delay" as a cast of characters that include the fossil fuel industry, right-wing partisans, and governments and others funded by oil. The newer deflection strategies are a "softer form of denialism," Mann writes. This tactic puts the burden of responsibility for climate action on individuals rather than on industry. Mann calls the campaign "masterfully executed," one that takes a page from the playbook of the tobacco industry and the gun lobby.[36] Want to reduce emissions? Stop flying. Go vegan.

Meanwhile, oil companies continue to produce fossil fuels while ramping up efforts based on "deception, distraction and delay."[37] In 2023, world leaders gathered for the annual Conference of the Parties in the United Arab Emirates, which is one of the biggest oil and gas producers in the world. In a blatant example of the fox guarding the henhouse, the fossil fuel industry had a massive presence at the complex for COP28.[38]

Climate Misinformation Gets Personal

A 2009 manufactured scandal called Climategate illustrates the way powerful interests try to orchestrate doubt by attacking climate science and scientists. Emails between climate scientists, including Michael Mann, were hacked from a university server in Great Britain. The emails were taken out of context and rearranged by "climate deniers to misrepresent both the science and the scientists." Climategate was a well-orchestrated narrative that was "foisted on the public and policymakers in a collaborative effort by fossil-fuel-industry front groups, paid attack dogs, and conservative media outlets."[39]

Mann himself was the subject of abusive attacks on his personal credibility when conservative writers at the *National Review* and at the Competitive Enterprise Institute likened him to a child molester, Penn State football coach Jerry Sandusky. In 2024, after more than a decade of litigation, Mann won his defamation case.[40]

"You have the right to challenge scientists, . . . to disagree with it in good faith," Mann said during an interview at the Society of Environmental Journalists conference after winning his case in 2024. "But when it crosses a line into ideologically motivated, the defamatory statements are not really about the science and its validity, but they are intending to discredit the science and the scientists to further you know, a potential political agenda."[41]

Climate Change Trolls

The campaign to delay and deflect action has added fresh tactics aimed at swaying people, such as deploying online bots and trolls to manipulate social media and the web.[42] Remember the story of Wilson Truong? His post on the social media site Nextdoor sparked a firestorm of debate. That prompted journalist Rebecca Leber to find out who he was. She discovered Truong wasn't a Culver City neighbor. He was actually an account manager for the public relations firm Imprenta Communications Group. One of their clients was Californians for Balanced Energy Solutions. Leber discovered as part of her in-depth investigation for *Mother Jones* that the group was "a front for the nation's largest gas utility, SoCalGas, which aims to thwart state and local initiatives restricting the use of fossil fuels in new buildings."[43] This tactic is known as microtargeting.

As these examples illustrate, climate misinformation and disinformation come in many forms. By understanding these tactics, journalists can more effectively identify climate myths and are better equipped to debunk the false narratives surrounding our warming world.

Debunking Misinformation and Disinformation

Debunking a climate myth can be overwhelming and raise questions. When does a misleading claim rise to the level of being corrected? How do journalists avoid amplifying false narratives? What is the most effective way to debunk a climate myth?

In this section, journalists will learn how to avoid the trap of unintentionally spreading climate misinformation via fact-checks, how to effectively debunk false climate claims by using a technique known as the truth sandwich, and how reporters can help inoculate their audiences to manipulation through a process called prebunking. With these skills, climate reporters can confidently challenge climate myths in ways that lead to a more informed public.

Researcher John Cook started *Skeptical Science* to debunk climate myths after trying to win arguments with his father-in-law, who was a climate skeptic. "I realized other people probably have annoying family members that think they know better than the world's climate scientists," Cook recalls.[44]

After a few years of debunking climate myths on his website, Cook had a moment of insight when a cognitive scientist asked whether he had considered the psychology behind debunking misinformation. The scientist shared a paper with Cook that highlighted a significant risk: *If misinformation is debunked incorrectly, it could backfire and reinforce the false beliefs instead of correcting them.* This revelation made Cook question his entire approach. He wondered whether, in his efforts to set the record straight, he had inadvertently been making things worse.[45]

Cook shifted his focus to search for the most effective ways to correct false information without reinforcing the myths. Thanks to the findings of Cook, Wardle, and other researchers, journalists now have three proven methods to confront misinformation and disinformation: Don't give oxygen to rumors, wrap falsehoods in a truth sandwich, and use prebunking to inoculate audiences to common climate myths.

Don't Give Oxygen to Rumors

Fact-checking and debunking wrong information is a foundational journalism practice and is obviously an essential part of correcting misinformation and disinformation. What's less obvious is how the journalistic instinct to fact-check and debunk falsehoods can be used against the profession.

The act of fact-checking can actually amplify awareness of a climate myth, Claire Wardle noted in a training at Arizona State University in 2020: "The whole way that journalism works—which is the paradigm of 'more sunlight is a disinfectant'—has been weaponized against the news media in the hopes that there will be more oxygen given to rumors."[46]

This kind of media manipulation is another disinformation tactic. Its purpose is to "sow division in this country," Wardle said. "So that means that they are trying to get newsrooms to give oxygen to rumors."[47] To avoid that mistake, newsrooms need to carefully choose what falsehoods to debunk so as not to spread the lie further and cause additional harm.

This chapter began with an example of a pervasive, important climate falsehood: In 2021, a deep winter freeze crippled the power grid in Texas. Millions of people lost their power. Republican Governor Greg Abbott blamed wind and solar for not being reliable. However, local reporting revealed natural gas pipelines and wells, which deliver the majority of the state's power, froze. The infrastructure couldn't handle the frigid temperatures.

Abbott is considered a newsmaker as governor. The journalistic practice is to report what powerful newsmakers say: "Governor blames renewables for power outages." This practice makes the media susceptible to manipulation by powerful interests. As this case proved, just because a newsmaker says something doesn't make it true.

Wardle suggests that the standard of covering what newsmakers such as Abbott say be reconsidered in light of the rise of misinformation and disinformation. "What do you do when a politician is repeating a conspiracy theory, which is more complex, and (reporting on) it requires giving more oxygen to the rumor?," she questions.[48]

Texas media covered Abbott's response to the power grid brilliantly. They reported his claim but didn't take the governor at his word and ultimately debunked the myth he and other Republican leaders were spreading. News outlets used reporting to correct his claim in the headline, which is what people read first. Here are a few excellent examples of those headlines:

- "Gov. Greg Abbott and other Republicans blamed green energy for Texas' power woes. But the state runs on fossil fuels."—*Texas Tribune*[49]

- "Fact check: Renewable energy is not to blame for the Texas energy crisis."—*NBC News*[50]
- "No, the blackouts in Texas weren't caused by renewables. Here's what really happened."—NPR[51]

In each headline, notice that the false narrative has been debunked with the correct information. However, some national media headlines *amplified* Abbott's message in favor of a more clickable headline:

- "Texas Republicans criticized for misleading claims that renewable energy sources caused massive outages."—*CNN*[52]
- "Millions of Texans are freezing and without power and Republicans are blaming . . . windmills."—*Rolling Stone*[53]

Both headlines repeat the myth that renewable energy is to blame, which keeps the myth alive. People who click past the headline and read further would learn what is wrong with Abbott's statement. But the harm has already been done.

In recent years, news organizations including the BBC, CBS News, and NPR have established teams dedicated to tackling misinformation and disinformation. However, journalists can't go after all the myths circulating in the zeitgeist. So how do reporters and editors know what to pursue? Wardle advises journalists not to chase every single falsehood but rather to focus on debunking myths that are most harmful and already in the mainstream, like the false assertion that renewable energy doesn't work in extreme weather.

Wrap Falsehoods in a Truth Sandwich

John Cook cautions that some myths can be difficult to debunk without repeating the lie. That's when journalists can deploy the truth sandwich. It's used when repeating the falsehood is unavoidable in order to explain what's true. How that information gets packaged matters.

American linguist George Lakoff, who has long studied how propaganda spreads, offered the truth sandwich idea as a way for the media to report on president Donald Trump when he lobbed lies at the media, calling them "fake news."[54] "Trump needs the media, and the media help him by repeating what he says," Lakoff told *The Washington Post* in 2018. That's not unusual for any president, but Lakoff argued that Trump's presidency was different.

"This situation is not normal—you have a sustained attack on the democracy and the news media."[55]

Journalists can refute such lies by wrapping the falsehood in truth. Through this method, audiences are presented first with what's true so they are prepared for the lie; then, along with the lie, they get the context behind the lie and why it's false; finally, they are again reminded of the truth.

The facts represent the sandwich "bread" that goes around the falsehood—the goodies in the middle of the sandwich. In *The Debunking Handbook*, John Cook details the four-step process of how to wrap a falsehood in a truth sandwich:[56]

FACT: Lead with the fact if it's clear, pithy, and sticky. Make it simple, concrete, and plausible. It must "fit" with the story.
WARN: Warn beforehand that a myth is coming. Mention the falsehood once only.
EXPLAIN: Explain how the myth misleads.
FACT: Finish by reinforcing the fact, multiple times if possible. Make sure it provides an alternative causal explanation.

Let's apply Cook's four-step method to the stories out of Texas during the winter storm to see how this works. That mid-February, conservative commentator Tucker Carlson said on *Fox News*, "The power grid in the state became totally reliant on windmills. Then it got cold, and the windmills broke, because that's what happens in the Green New Deal."[57] Shortly thereafter, Governor Abbott claimed that the failure of the grid "shows how the Green New Deal would be a deadly deal for the United States of America." Disinformation spread widely in the days afterward.[58] The falsehood that renewable energy failed circulated in the mainstream, rising to the level of needing to be debunked.

Now for the facts: By choice, the Texas power grid is independent from the rest of the country, so it can't tap into other power sources to help. It also wasn't prepared to handle such cold weather. Most of the state's power comes from natural gas, and the pipelines and wells froze. Some wind turbines also did freeze, but they accounted for only a fraction of the power outages.

NBC's report on the Texas grid failure stands out as an excellent example of how to apply the truth sandwich approach to debunking a climate myth. Their story, "Fact check: Renewable energy is not to blame for the Texas energy crisis," begins with what happened during the storm and then mentions that the power woes led to "politicians and media personalities" blaming renewable energy. In the second paragraph, reporter Kevin Collier states the fact: "And while frozen wind turbines have contributed to the state's energy crisis, that type of energy has only slightly underperformed against published expectations for winter output. Natural gas, the state's dominant energy source, has provided drastically less energy than expected, according to experts and industry data."[59]

Collier then brings in the expert: an energy power consultant who backs this fact up. "'Wind was operating almost as well as expected,' said Sam Newell, head of the electricity group at the Brattle Group, an energy consulting company that has advised Texas on its power grid."[60]

Next, Collier warns that the myth is coming: "Efforts to pin the ongoing crisis on renewable energy gained steam in recent days."[61]

Within four paragraphs, the reader knows what's true, and they have been prepared for the falsehood that's coming. Collier recaps the comments made by Carlson and the governor. He points out that when Governor Abbot spoke to a Dallas TV station, he explained the challenges of processing natural gas in the cold. However, when he talked with Carlson, Abbot's message shifted for the national conservative audience of *Fox News.* Collier puts that shift into perspective by detailing the "politicization of the Texas crisis," which underscored the ongoing battle between political parties over "how to address climate change, as well as previous battles over the energy industry."[62] With that context, Collier pivots the reader back to the truth, having fully unpacked the fallacy. "Data from Texas makes clear that renewable energy failures have played only a small part in the crisis."[63]

The story continues to show how wind actually performed on par with predictions in Texas during the blackout and, in some cases, excelled. Collier's approach is textbook: **fact → myth → fallacy → fact.**

Fact-checking and using the truth sandwich can only go so far. Misinformation travels fast and reaches more people than any of our best efforts to debunk. Facts alone sometimes are not enough to erase the myths. Research indicates that even when people know something is wrong, a falsehood still influences their thinking, so choosing what to debunk can be quite difficult. What if journalists could get out ahead of misinformation and disinformation *before* it gains traction in the mainstream?

Inoculate Against Misinformation

Every fall, doctors encourage us to get a flu shot to inoculate us against the worst effects of the virus. We do these shots hoping to stave off the worst sickness, and our immunity increases collectively. A similar theory applies to confronting the misinformation and disinformation landscape. The "shot" is truthful information that helps people understand what's right and what's not *before* falsehoods take root.[64] The prevention comes by getting out *ahead* of falsehoods—prebunking them—*before* they go viral on social media and online platforms.

> **Hot Take:** *Climate misinformation and disinformation spread faster than truth. Journalists have an important role in fact-checking such myths, but facts alone are not as powerful as being ahead of falsehoods. Prebunking—getting ahead of potential lies—helps arm the public with the truth so they can spot misinformation and disinformation.*

People's immunity to manipulation increases when they know the tactics used to mislead.[65] A dose of truth prepares people so they are less susceptible to myths. Election cycles are ideal for prebunking because misinformation tactics are often reused from one election to the next. During the 2020 election, reporters wrote articles preparing people to avoid falling victim to election scams and misinformation that might circulate ahead of the election.[66]

Common tactics from bad actors to discourage voters have included disseminating false claims suggesting people could skip in-person voting by casting their ballot by text, raising questions about mail-in ballot security, and posting false or misleading images and stories about long lines or dangerous conditions at polling places.[67]

Climate journalists can use this same method to prebunk common climate misinformation tactics. For example, reporting by NPR's Michael Copley and *Floodlight*'s Miranda Green documented a playbook frequently used in local communities across the United States when someone proposes building a new renewable energy facility.[68] A reporter could prebunk the tactics used by activists who oppose renewable energy, enabling people in a community to develop immunity to such manipulations.

John Cook has spent years researching how to inoculate people against falsehoods. There are three main methods journalists can use:[69]

- **Fact-based:** correcting a specific false claim or narrative
  Example: False claims that wind isn't reliable in extreme weather.

- **Logic-based**: explaining tactics used to manipulate
Example: Stoking range anxiety to discourage electric vehicle adoption.

- **Source-based:** pointing out bad sources of information
Example: Someone poses as a neighbor on social media but is actually employed by a public relations agency.

Journalists might mix and match these tactics when getting ahead of a myth in a prebunk.

The Power of the Prebunk

Taking on misinformation and disinformation before it goes viral can be challenging. Generally reporters can get ahead of misleading or wrong information when they have advance notice of a planned event. For example, scheduled elections or a public meeting on siting a solar project give reporters time to prepare for and anticipate audiences' questions. Even hurricanes, which can be predicted days in advance, offer the opportunity to inoculate audiences against misinformation and disinformation. Hurricanes Helene and Milton in 2024, for example, fueled conspiracies about the government and forecasters controlling the weather. Warning audiences in the path of an oncoming hurricane of previous deceptions is one way to help protect communities from misinformation about extreme weather. There are also a host of other tools to prebunk a variety of misinformation and disinformation.

Here are John Cook's ten points to consider when doing a prebunk.[70]

What to prebunk:
- What information do people need to know?
- Choose what myth (fact, technique, source) carefully.

Design the prebunk:
- Wrap the myth in truth.
- Warn the audience that it's coming.
- Add context (details and facts).
- Draw out the tactic being used to spread the misinformation and disinformation.
- Be transparent: Journalists need to show how they know.

How and where to share the message:
- Keep the prebunk simple.
- Make the story shareable.
- Know where the audience is at, and put the story there.

Climate journalist Amy Westervelt's reporting about the anti-wind movement in the United States is an excellent example of prebunking. Massive investments and progress have been made in the United States in developing renewable energy since the country's first climate policy came into law in 2022. All that growth has sparked an "uptick in anti-renewables activism, especially when it comes to offshore wind projects," Westervelt reported.[71]

In her 2024 story "The U.S. Anti-Wind Movement, Explained," Westervelt identifies a growing area of misinformation and disinformation in renewable energy. She explains to readers the tactics being used—the inoculation so people can be prepared as the industry develops and pushback continues. Here's how Westervelt does this: "There are some new groups too, and they're deploying some new tactics, especially around conservation and the idea that wind turbines are bad for birds and whales. There's no science backing up these claims, but that hasn't stopped them from taking hold. Still, it's a tricky situation. We're not just talking about fossil fuel backed resistance here."[72]

By the second paragraph, Westervelt has warned readers about the rise in misinformation and disinformation as the wind industry gains momentum. Then she lays out the tactics being used so people aren't susceptible to what they will surely hear in the future and then she explains the fallacy.

Misinformation researcher Claire Wardle describes prebunking this way: "In the context of information disorder, if you get people to think about the tactics and techniques that they might expect to see, when they see it, they are more likely to say, hang on, there's something about this that resonates. I remember this."[73]

An old saying famously quipped, "A lie can travel halfway around the world while the truth is still putting on its shoes."[74] The harsh reality is that fact-checkers can't keep pace with the flow of climate falsehoods. Prebunks are far more effective in equipping audiences to better spot myths and manipulation.[75]

Pick Your Battles

Climate journalists won't be able to debunk or prebunk all the misinformation and disinformation swirling around climate change and climate solutions. An ever-evolving array of tactics make it nearly impossible. There's simply too much false information in the universe. I have likened it to reporters as playing a game of nonstop whack-a-mole.

I am increasingly part of conversations with reporters and editors who will flag a study, a troubling headline, a story, or a social media post about climate change. It could be greenwashing about gas stoves or a climate-friendly spin on coffee pods. We discuss what rises to a fact-check or a debunk and how best to do that. Often the answer is that the myth will continue to spread, and we owe it to our audiences to debunk significant falsehoods.

"Exxon: The Road Not Taken" is arguably the holy grail of debunking. A team of journalists at *Inside Climate News* worked for nearly a year gathering hundreds of documents and filing requests for information to understand how Exxon, once on the leading edge of climate science, became a leader in manufacturing climate denial. The team took months to unravel and explain the multilayered strategies of deception and manipulation used by the oil giant to sway policy and mislead the public. That kind of deep investigative debunking is uncommon. Most reporters will serve their audiences by regularly applying the truth sandwich, avoiding giving oxygen to mere rumors, and prebunking to inoculate against common climate myths.

As an editor, I have found simple prebunks and debunks on social media and traditional platforms helpful because they happen where people get their information. Such valiant efforts can boost the public's resilience to climate misinformation and disinformation so they can be informed and armed to resist climate conspiracies, greenwashing, and bad information.

Together, we can create a truth movement to deflect falsehoods about our warming world and, in the process, inform people about what is factual and what is not.

Want to Learn More?

John Cook developed an app called Cranky Uncle, which is an excellent way to up your game in spotting misinformation and disinformation. Cranky Uncle is the ultimate curmudgeon of a character bent on denying science by spreading conspiracy theories and lobbing fake experts at you. The game starts with the question, "Do you want to be a Cranky Uncle and deny science?" asks the cartoon character. "Of course you do!" Cranky Uncle then explains the tactics used to deny science: "conspiracy theories, impossible expectations, cherry picking, fake experts, logical fallacies which 'commit the error of jumping to conclusions, also known as a non sequitur.'"

Spoiler alert: Cranky Uncle is fun to play, and I've found it useful in boosting my own detection of misinformation and disinformation.

Essential Reading and Resources

The Merchants of Doubt: How a Handful of Scientists Obscured the Truth on Issues from Tobacco Smoke to Global Warming, by Naomi Oreskes and Erik Conway: This definitive book traces the roots of today's climate disinformation back to the original playbook developed by the tobacco industry to misinform the public about the dangers of smoking tobacco products.

The New Climate War: The Fight to Take Back Our Planet, by Michael Mann: This must-read provides a deep dive on politics as well as misinformation and disinformation battles surrounding climate change.

The Consensus Handbook: This handbook gives an overview of the history and research of scientific consensus on climate change. It also explores the public's misconceptions about climate change due to misinformation campaigns and offers strategies to counter misinformation and disinformation effectively. https://www.climatechangecommunication.org/wp-content/uploads/2018/03/Consensus_Handbook-1.pdf

The Debunking Handbook: This is an essential and quick read about what misinformation and disinformation are and how journalists can put fallacies to rest. https://skepticalscience.com/docs/DebunkingHandbook2020.pdf

A Guide to Pre-bunking: A Promising Way to Inoculate Against Misinformation: This guide explains how to prebunk misinformation and disinformation successfully. https://firstdraftnews.org/articles/a-guide-to-pre-bunking-a-promising-way-to-inoculate-against-misinformation/

Inside Climate News' Exxon: The Road Not Taken series: This in-depth series is an exceptional example of investigative climate journalism. https://insideclimatenews.org/project/exxon-the-road-not-taken/

We Tracked Down a Fake-News Creator in the Suburbs. Here's What We Learned: This NPR story shows the depths of misinformation and disinformation in our world. https://www.npr.org/sections/alltechconsidered/2016/11/23/503146770/npr-finds-the-head-of-a-covert-fake-news-operation-in-the-suburbs

Your Turn

Exercise 1: Spot the misinformation and disinformation. Do an internet search to find up to three examples of what you identify as a climate-related myth. Identify what is inaccurate and explain why.

Exercise 2: Write a truth sandwich. Take one of the examples you identified as misinformation or disinformation and write a story with a headline no longer than 400 words that correctly explains the truth using the **fact → myth → fallacy → fact** method.

Exercise 3: You are preparing to report on the latest international gathering of world leaders, where they will discuss how countries are doing to draw down planet-warming pollution. What common climate myths might surface ahead of the conference? Identify one potential falsehood and explain how you would prebunk it.

CHAPTER 5

The Objectivity Illusion

"What is our role as journalists, if not to play a proactive and intentional role in trying to alleviate the suffering by bringing about solutions?"

—Sammy Roth

Los Angeles Times climate columnist Sammy Roth sat in his Los Angeles apartment with no air conditioning, sweltering in the August heat. "It was freaking hot," he recalled.[1] It was 2020, and California was in the middle of an epic heat wave. Power demand strained the electric grid as people struggled to stay cool. Then, the lights went out for hundreds of thousands of California residents. The state had imposed rolling blackouts to conserve energy.

Roth's electricity stayed on, but seeing so many people affected that Friday night in August, he said it felt like something from a history book. "Like this was some weird blast from the past that like, how is this happening in the present that we're now dealing with a crisis like this."[2] Indeed, California hadn't had blackouts due to energy demand in nearly twenty years.[3]

The heat wave and the blackouts came amid devastating wildfires that year. The sky turned orange in the San Francisco Bay area from wildfires, and the air was saturated with smoke. In California that August, hundreds of thousands of people were home, isolated by the COVID-19 pandemic. Many didn't have air conditioning. Then the power went out. Life felt apocalyptic.

Roth reported on the aftermath of that insufferably hot weekend, trying to understand why the power went out. That Monday morning Roth covered a press conference where the head of the California Independent System Operator, which oversees one of the world's largest power grids, blamed the Public Utilities Commission for the power shortage.[4]

Roth described the situation as a "cluster."[5] Why did the blackouts even happen when there were alternatives? That question guided his reporting for the next day: How could the state set clean energy goals to address climate change while keeping the lights on?

"We have not solved this issue [or] come up with the clean energy resources to keep the lights on after sundown when it's super hot," Roth said. He learned that the state planned to extend the life of gas power plants even though they contribute to planet-warming pollution. "It was the cherry on top of the week," he recalled. "This is what we're reaping for ourselves now, and it's just going to keep making the problem worse."[6]

By Wednesday, Roth was mentally and physically exhausted from the weekend and scrambling to report stories to help readers understand what happened and how to move forward. He opened up to readers of his newsletter, *The Boiling Point*, about the wild times they were all living through.

People have asked him how he keeps hope alive on a beat that can breed despair. Roth wrote that he's an optimistic person who covers energy, an area under the climate change story umbrella that has seen positive developments. That reporting can be invigorating, he told his readers. Roth also wrote that sometimes he has felt scared about the future, given the trajectory of human-caused climate change. "The optimist in me—the kid who truly believes every October that the Dodgers are finally going to win the World Series—can't fathom the idea that humanity won't eventually get its act together. The rational journalist in me peers into the middle distance and has trouble making out a future that looks any better than the present," he wrote in his August 2020 newsletter.[7]

Roth put himself and his opinion into his reporting. Some journalists and editors would say he crossed a line by not being "objective"—the age-old idea in journalism that reporters must remain neutral and unbiased. However, younger journalists have grown up immersed in an environment where people express themselves transparently and authentically on social media. For many younger journalists, the traditional concept of journalistic objectivity seems outdated. Some have decided it doesn't serve the audience. They view it as a holdover from bygone days when the ethics of journalism were established largely by White men in positions of power.

Roth says he adhered for years to the expectation that he'd keep his opinions out of his reporting—that reporters never give "any indication of what your view is of the thing you're writing about."[8]

Now, like many journalists today, Roth sees objectivity differently because the science of climate change reveals the urgent need for responses to drastically reduce planet-warming pollution. He feels his audience needs to know this to make the climate connection personal and relevant.

As an editor and a former professor of practice, I dealt with objectivity mainly when a story appeared to cross into advocacy—championing a movement, for example. Especially in climate reporting, I have talked with student journalists who want to cover climate change to urge action. "Is that our role?," I'd ask them. We had philosophical debates over the answers to that question. Where is the line between journalism and advocacy? There isn't an easy answer. It depends (my other favorite phrase for journalism besides "it's complicated"). I grew up with capital "J" journalism, and I would go out of my way to be fair, balanced, and impartial. I refused to declare a political party for years out of fear that someone would call that into question. Was that too far? Probably. However, my views of objectivity have evolved, like Sammy Roth's. In this chapter, we'll unpack the complexity of journalistic objectivity, beginning with where this concept came from, why it's persisted, and how it affects reporting on human-caused climate change.

Objectivity Then and Now

For decades, objectivity has been considered a guiding principle of journalism. The Merriam-Webster dictionary defines *objectivity* as "the quality or character of being objective; lack of favoritism toward one side or another; freedom from bias."[9] Put another way, journalists should report stories impartially, those stories should be "balanced" and "fair," and the reporting should be free of personal or political persuasion and opinion, allowing readers to decide for themselves what conclusions to draw.

The expectation of objectivity isn't limited to journalism. We ask judges to be unbiased. We want scientists to rely on their research and experiments to draw conclusions. We want teachers to be fair in their classroom lectures and their grading.

Martin Baron, former executive editor of *The Washington Post*, wrote in an editorial in 2023, "We want medical researchers and government regulators to be objective in determining whether new drugs might work and whether they can be taken safely. We want scientists to objectively evaluate the impact of chemicals in the soil, air, and water."[10]

Baron argued judges and doctors don't always get objectivity right, and neither do journalists. His defense of objectivity lies in the original definition, when journalists were expected to follow a meticulous reporting method, similar to how scientists approach research by interrogating a thesis. His argument raises two questions: What is the history behind "journalistic objectivity"? And does that concept still serve audiences and journalists today?

Origins of Objectivity

Objectivity's roots are generally traced back to American journalist Walter Lippman. In the late 1800s and early 1900s, newspapers focused on sensational stories espousing polarizing and opinionated views to sell papers. In 1922, Lippman penned *Public Opinion*, which explored the complex relationship between media, public opinion, and democracy's future. He emphasized, among other ideas, that journalists needed to be more detached and scientific in reporting the news.[11]

Lippman tried to define what truth in reporting meant, hoping readers would get an unbiased rendering of the news. "The cardinal fact always is the loss of contact with objective information," Lippman wrote two years later in *The Atlantic*. "Public as well as private reason depends upon it. Not what somebody says, not what somebody wishes were true, but what is so beyond all our opining constitutes the touchstone of our sanity."[12]

Lippmann's ideas elevated objectivity as a journalistic ideal. The goal? Build truth and credibility in journalism through rigorous fact-based reporting. The noble pursuit of truth cascaded through newsrooms and press agencies as journalists focused on fairness, balance, and fact-based information. American universities integrated objectivity into journalism curriculums as the field further professionalized.

Whose Truth?

Fundamental questions exist over objectivity in journalism: What is truth *really*? Who defines it? Whose truth gets presented? How does truth get intermediated by the journalist reporting a story, and whom do they choose as sources? "Journalism by nature is reactive and practical rather than philosophical and introspective," wrote Bill Kovach and Tom Rosenstiel in their preeminent book *The Elements of Journalism: What Newspeople Should Know and the Public Should Expect*.[13]

For decades, White journalists and editors, largely men, held leadership positions that shaped the "truths" reported in the mainstream media. As a result, underrepresented communities have questioned the validity of claims of journalistic objectivity.

In the 1900s, Lippman acknowledged the limitations and potential challenges of objectivity. I seriously doubt, though, that he imagined a media landscape like today's, with so many ways to access news, from social media and digital publications to multiple news channels.

The nature of daily news, for example, has led to quick-turn stories with quotes from both sides of a story—a stenography of a first draft of history. Journalists didn't let readers know how they reported a story or how they arrived at their reported "truth." Kovach and Rosenstiel wrote, "Journalists tended to deny that they (reporting techniques) existed—let alone that their subjective experience, culture, age, gender or race had any hand in the choices." Some journalists chose not to vote in elections or refrained from civic engagement for fear of appearing biased. Such an extreme view of objectivity has left readers "suspicious that the press was either deluding itself or hiding something."[14]

Objectivity's Evolution

Journalists practiced reporting both sides of a story for decades. The practice of remaining "neutral and unbiased" really came into question in the early 1950s when Senator Joe McCarthy, a Republican from Wisconsin, rose to unexpected prominence. He claimed to have a list of Communist Party members who worked in the US State Department, and he incited what became known as the Red Scare.

At the time, Elmer Davis, a radio commentator, acknowledged journalism's adherence to remaining unbiased: "Let the public be imposed on by the charlatan with the most brazen front." In 1953, Davis said that McCarthy's domination of headlines perpetuated lies and fear.[15]

The McCarthy years signaled a shift in journalism's long-held views on objectivity. By the 1950s and 1960s, journalists brought heightened skepticism and questioning of government officials. Sources and context, along with facts, were needed. Daniel Hallin, a journalism historian and a distinguished professor emeritus at UC San Diego, said this period signaled a move toward "critical professionalism" in journalism.[16]

The Vietnam War, for example, required journalists to contextualize and investigate claims. No longer could reporters just print what government officials said because their words couldn't be trusted. To confront government propaganda, reporters needed to investigate and develop sources to discover the truth behind government messaging.

Investigative journalists in the 1960s especially questioned objectivity if "it did not challenge power, privilege, and inequality."[17] In 1971, *The New York Times* published excerpts of top-secret information about America's involvement in Vietnam. The Pentagon Papers generated more investigative reporting, challenging the objectivity norm.

Then, a year later, America experienced Watergate. This political scandal rocked the presidency of Richard Nixon in the early 1970s and changed journalism. Investigative reporting by Bob Woodward and Carl Bernstein of *The Washington Post* showed the power of investigative journalism to expose how far government officials would go to deceive both the public and the press. The Watergate scandal ended with Nixon's resignation and marked the rise of investigative reporting as a noble pursuit.

The idea of journalistic objectivity further evolved as Congress began to deregulate cable television in the 1980s and into the mid-1990s. That paved the way for programming to increasingly lean conservative or liberal.[18] Conflict-powered cable news viewership and programs typically showcase debates between "two sides" as a way to achieve fair and balanced reporting. Cable news networks such as MSNBC and Fox News offered viewers news tailored to their political worldview.

By the early 1990s, access to the internet had become more widespread, further reshaping the media industry. Social media further disrupted media by increasing the speed and spread of misinformation and disinformation. Bias and opinion blur with facts and a traditional take on objectivity in today's crowded media landscape. Objectivity, as Walter Lippman imagined it, means something different in this modern news world, and its role continues to be a flashpoint in journalism debates.

Differing Opinions

Journalists and editors have long debated objectivity and today increasingly question its relevance.[19] Some see the idea as a symbol of fairness, a flag of credibility to news consumers. Others believe objectivity leads to "both-sides-ism" which too often suggests false equivalencies. Some news organizations have defaulted to automatically presenting "both sides" of an issue. In practice, that's resulted in climate deniers getting equal time with climate scientists despite a consensus among scientists on the truth of human-caused climate change. This misapplication of objectivity as "equal time for both sides" has given audiences a false impression of the facts about climate change. The one thing most journalists, including me, can agree on is that objectivity was instilled early in our careers.

However, a generational shift is under way as new journalists recognize the complexities of the media landscape today. There's growing recognition that the concept of objectivity remains as elusive as a unicorn. It's useful to understand differing viewpoints as journalists develop their own approach to reporting.

The newsroom culture that exalted objectivity as a value developed at a time when predominantly White men were in charge, and there were fewer sources of news. Rosenstiel argues that "open-minded inquiry" gets closer to what journalists are after. "If we could start there and lose the term objectivity altogether," he says, "we'd be in a better starting spot."[20]

Christiane Amanpour, a long-time international journalist, pinned a video clip of her reporting in conflict zones over the years on her X page (formerly Twitter). She wrote, "Truthful, not neutral."[21] In an interview with Poynter, Amanpour explained that journalists must practice pursuing truth as a form of objectivity. "Objectivity is not whataboutism, it is not about drawing false equivalencies, either factual or moral," she said. "I do believe that, when we seek the truth, we are being objective."[22]

Hot Take: *Journalists' views on objectivity are evolving. The profession's gold standard is being redefined by transparency, authenticity, and fairness rather than the traditional interpretation, which has historically led to a false balance in climate reporting.*

Amanpour found that trying to report "both sides" of the Bosnian War in the early 1990s, for example, didn't align with what she witnessed: ethnic cleansing and genocide. "I could not equate those two sides, and I refused to equate those two sides," Amanpour said. "I was just doing my job: telling the truth and bringing the facts." Amanpour was criticized for not being objective. That experience, she said, made her focus on being truthful in reporting—her definition of objectivity.[23]

Objectivity "leads to a fundamental misunderstanding of what journalism is," said Nikole Hannah-Jones, a Pulitzer Prize–winning reporter who covers racial injustice for *The New York Times Magazine* and created the landmark *The 1619 Project*. She is also the Knight Chair in Race and Journalism at Howard University, where she is the founding director of the Center for Journalism & Democracy. "Journalism is not stenography.... That should not be our role," Hannah-Jones said on the *1A Podcast*. "Our role should actually be to get at the truth and provide context and analysis so people understand what this means."[24]

A Defining Moment

In 2020, a racial reckoning swept across the United States after George Floyd was murdered by Minneapolis police. Difficult discussions ensued in newsrooms across the country.[25] Objectivity was being called into question. How was it that major news publications weren't calling out the injustice being done? Why couldn't journalists take a stand on their social media platforms or participate in marches? Why did the media refuse to call George Floyd's death "murder"?

My students at Arizona State University asked those questions in the days after Floyd's death in late May 2020. Why shouldn't "we"—the media—stand up for what was right? Shouldn't "we" be doing more to diversify our sources and better reflect our audiences? They didn't see why it was "wrong" to post about what they saw and felt. The professional program I taught in, Cronkite News, took a traditional stance: Student journalists could not post on their social media accounts or participate in marches. They needed to adhere to the journalism standard of objectivity. The message to the students was they needed to learn the lesson I and so many veteran journalists had grown up with: Remain neutral, detached, and unbiased. Many newsrooms across the country took a similar stance.

George Floyd's murder marked a tipping point for many journalists to directly question what they saw as an outdated concept of objectivity.[26] For example, Pittsburg was one of many cities where protests occurred in the wake of Floyd's murder. Alexis Johnson, a Black journalist at the *Pittsburgh Post-Gazette*, posted photos of trash heaps in a parking lot: "Horrifying scenes and aftermath from selfish LOOTERS who don't care about this city!!!!!. . . . oh wait sorry. No, these are pictures from a Kenny Chesney concert tailgate. Whoops."[27] Johnson's tweet went viral, yet she was told by news management that she had "violated social media policy and could not be objective."[28] She was removed from reporting on protests.

Poynter reported that a White male reporter had a similar social media violation during this same period.[29] He was not removed from covering the protests. "The implication here is that his violation was an anomaly, while hers was inherent to her being," wrote Gina Baleria, an associate professor in communications at Sonoma State University.[30]

Johnson's photos and tweet gave context in the wake of protests. "She was illustrating how the same behavior is condoned when perpetrated by White mainstream society and vilified when undertaken by people of color," Baleria continued. "Her perspective is actually needed as we navigate coverage of this important and ongoing story—her personal objectivity isn't."[31]

This example illustrates that every decision made in reporting a story—from the photos used to the headline—is subjective. The fact that a reporter is interested in reporting about climate change, for example, says something about them. How can—or can—journalists be objective in reporting on the scientific fact that our world is warming at a rate that endangers our very survival?

Consequences of Objectivity

Journalists have tried to maintain objectivity while reporting on climate change for years. They talked with climate scientists who said Earth was warming and that burning fossil fuels was the cause. They interviewed those who denied the science to tell the "other side" of the story. That approach—now criticized as both-sides-ism—created a false and damaging narrative that fed misinformation and disinformation. In the early years of reporting on climate change, a sense of duty to objectivity led to coverage that stoked debate over whether global warming was real and whether humans were to blame.

Journalists gave climate deniers credibility by including them prominently in stories that deepened and delayed climate action despite the science clearly showing that human-driven climate change was under way.

In hindsight, this default toward "giving both sides" made journalists susceptible to misinformation campaigns from the fossil fuel industry and other climate deniers. Climate coverage in the 1990s and early 2000s helped sow doubt about climate science information. "The disinformation campaign was so powerful, well-funded, widespread, and they were successful in casting doubt on science that was already pretty darn solid," says climate change science communicator Susan Hassol.[32]

Giving climate scientists and climate deniers equal billing in stories has had lasting consequences. The intense political debates over the cause of global warming were enabled by the lazy journalism practice of giving equal time to both sides as so-called proof of objectivity and fairness. The result is a continued argument over the cause of climate change, delaying the clean energy transition.

Climate journalists today are reporting at a time when the overwhelming majority of scientists agree that global warming is happening and it's caused by humans. Climate deniers rarely appear in stories now. But as the focus shifts to solutions aimed at reducing emissions, reporting often falls into this same false objectivity, both-sides reporting. That's why it's important to know the role of objectivity in the past so journalists today can champion fresh ways of reporting. Stories are multifaceted and require multiple sources. It's not one side and the other. It's not good or bad. Such old paradigms are simplistic, and as an editor, I welcome new iterations in our field to get at the immense complexity in this warming world.

Where's the Line?

Let's say a reporter writes a story that calls climate change the "climate crisis." The editor questions the use of "climate crisis," arguing the reporter has injected their opinion. Have they? If scientists call climate change a crisis, is it okay to use that phrase?

The British global news organization *The Guardian* decided that writing "climate crisis" was perfectly appropriate. In 2019, the paper explained to readers why it preferred the terms "climate crisis," "climate emergency," or "global heating" instead of climate change. "We want to ensure that we are being scientifically precise while also communicating clearly with readers on this very important issue," said Katharine Viner, *The Guardian*'s editor-in-chief. *Climate change* sounds passive when scientists discuss a "catastrophe for humanity," Viner said.[33]

The Guardian's decision came after prominent leaders, including scientists and the Pope, expressed the urgency of climate change. For instance, the United Nations secretary-general had already used "climate crisis" to describe the global impacts of a warming planet as "a direct existential threat."[34] Scientists, too, had already labeled climate change a crisis. *The Guardian*'s decision sparked internal discussions in newsrooms in the United States about whether climate change was the universally acceptable way to talk about a global crisis. Did using the term "climate crisis" or "climate emergency" cross an objectivity line? Would they be seen as biased for using such language?

Major news publications use variations on the term, but some organizations, such as the Canadian Broadcasting Corporation (CBC), have been more cautious. It noted that using "climate crisis and climate emergency" is sometimes legitimate but not always.[35] The public broadcaster left it to journalists to decide what language to use. "Neutrality is an important principle in our journalism," said Paul Hambleton, the CBC News standards editor. "'Climate change' and 'global warming' offer a neutral starting point for that debate, but as with all our journalistic decisions, context matters."[36]

The CBC offers an example of how a news outlet might address the objectivity question: Does using "climate crisis" or "climate emergency" in stories leave readers thinking the reporter or publication is advocating for reducing planet-warming pollution? Would that be wrong when the solution to global warming is to reduce emissions?

For *The Guardian*, the answer was to do even more reporting on climate change, including recognizing a need for climate journalism that didn't pull punches. The paper became a lead partner with the initiative Covering Climate Now—founded in 2019 by the *Columbia Journalism Review* and *The Nation*—to "address the urgent need for stronger climate coverage." Before Earth Day in 2021, *The Guardian* and other news organizations, all part of Covering Climate Now, publicly declared "what has long been evident: the climate emergency is here."[37]

News outlets that uphold objectivity would probably call *The Guardian*'s decision a journalistic overreach. It takes a clear position, albeit a position grounded in scientific fact. Other media might see this decision as transparent, fair, and truthful reporting. As an editor, I recommend reporters discuss the matter with the publication they are working for to understand the outlet's guidance.

Climate journalists are increasingly comfortable engaging in rigorous journalism while also clearly stating the reality of climate change. That's been an evolution for *LA Times* climate columnist Sammy Roth, who remembered having objectivity instilled in him early in his career at *The Desert Sun* in California. He never would have written in the *Sun* that solutions were desperately needed to lower emissions by half by 2030 and by zero by 2050 to avoid the worst impacts of climate change. At that time, he worried he or his editor would be criticized by people who denied climate science. "That's just not a good reason not to say reality," Roth said.[38]

Roth's comfort with accurately stating the reality of climate change and the effective responses has grown over the years. He said it's obvious to him that solutions are needed quickly and that suffering from climate change is under way. "What is our role as journalists," he asks, "if not to play a proactive and intentional role in trying to alleviate the suffering by bringing about solutions?"[39]

Climate journalist Emily Atkin, who founded the digital newsletter *Heated*, doesn't mince words about the urgency of addressing climate change. Some might find her approach refreshing, while others might see it leaning toward advocacy. Atkin focuses on the facts—the science, the data, the lived experiences of people—to help people understand the complexities of climate change and what is at stake. "It is not your fault that the planet is burning," she wrote on the *Heated* site. The blame for the climate emergency rests with the "greedy; the cowardly; the power-hungry; the apathetic." It's why Atkin created *Heated*: "to expose and explain the forces behind past and present inaction on the most existential threat of our time."[40]

Beyond Objectivity

A new generation of journalists is questioning traditional objectivity, having witnessed the false equivalencies that can emerge in coverage of issues such as racial injustice and climate change. For these journalists, the goal is to be accurate and fair in reporting while acknowledging the reality of what's happening. This perspective can sometimes clash with seasoned journalists and editors who remain committed to objectivity and may view this approach as veering into advocacy. However, several strategies can help maintain rigorous journalism without falling into the traps created by objectivity.

Acknowledge Bias

We all have biases. As an editor, I specifically wanted to focus on human-driven climate change because I care about the planet's future, and I believe journalism has a center stage role to play in informing people about our warming world. Should I refrain from climate coverage because I hold this viewpoint? I don't think so, given that I can bring valuable perspectives and critiques to many climate issues because of my interest and experience. The key is to acknowledge bias and talk it through with an editor.

Journalists do need to avoid clear conflicts of interest. For example, reporters may have volunteered on a campaign to raise awareness about climate change, helped build trails, planted trees, or participated in Earth Day activities. Such lived experiences can aid reporting and potentially connect journalists with sources. Far from disqualifying a reporter from covering this beat, such experiences might better inform their work.

But let's say a reporter organized and led a youth climate march. Would it be okay to cover future climate activism or interview someone at an environmental organization that was involved? If a reporter did that, they should recuse themselves from covering future events. Instead, they might pass their knowledge on to another colleague to cover the story. Each situation is unique and merits a conversation with an editor.

Here's a different scenario: A reporter has a childhood friend who now works for an offshore wind company in the United States. The friend says the company plans to halt a proposed project. That's an interesting story because it helps explain the challenges a young industry has had getting started in the United States. Should the reporter cover this story? There's a conflict of interest at work here. The reporter knows about the story only from the friend, and covering the story could benefit the company where the reporter's friend works. Political actors who oppose renewable energy might spot the connection and call out the reporting and the journalist's credibility.

These scenarios aren't uncommon. When journalists encounter them, it's best to discuss them with an editor to avoid pitfalls. As a journalist who grew up with objectivity as the standard, I have historically taken a more conservative approach to these questions. But other journalists will have a different comfort level, so the key is to be clear on each media organization's practices and policy.

Avoid the "Both Sides" Framework

A major pitfall of traditional objectivity has been to report stories by getting "both sides," which frankly is lazy journalism. This chapter illustrated how reporting on climate change fell into this trap, giving climate deniers an equal voice alongside climate scientists in the name of being "fair" and "balanced." That fueled false narratives and a political divide over whether climate change was real and human-caused.

Stories should include multiple perspectives from various sources, but those perspectives should be interrogated and compared with hard data and facts. That could mean getting the oil and gas industry's perspective on what it claims to be doing to reduce planet-warming pollution, but it doesn't mean simply reporting those claims as objective truth. For example, if a company representative says they have dramatically reduced their emissions, a journalist should find out what "dramatically" means numerically. By what percentage? Over what time period? Has an outside source verified those figures?

Most climate stories will include perspectives from academic researchers and scientists. As we discussed in an earlier chapter, it's important to know those scientists' credentials and where their work has been published. Reporters will probably also need to explain any science terms and provide context rather than simply repeating words and phrases used by the scientists.

Including various perspectives also means interviewing those directly affected by climate change because they are experts on their own experiences. Journalists will need to provide context and facts after hearing someone share their general perspective and emotions about what has happened. For instance, if someone says they feel like more hurricanes have hit their hometown in recent years, reporters can look at weather data over time to see whether that feeling is borne out by the data. Maybe storms are becoming more frequent in that area, maybe they're not more frequent but more intense, or maybe failing infrastructure makes them feel more intense. That is excellent context to bring into a story.

The key is to take the time to find diverse experts and sources who will bring valuable perspectives to the audience—and then to examine those perspectives. How do they stack up against one another and other sources of information? Ultimately, getting multiple diverse perspectives can help determine the accuracy of sources' statements, serving as a reliable method to present an honest view. It's what long-time investigative journalists Bob Woodward and Carl Bernstein call "the best available version of the truth."[41]

Be Transparent

Being open about the reporting process—how a journalist arrived at the best "version of truth"—is an excellent way to win over skeptical readers and build credibility.

Climate journalists, including Sammy Roth with *The LA Times*, are increasingly transparent about how they approach stories—a far cry from capital "O" objectivity. In Roth's *Boiling Point* newsletter, he made his approach clear from the beginning. He described his tone and approach to readers of his newsletter as "'Hi I'm Sammy. I cover this stuff. I care about this stuff.'" It's a conversation he's established, and each week he covers what's important in the climate space and why it matters. "In the same way that journalists ought to be comfortable denouncing systemic racism and pushing politicians to tackle homelessness," Roth wrote in an issue of *The Boiling Point*, "we need to get comfortable decrying the horrors of the climate crisis and demanding solutions."[42]

Roth says his audience responded when he started sharing more about his perspective. When he wrote in 2020 about how he experienced the heat wave that crippled California's electric grid, he says, "I got more response to that piece than anything I had ever written basically."[43]

I've written stories where I explained that I tried to get a comment from a particular federal agency, but that the agency either didn't return my messages in time or simply said "no comment." That's transparency. So is taking readers along for a reporting adventure to understand the great lengths it took to get a story. A news organization's mission might also need to be shared in a story. Journalists and editors should also own mistakes and clearly state corrections to the audience. All of this helps people understand the journalism process while boosting credibility. Being transparent is the antidote to traditional objectivity, which instills skepticism in news consumers.

Newsroom Policies

Most news organizations have established guidelines defining acceptable participation in everything from political activities to social media. Generally, news leaders frown upon placing a yard sign or a bumper sticker on a journalist's car for a political candidate because it can show bias. Marching for a cause could also be a concern. Social media policies also vary between news organizations: Some are more comfortable with journalists expressing views, and others aren't. Journalists don't want to say or do something that can erode "the perception of fairness and open-mindedness—of 'trustworthiness.'"[44] When in doubt, discuss with your editor.

Accuracy

If modernized objectivity is about fairness and accuracy, the oldest principle—accuracy—remains essential and timeless. Journalists who want to earn the audience's trust will stay laser focused on accuracy. Nothing hurts credibility more than getting something wrong in a story. Errors happen. But when they do, it's best to own and be transparent about them through a correction.

Noting fact-checks in the margins of a story creates a breadcrumb trail that will help the editor double-check facts. Running facts by sources is standard and excellent practice. Similarly, an investigative piece might undergo a legal review by a lawyer to make sure a journalist doesn't cross the line into conjecture or attribute motives (which you cannot know) to the sources in a story. For instance, finding evidence that a carbon storage facility is leaking emissions does not mean that a reporter can assert that the company was intentionally trying to poison the surrounding community. That requires serious reporting and fact-checking. Journalists' credibility skyrockets when they're meticulous about accuracy, and reporters meet a more modern definition of objectivity.

Any journalist who reports on climate change will find themselves confronting the complexities of fairness and objectivity. Historical conceptions of objectivity have led to false equivalencies and both-sides-ism. Such practices have fanned climate misinformation and disinformation. Some reporters today feel compelled to convey the dire nature of the climate crisis because they recognize the urgency of climate change and the scientific evidence behind it. Unlike those of us who were raised with objectivity as a guiding principle, these reporters are also driven to share their personal experiences and passion for the subject.

Although objectivity was once the gold standard in journalism, today's pursuit of fair and accurate reporting emphasizes transparency and authenticity. Reporters who embrace these practices are most likely to earn audience trust and get the climate story right.

Essential Reading and Resources

Beyond Objectivity: Leonard Downie Jr. and Andrew Heyward wrote an insightful report on journalism beyond objectivity. Their insights helped shape my thinking on this chapter, and they will help you too. https://cronkitenewslab.com/wp-content/uploads/2023/01/Beyond-Objectivity-Report-1.pdf

The Elements of Journalism: What Newspeople Should Know and the Public Should Expect: Bill Kovach and Tom Rosenstiel have created this must-read for a deeper understanding of journalism principles.

Trusting News: There's a trust gap between news consumers and media organizations. If you're interested in improving understanding and trust with audiences, check out Trusting News.org. https://trustingnews.org/

CHAPTER 6

Unequal Burdens

"Climate justice journalism is just journalism."
—Ezra David Romero

In 2022, Ezra David Romero reported a series of stories for public media outlet KQED about how communities throughout the San Francisco Bay area were responding to climate change, particularly to sea level rise. His first piece centered on Bayview Hunters Point, a neighborhood of some 35,000 people, largely people of color, that is located next to one of the country's worst Superfund sites: the sprawling Hunters Point Naval Shipyard. The complex opened for business in 1945, housing ships that had been used to test atomic bombs in the open ocean. The vessels were cleaned in the shipyard, often by Bayview residents. When the facility closed in 1974, it left a legacy of radioactive and toxic materials that had leached into the soil.[1] Residents worried that rising seas would bring that pollution ever closer to their community. They pushed for faster site cleanup and fought against plans to build new housing there.

Romero's radio story opens by explaining why he chose this location, this community: "I started off in Bayview Hunters Point because this whole project was based off of listening to people around the Bay. And when I listened to a bunch of community members, Bayview Hunters Point stood out because there's all this work happening there, and they're also worried about sea level rise."[2]

The audio then cuts to Arieann Harrison, a fifth-generation resident who founded an environmental justice group after her mother died of lung disease—a disease her mother attributed to pollution at Hunters Point, where she worked. Harrison said matter-of-factly, "I want you to know that this community is super inundated with toxicity. We were always claiming that we were sick. You know, that a lot of people were dying of cancer."[3]

Romero also interviewed a scientist, Dr. Ahimsa Porter Sumchai, who had studied the chemical levels in residents' bodies. The story he told was not only about a contaminated shipyard but about health, climate change, race,

133

and actions to protect the community. As Harrison told Romero, "Climate justice is a real thing. Sea level rise is real. This is the opportunity to stand up and do the right thing by the people."[4]

In his reporting, Romero carefully presented Harrison as an expert who provided context and helped listeners understand the stakes of the story rather than merely as a victim. "As a person of color myself covering communities of color, I often see myself or my family having gone through similar things," Romero says. "I want to make sure that I'm not just tokenizing them [sources] or hurting them in the process [of reporting]."[5]

Romero grew up in California's Central Valley, the state's agricultural heartland. His parents worked on a peach farm in the mountains near the Sierra Nevada range and Yosemite National Park. They were also missionaries whose evangelical Christian group provided food to countries around the world. The farmers, farmworkers, and rural residents of his hometown stayed with Romero even after he left for college. After graduation, Romero landed back in the Central Valley in 2012 at Valley Public Radio in Fresno with his first radio reporting job.

He consistently pitched stories to his editor that drew on his childhood roots: the environment and farming. By 2013, Romero became the station's full-time environmental reporter. Wildfires ripped through the Sierra Nevada mountains that year. Drought gripped the Central Valley, and farmers struggled to grow crops. Romero recalls that climate change's effects seemed to saturate the land wherever he went.

"I was just reporting on what the communities around me were dealing with and they just happened to be lower income, mainly Hispanic or Hmong," Romero remembers.[6]

Climate justice is a core focus in Romero's stories, but he disagrees with being labeled a climate justice reporter. "I didn't think of my role as a journalist with climate justice ingrained," he says. "It was just like, that's what's happening."[7]

For Romero, reporting on climate justice is like covering any other aspect of the climate crisis. "These are people who are affected by the worst of climate change in our world," he says. "And it's just journalism." He worries that defining climate justice as a journalism beat can have the unintentional consequence of further marginalizing communities. "We put this category to it that makes it its own thing. And so only certain people can do it," Romero says. "But I think it's everyone's job because we're all human. And we all live in the world."[8]

Romero makes an excellent point: It is all of our responsibility to cover climate justice issues. So we begin by learning about where some of the largest inequities, globally and locally, persist. What has driven those inequities? How is that changing through climate justice movements? Then, in the pages ahead, we'll look inward at journalism and its responsibility to reflect the audiences we serve and how that shows up in the newsroom. Finally, we'll explore practical reporting tips that can help journalists cover communities that are not their own.

From Global to Local

Whether or not a newsroom defines climate justice as a separate beat, journalists will discover the disproportionate impacts of climate change everywhere. Although climate change is global, it does not affect everyone equally or in the same ways. Where people live matters; so do income, race, and ethnicity. In a particularly cruel irony, the people and communities who have historically contributed the least to global warming often experience its most severe consequences.[9]

"The impacts of climate change will not be borne equally or fairly between rich and poor, women and men, and older and younger generations," according to the United Nations. "Consequently, there has been a growing focus on climate justice, which looks at the climate crisis through a human rights lens."[10]

Observing the world through that lens gives reporters a different perspective on all types of climate stories, from the local (storms, wildfires, extreme heat) to the national (federal policy and programs) to the global (international climate accords and adaptation financing). Such a big-picture view helps local journalists connect what's happening at a massive scale with what's happening in their communities.

Penn State University atmospheric scientist Greg Jenkins has spent most of his career researching the impacts of climate change on people, including in African countries. He went to Niger as a postdoctoral student and saw how vulnerable that population was to the shocks of a warming world. What's alarming, he says, is the lack of systems to predict major storms or warn people about torrential rains that could lead to catastrophic flooding. "This is injustice at the root of it and it's not being addressed," Jenkins says.[11]

It's not just the risk of floods that can devastate communities but also the environmental harm that's already been caused by oil extraction in African countries. Jenkins reminds students about this connection in class. He asks his students whether they consider where their fuel comes from when they gas up their cars. They might say the gas came from an oil well but not make the connection with extractive drilling. "The things that get me in places like Africa, like Nigeria and Angola, they're pumping out a lot of oil…but they're gonna get a double whammy," he explains.[12]

This, for Jenkins, represents the intersection of climate, environmental, and social injustice. It's not just happening in Africa. It's also happening right down the street. "I grew up in Philadelphia in a very rough neighborhood with poverty and a lot of inequity," Jenkins says. When he asks young men in similar circumstances about climate change, "They're just like, 'Man, I can't even deal with that. I don't have money. I might get killed from gun violence. And if the police pull up behind me, I might not survive the encounter.'"[13] That's social injustice.

The truth is that those young men are also dealing with climate and environmental injustice. Their neighborhoods are disproportionately affected by heat waves, air pollution, lack of basic infrastructure, and other ills from which the affluent can buffer themselves.

Robert Bullard, known as the "father of environmental justice" because of his long history of activism and scholarship, says the particulars may vary from community to community, but "climate change will impact every region of the country, and every aspect of our lives."[14] Our job as journalists is to help explain those changes: Who is most affected, what are the specific impacts, where is this happening, when did it begin, and why does the disparity exist?

Extreme Weather and Natural Disasters

The impacts of climate change look different across the country. Catastrophic wildfires and extreme heat dominate the western United States, and hurricanes and floods threaten the East Coast and Gulf states every year. Some regions, explains Bullard, are more vulnerable than others.

An Environmental Protection Agency (EPA) study from 2021 reveals the disproportionate repercussions of climate change on socially vulnerable populations in the contiguous United States, accounting for education, income, race, ethnicity, and age. The peer-reviewed study found that socially vulnerable communities are less prepared for heat waves, floods, and droughts exacerbated by climate change. Their ability to respond after a disaster also lags.

Climate justice stories exist in each of those communities, but too often, they go underreported or are missed. Take, for example, the extreme winter

Vulnerabilities to Climate Change

An analysis by the US Environmental Protection Agency identified critical areas of vulnerability among Americans. Researchers found that not all populations experience the impacts of climate change the same. Income, education, race, and ethnicity all play a role.

Minority communities in the United States are more likely to live in places that are projected to experience the worst impacts of human-caused climate change with a 2°C (3.6°F) increase in global temperatures.

Black and African American Communities
- 40 percent more likely to live in areas with the largest predicted increases in death rates from extreme heat due to climate change
- 34 percent more likely to live in places with the highest expected rise in childhood asthma cases, linked to worsening air pollution from climate change

Hispanic and Latino Communities
- 43 percent more likely to live in regions where weather-exposed jobs are expected to lose the most work hours because of more frequent high-temperature days
- 50 percent more likely to live in coastal areas facing the biggest increases in traffic delays due to higher tides and flooding caused by climate change

American Indian and Alaska Native Communities
- 48 percent more likely to live in areas most at risk of losing land due to sea level rise
- 37 percent more likely to live in regions where jobs in weather-exposed industries will suffer the largest loss in work hours due to rising temperatures

Asian Communities
- 23 percent more likely to live in coastal areas where traffic delays from high-tide flooding are expected to worsen the most because of climate change

Source. Courtesy of the US Environmental Protection Agency. *Climate Change and Social Vulnerability in the United States: A Focus on Six Impacts.* EPA 430-R-21-003, 2021. Accessed September 22, 2024. https://www.epa.gov/cira/social-vulnerability-report.

rains called atmospheric rivers that deluge Los Angeles, San Diego, and other West Coast cities every year. News outlets will cover the weather, focusing on whether infrastructure works or fails. After all, levees, dams, storm drains, and other infrastructure aren't built for 10 inches of rain falling in a short period of time. Reporting may also look at the science of how these rivers of moisture form. These are all valid and necessary stories. However, an equity component looms large in such stories of extreme weather.

Ezra David Romero focused on the human toll when covering the aftermath of one of the devastating winter storms in 2023. During his reporting, he met then-eighteen-year-old Denia Escutia through a climate justice organization. Escutia, a senior in high school at the time, stood in her bedroom with bags of clothes and belongings, flood damage everywhere. Through Escutia's eyes, Romero tells the story of a family trying to decide whether to rebuild or leave the community where they had lived for years. Escutia and her family ultimately decided to move, only to return in 2024 to an apartment in the same area that flooded.[15] Rents were too expensive elsewhere.

Romero met with Escutia periodically for months. There was "a connection," he remembers. The initial radio story focused on Escutia and her family. Many meet-ups and interviews later, their story became part of a podcast called *Sold Out* about climate change and housing. "You take the time to figure out who's the best person for this story," Romero says. "Then you get to know them really well for a feature."[16]

Finding people willing to share their experiences in historically marginalized communities makes the intangible tangible. Romero could have framed his reporting differently, focusing on the levee and the people tasked with maintaining or rebuilding it. Instead, by zeroing in on one family's difficult decision, he humanized the vast injustice of climate change.

"There's never enough reporting on the issues around which communities are better able to adapt and cope with these disasters, whether it's a flood, whether it's a hurricane, or whether it's a drought, or whether it's even a winter storm," explains Bullard.[17]

Heat

Extreme weather or disasters almost always have a climate justice component. Summer temperatures are hotter in densely concretized sections of any city than in its more shaded suburbs. The National Oceanic and Atmospheric Administration has a program to map urban heat islands in select cities every summer that enlists the help of residents to record temperature and air quality data.[18] The data can help lead reporters to climate justice stories.

Journalists don't have to look far to find inequity where they live. Take something as seemingly simple as the trees in a community: They are an outstanding way to begin investigating climate justice. Tree canopy can help reduce hot summer temperatures. In places where few trees thrive, temperatures can be 15°F higher than in shaded neighborhoods.

Some cities, such as Chicago, Phoenix, San Francisco, and Seattle, have mapped the tree canopy. By overlaying the data onto a map of city neighborhoods, reporters will probably find something newsworthy: Low tree canopy is usually found in historically marginalized neighborhoods. When heat waves strike, these communities suffer the most.

Another climate justice angle is to find out where cooling centers are located. Are they only in affluent neighborhoods? Are they where they need to be? Are they accessible, and for how long?

That reporting can lead to heat-related mortality figures. How many heat deaths were reported in a city, and how many have occurred during the last five years? What is a city doing to address those health risks? Asking these questions can help inform city officials, policymakers, and community organizations about how to respond to the inequities of climate change.

Air Quality

Similar statistics about air quality reveal societal inequities exacerbated by climate change. The American Lung Association's *State of the Air* report in 2024 found that more than 131 million people in the United States live in counties with unhealthy levels of air pollution. People of color are 2.3 times more likely than White people to live in communities that have failing grades for ozone and other types of fine particle pollution.[19] That translates to more cases of asthma and respiratory illnesses.

Breathing other people's pollution is "a problem of justice and equity," Bullard says. "Blacks and Latinos are disproportionately burdened with breathing bad air that has been polluted by White people. Blacks, for example, are exposed to 56 percent more pollution than they cause. Latinos are exposed to 63 percent more pollution than they cause. On the other hand, Whites enjoy a pollution advantage. We would say that's equivalent to White privilege, meaning they breathe 17 percent less pollution than they cause."[20]

Air quality issues translate to hospitalizations and deaths. African American adults, for example, are nearly three times more likely than White people to die of asthma. Black and Hispanic children are nearly five times more likely to be admitted to the hospital for asthma than White children. Black children have a national death rate that's more than seven times that of non-Hispanic White children.[21] "These statistics are not acceptable," Bullard says. "Climate change will make it worse."[22]

Reporters can find out the specific statistics in the communities they cover: Where are the industrial plants and highways located? Near which communities? How were decisions made about the location of these facilities, and what are officials doing to ameliorate the health risks? These questions often lead to compelling climate justice stories.

Roots of Inequity

Infrastructure might not seem directly related to climate change. However, inequality in infrastructure between communities of color and White communities exacerbates the harmful effects of climate change. Freeways and levees, for example, can be found near communities of color. That infrastructure can also be vulnerable to extreme weather influenced by climate change.

The most recent report card on US infrastructure produced by the American Society of Civil Engineers gave the country a C− for its overall infrastructure.[23] The report gave a grade for eighteen unique infrastructure areas in the United States, including dams, bridges, schools, and drinking water.

"Many of the communities that are on the front line and the fence line," explains Bullard, "are the same communities that are getting C and D minuses when it comes to those infrastructure items."[24] These communities are in the path of potential climate disasters.

Such inequities are rooted in another grading system created by the federal government in the 1930s to map neighborhoods in every major city in the country. The grades identified the "residential security," or the risk a bank took by lending to homebuyers in that neighborhood.[25] An "A" grade meant the neighborhood was considered safe and best for a mortgage, and a "D" rating on the maps indicated risk. The term *redlining* comes from this practice.

A federal agency determined what sections of a city were labeled desirable and safe or risky and unsafe, deeming African Americans and immigrants a "threat to the stability of home values."[26] The practice created huge economic disparities between communities. "A" grade neighborhoods were largely affluent and White, and "D" rated communities were typically Black, Latino, or low income.

The decades-long fallout from redlining defined marginalized and vulnerable neighborhoods. Many communities today still bear the brunt of this racist practice; formally redlined neighborhoods are the same places where industry has been allowed to build and pollute.

Redlining from the 1930s, says Penn State University professor Greg Jenkins, connects to the effects of climate change today and will have a ripple effect for decades. "The background issues of a community need to be at least understood before the story's written," says Jenkins.[27]

Past housing practices in a city are an excellent way to find potential local environmental and climate justice stories. Environmental and community organizations can help journalists learn about inequities people face and connect them to invaluable experts: the people who have experienced environmental injustice and who historically have not had a voice. Their stories and their solutions offer critical insights into what climate justice can mean.

Hot Take: *Breathing other people's pollution is "a problem of justice and equity," explains the "father of environmental justice," Robert Bullard. Want to understand a city's history of environmental inequities? Check out the University of Richmond's "Mapping Inequality: Redlining in New Deal America" to find digitized maps of major US cities that have historically redlined neighborhoods. It's a starting place for future reporting.*

Climate Justice as a Movement

Around the world, a diverse coalition of groups and individuals have joined together to address climate change as an environmental issue and a complex social, economic, and ethical challenge. Organizations such as 350.org, Robert Bullard, and youth climate activists including Greta Thunberg and Xiye Bastida have all influenced this growing movement. Bastida, who grew up in Mexico City and is a descendant of the Otomi and Toltec people, describes the climate justice movement as led by young people from all races and ethnicities who recognize that "addressing the climate crisis is a survival issue for everyone. Climate change doesn't discriminate, but the ability to respond to climate disasters does."[28]

Greg Jenkins believes this type of intergenerational global grassroots effort will lead the way toward climate solutions more than governments or industry. "You're really looking out for everyone," Jenkins says. "You're connecting, whether you're in rural zones or the city, you're bringing the important constituents to the front. And those constituents generally have not had any voice in this thing."[29]

Although much coverage of climate justice is bleak, countless hopeful stories exist about everything from demonstrations and marches to advocates successfully pushing for policy change. One way to learn about progress is to talk with grassroots groups and advocates. Perhaps a community has rallied to get an industrial plant to reduce emissions that have historically been linked to escalating asthma cases in a low-income or marginalized neighborhood. Reporters might discover how a community organization worked with a neighborhood church to create a cooling shelter. From gardening programs to community solar farms, journalists will find plenty of exceptional stories to report that shift the narrative away from a helpless community—a victim narrative—to one empowered to help its neighbors.

Government Programs and Promises

Along with reporting on policies that created injustices, journalists are uniquely positioned to investigate the government programs that are designed to right historical wrongs. As environmental justice initiatives become more common, examining their benefits and weaknesses is important. How is a program being rolled out in communities? How does the money get spent, and where does it go? What programs are supported, and how are they working? Such questions lead to stories of accountability that can be followed over time.

"I found that a lot of the EJ [environmental justice] coverage, especially of the Biden administration, was not as skeptical, not as rigorous," says Naveena Sadasivam, a senior staff writer for *Grist* who covers energy, environment, and climate change.[30]

Stories about the Justice40 Initiative, for instance, help unpack why investigating federal programs is critical. Justice40 promised that 40 percent of all environment and climate investments would go to communities of color that have historically shouldered the brunt of environmental pollution.[31] That's a massive influx of money: billions of dollars to be spent across 518 programs by nineteen federal agencies.[32]

News stories initially celebrated the initiative but failed to examine its implementation: Did the money go where it was promised? *The New York Times* reported in 2023 that the administration's "signature environmental justice program may not shrink racial disparities in who breathes the most polluted air, partly because of efforts to ensure that it could withstand legal challenges."[33]

After the US Supreme Court ended race-based affirmative action for college admissions, the Biden administration decided race would not be considered when deciding who could get the funds. "Unless carefully implemented," *The New York Times* reported, "the program may not work as hoped and could even widen the racial gap by improving the air in Whiter communities, which may also be disadvantaged in some ways, faster than in communities of color."[34]

The White House created the Climate and Economic Justice Screening tool to help determine where investments would go. It accounted for numerous indicators of environmental justice, including income, exposure to tiny particles of pollution known as PM2.5, education, housing, and climate change, but not race or ethnicity.

Subsequent news coverage looked primarily at the question of whether race should be an explicit factor used in the tool. "We decided that we wanted to kind of push that story further," recalls Sadasivam.[35]

Sadasivam and data reporter Clayton Aldern at *Grist* downloaded the publicly accessible data. They compared it with maps that accounted for race to determine whether the investments reached communities of color. They discovered that "the tool confirms what environmental justice advocates have long argued: Race is one of the most potent predictors of pollution burdens. By prioritizing communities with the greatest pollution burdens, it has automatically prioritized communities of color as well."[36]

The future of initiatives such as Justice40 will probably change as new administrations with different priorities take office. Reporters should continue to monitor such programs, following the money to see what happened and also to report on what happens to them in the future. For example, Justice40 was meant to move resources to those who needed them the most. Robert Bullard remained cautious, especially as federal dollars transferred to states. Bullard points to Hurricane Harvey, which struck in 2017, devastating parts of Texas and Louisiana, as an example. Texas received federal funds to aid in the recovery, but according to Bullard, the money did not reach the hardest-hit communities. "That's the kind of injustice and inequity that we have to correct," Bullard says. "Money should follow need, as opposed to the strategy for those who have the most political power, most economic power to force money to go in that direction."[37]

Journalists have an important accountability role. Several ongoing tracking efforts can help them find out whether an organization in their city or state received federal aid. Harvard's Environmental and Energy Law Program, for example, provides regular updates on administration environmental justice commitments, including Justice40.

Legal Planet, a blog that follows climate policy and environmental law, breaks down grant programs related to the first major climate policy in the United States, the Inflation Reduction Act. What program or initiative has been developed with the money? Reporters might discover dollars were awarded, but there's nothing to show for the investment; then they can ask why. Or journalists might find a tremendous success story of a grassroots effort funded by federal investments. Either way, it's critical to follow the money and to follow what happens to federal initiatives such as Justice40 when new administrations come into office.

Legal Requirements

Title VI of the landmark 1964 Civil Rights Act prohibits any program or activity that receives federal funds from discriminating against individuals based on race, color, sex, or national origin. The statute has major implications for righting past wrongs and is essential to understand when investigating environmental injustices.

Communities across the country have filed Title VI complaints because of disproportionate exposure to pollution. Let's say an environmental organization discovers a state agency being lax in its pollution permits for an industrial complex. That facility is on the edge of a historically low-income community. That state agency gets funds to regulate air quality from the EPA. The environmental organization, citing Title VI, can file a complaint directly to the EPA to investigate what's happening.

However, the Center for Public Integrity found that fewer than twenty claims are filed each year (possibly because many who experience these injustices are unfamiliar with the process), and most are rejected.[38] The EPA maintains a list of complaints from 2014 to the present, which is worth searching periodically. A call to the local or state agency listed on the complaint is a simple way to learn more. Don't be surprised if the agency doesn't want to talk, especially if there's pending legal action. It's always worth asking, though. Such reporting is essential to hold agencies to account.

Global Inequities

So far, we have focused on inequities between communities within the United States. But when we zoom out to look at the global picture, we find an even starker contrast between rich, industrialized nations such as the United States, which have contributed the most to global warming, and poorer countries that have contributed the least. Countries including Pakistan, Nepal, Bangladesh, Haiti, and Somalia have emitted the lowest amount of greenhouse gases, yet their residents suffer from the extreme impacts of warming temperatures.

At one point in 2022, more than a third of Pakistan was underwater because of extreme rainfall.[39] Millions of people were displaced, and hundreds died. The cost to rebuild? About $30 billion.[40] That's on top of the ongoing debt the country has accumulated over the years.

In Bangladesh, rising sea levels threaten to displace millions of people, and in Sudan, ongoing conflict is only heightened by climate change, where people rely on agriculture to survive. Drought, coupled with erratic rainfall, stresses already tenuous livelihoods.

In 2023, the world witnessed the hottest year in recorded history at the time.[41] Migrants from Central America died from heatstroke trying to make it to the United States during record-breaking temperatures.

"We are living in a total climate breakdown," Guadalupe Cobos Pacheco, a resident of El Bosque, Mexico told *The Guardian* from an emergency refuge. Her community is disappearing because of rising sea levels. "It is a constant worry. . . . We don't know what to do," she said.[42]

Climate change carves a deep chasm between countries with the resources to adapt to warming temperatures and those without. Nations without adequate resources are stuck in a loop of constantly responding to the latest disaster and then trying to recover. Every disaster changes a place and its people. There's no recovery in the truest sense of the word.

World leaders have debated this dilemma for decades through international talks, with limited success. As part of an international climate accord in 2009, wealthy countries agreed to mobilize $100 billion by 2020 to help poor countries that bear the brunt of climate change.[43] Yet they repeatedly failed to deliver on that promise until 2022, and poor countries have historically called that figure inadequate.

The UN estimates the need to be near $300 billion by 2030 and in the trillions of dollars by 2050 for countries to adapt to global warming.[44] At COP29 in Azerbaijan, climate negotiations culminated with wealthy countries agreeing to pay $300 billion a year to poorer countries starting in 2035. However, real questions remain about whether countries will make good on their finance promise, what type of funds will be given, and how the money will be distributed.[45] Climate finance will continue to be an emerging area for journalists to pay attention to.

Covering climate finance amounts to accountability journalism. By understanding the inequities in funding, journalists can track what happens with distributed funds and the projects that are created, or not created. Momentum will continue to grow internationally to increase financial support and put mechanisms in place to distribute funds.[46] Those discussions happen at international gatherings such as the annual UN Conference on the Parties (COP).

Reporters can monitor the Loss and Damage Fund, which was established at the UN climate talks in Sharm El Sheikh, Egypt, in 2022 to help countries most vulnerable to climate change.[47] At COP28 in Dubai, some countries agreed to contribute to the fund, including Germany and the United Arab Emirates, which each pledged $100 million, and the United States gave $17 million.[48]

"The Loss and Damage Fund will be a lifeline to people in their darkest hour," explained Ani Dasgupta, president and CEO of the World Resources Institute.[49] He pointed to the money helping families rebuild their lives after a climate disaster and those needing to relocate because of sea level rise.

Dasgupta called the money promised at COP28 "a down payment to the far greater resources to help people reeling from losses and damage from climate change." However, he urged countries "to step forward with much larger pledges as well as mobilize innovative funding sources such as taxes on fossil fuels and shipping."[50]

The Adaptation Gap

Adaptation refers to how people and communities adjust and prepare for current and future problems brought on by human-driven climate change. That future will bring more intense, more frequent extremes that will stress and destroy infrastructure meant to protect people. Some countries have the necessary funds to adapt, but others do not. Climate-prone countries especially face an adaptation finance gap, and world leaders have long debated how to meet growing needs.

The UN Environment Programme releases a yearly adaptation gap report, and in 2023 it revealed how underfinanced adaptation efforts are in poor countries. The program found that "the adaptation finance needs of developing countries are 10–18 times as big as international public finance flows." That's more than 50 percent higher than any past estimate.[51]

Ephraim Mwepya Shitima, from Zambia, led a group of negotiators from Africa at COP28. Shitima told *The Guardian*, "We are in an adaptation emergency and our vulnerable populations are suffering." Countries must close the adaptation financing gap "so that Africans do not get left behind." Severe droughts, catastrophic storms, and sea level rise threaten "our very lives."[52]

International climate talks have historically deferred resolving thorny questions about climate finance for later discussions, opting instead for further discussion and study. That's increasingly frustrating for developing nations that need funding now as climate change accelerates. That makes the need to respond even more urgent.

Such gaps get overshadowed by broader negotiations over reducing emissions, but the issue is an important piece of the climate change puzzle and worth reporting on. Consider the growing number of national adaptation plans and whether and how they're funded. Take the Marshall Islands, a country of small islands that together are equal in size to Baltimore. These islands have contributed little to global warming. The nation's adaptation plan would bolster water supplies to stave off drought and prepare the islands for rising seas. The plan is considered comprehensive and forward thinking, a model to emulate. Yet the price tag to implement the plan is $35 billion, an extraordinary sum for such a small country.[53] Coverage of the plan and how to finance it is important not only to one set of islands but to every nation facing similar challenges.

The Just Transition

The legally binding Paris Agreement has a vital line tucked into the twenty-seven pages of text agreed to by nearly 200 countries: Consider the "imperatives of a just transition of the workforce and the creation of decent work and quality jobs in accordance with nationally defined development priorities."[54]

As economies shift from reliance on heavily polluting fossil fuels to a green, net-zero (emissions) future, the workforce will be dramatically disrupted. Jobs will disappear in the oil, gas, and coal sectors. New jobs will be created to manufacture solar panels, install heat pumps, and build wind turbines. Such tectonic shifts in economies tend to disadvantage people of color and developing nations, and those concerned with a "fair and inclusive" transition are keen to avoid past mistakes.[55] It also matters who gets hired, how well green jobs will pay, and where renewable companies will operate.

Stories about a just transition require a long view and tenacity. They are meant to be followed and reported on over time. Journalists who follow the money, especially, can identify and report on who gains from a green economy and who is put at risk.

Some international mining companies, for example, operate in poorer countries. They have historically paid subpar wages and expect employees to work long days in unsafe conditions. In recent years, mining companies have focused on extracting the necessary minerals for batteries to power electric cars—spelling an unjust means to a more just and green end.

For developing countries, such as the Congo, where minerals such as lithium and cobalt are found and used to make batteries to power electric vehicles, a new "gold rush" has exploited people working in the mines. That's not a just transition. Such stories remain underreported, in part because they are happening in places that are difficult to report from and potentially dangerous. Yet such operations represent a rapidly growing injustice: mistreatment of the workforce of poor nations for the benefit of wealthy ones.[56]

When covering the economic transition, May Thazin Aung with the International Institute for Environment and Development recommends journalists keep a basic question in mind: How just are the policies that govern the transition, and who benefits from them?[57]

Reporters can examine stories about job security, ranging from people and companies that do not want to leave the work they know to others who are eager to start learning new skills for a green economy. In states such as West Virginia, Minnesota, Tennessee, and Colorado, communities that have long relied on coal mines as their economic backbone have less demand, or their mines have completely shuttered. In Colorado, for example, the state established a government office focused on the "Just Transition" to help workers whose livelihoods were tied to the coal mines.[58] The program can retrain, relocate, and, in some cases provide an early retirement. Some Colorado cities and towns have encouraged wind and solar development, shifting coal-related jobs to new energy. Similar stories can be found across the United States and abroad.

New industries that generate significant numbers of jobs are also worth covering. Take the young offshore wind industry in the United States, which the Biden administration made a key piece of plans to reduce carbon emissions. Vineyard Wind off the Massachusetts coast has created hundreds of jobs, and it's just one development out of dozens planned along the country's coasts.[59] Who gets these jobs? How sustainable is the industry for the surrounding community? Such questions can hold powerful interests accountable while representing voices of those directly affected by changing economies.

Diversity of Sources

Sources will fundamentally shape and inform climate stories, and excluding voices will lead to contextual misses. As I reflect on my past reporting, my heart hurts when I read stories I reported on climate change. That hurt isn't over the topic but over who was in the story or, rather, who wasn't included.

For instance, I reported a story for the audio program *Living on Earth* in 2007, when climate change science was hotly debated. In northern Arizona, a scientist studied dried nests of urine, feces, and detritus known as middens. The middens were thousands of years old and contained a record of the region's climate history, illustrating how much the area had warmed. I interviewed four primary sources for the story, all White and all male. Not a single woman. Not a single person of color. And no Indigenous sources.

As a young journalist, I had a blind spot, an unconscious bias to interview scientists and academics, the lead authors of major studies. And since most fields of science have historically been predominantly White, so were my sources. I wish an editor or colleague had pushed me to diversify my sources. I imagine if I had, the midden story would have been richer and more nuanced, perhaps providing context from an Indigenous perspective, for example.

Contrast my story with Ezra David Romero's approach in *Sacrifice Zones*, the radio series described in the opening of this chapter, about communities vulnerable to climate change and toxic exposure. Like me, Romero found that many prominent scientists who studied toxins and the implications of climate change were White. But that didn't deter him. Romero widened his source pool and located, among other sources, a Black researcher studying reparations and climate change. "I found these adjacent people who may not be specifically covering the exact topic of toxic contamination, but who have written about and who are thinking about race and color," recalls Romero.[60]

The series that resulted from his reporting helped listeners understand why specific communities are more prone than others to climate disasters and toxic exposure. Romero could have included only the scientists who provided a clinical viewpoint, but his additional sources explained how redlining in parts of Oakland, California, had created a hazardous situation.

Along with interviewing academics from diverse backgrounds, Romero treated community members as experts; they had witnessed and lived through injustice. Not every resident had all the pertinent statistics and data at their fingertips. Still, they could share their experiences and the history of the community, along with their perspectives on the economic and racial dimensions of the story.

Romero's series didn't happen on a tight deadline. He took months to develop relationships, interview, and investigate the stories. He engaged with the community, and community members responded.

Two women Romero profiled in the series later told him how much they valued his reporting. "A lot of these community members have to fight everywhere they go to have anyone listen to them," Romero says. The series amplified their voices—voices that had too often been ignored.[61]

Ultimately, reporting environmental justice stories is simply about practicing good journalism: listening, avoiding preconceived ideas, and taking time to tell the whole story through diverse perspectives. Below are specific points to keep in mind as reporters go about covering climate justice-related stories.

Track Sources

Newsrooms increasingly invest in tracking the diversity of sources in stories, including using databases that make it easy for journalists to add source information. Such data can show how well a newsroom reflects its audience.

How old are the sources in the story? How do they identify racially or ethnically? What are their pronouns? Income bracket? Where are they geographically located? These are all questions journalists must commit to asking. Regular reviews of the answers, newsroom-wide, will help journalists see blind spots in their reporting.

Independent journalists don't need expensive software to track this information and can develop simple methods to document sources. That data reviewed throughout a year can help identify people of color, for instance, and help reporters shift their sourcing. Ask: Are you truly building relationships with the community you report on? If not, why?

Participate in Diversity Trainings and Journalism Groups

I cannot emphasize enough how eye-opening diversity training can be. I've been through several programs, including in-depth training, when I was president of the Society of Environmental Journalists board. It helped me to recognize my blind spots and to expand my perspective as an editor. Diversity, equity, and inclusion (DEI) training can help reporters develop new skills and ways to connect with communities that reporters may not be familiar with.

Similarly, journalists can join organizations that support reporters of color, who have historically been underrepresented. The Uproot Project, for example, was formed specifically for journalists of color covering environmental issues. The National Association of Black Journalists, Asian American Journalists Association, Indigenous Journalists Association, National Association of Hispanic Journalists, and NLGJA: The Association of LGBTQ+ Journalists are a few organizations dedicated to supporting journalists through mentorships, professional development workshops, conferences, scholarships, and more.

Interact with Communities

Nothing can substitute being present in the community that a reporter wants to cover. Many journalists, including my student journalists at Arizona State University, learned this during the early months of the COVID-19 pandemic. Most of us were forced to do our jobs remotely, removed from direct contact in our communities. It's hard to build trust and rapport that way, let alone sources. For a journalist and an editor, nothing can replace being in person at events, organizational gatherings, and city council meetings. This builds trust and helps develop sources over time. Journalists can listen and get to know people over time without the pressure of a deadline.

Treat Community Members with Respect and Care

Anyone who has survived a catastrophic hurricane, lost a home to wildfire, or suffered the loss of a loved one in a climate disaster qualifies as an expert with lived experience. Many are part of communities that have been ignored or marginalized and know what climate injustice represents. These sources understand their own arc of history and have probably heard stories passed through the generations of inequities that shaped their lives. Such perspectives provide much-needed context and are invaluable in climate reporting.

Although community members are experts, unlike lawmakers or agency officials whose salaries are paid by taxpayers, they have no obligation to talk to the press. Reporters will meet people who have experienced pain and trauma; some will want to share their experiences, but others will not. In Chapter 9 we'll examine what it means to do trauma-informed reporting and how to interact with people who are suffering from trauma. The takeaway is that journalists need to approach climate justice stories and the people in them with care and represent them thoughtfully, as Ezra David Romero does in his reporting. "At the end of the day we're telling stories about people's lives," Romero says. "These are not gotcha stories. . . . We're trying to tell a story about someone who's devastated by everything around them."[62]

Avoid "Parachute" Journalism

Parachute journalism is the practice of a reporter, usually a national or international journalist, flying in to cover a breaking news story without any advance legwork and then disappearing as soon as they've filed their story. There's unfortunately a long history of this behavior, which comes from a legacy journalism culture, and it is fundamentally extractive. Communities can feel victimized, taken for granted, or misrepresented, which in turn generates ill will toward journalists.

Instead, reporters can prepare *before* weather- and climate-related disasters strike and become familiar with issues such as historical redlining and where infrastructure (dams, sewage systems, major freeways) is located. By identifying communities ahead of a potential disaster, reporters can spend time talking with community planners, leaders, and neighbors. That way, journalists have already established relationships within the community when something happens, so rather than "parachuting in," they are reporting with thought and care.

Learn History

Reporters need to study and understand the history of systemic injustices faced by the communities they cover. Oscar Perry Abello, a senior economic justice reporter for Next City, believes journalists must help people recognize how communities became oppressed. History provides that context. When Abello wrote about community land trusts in New Orleans providing Black communities affordable housing and job opportunities, he brought in the history of redlining in the city, which excluded the city's African American population from economic opportunities.[63] Such context is essential to understanding the current situation a community is confronting and helps journalists report accurately and empathetically.

Avoid Victim Narratives

Describing a history of injustice does not mean representing people as helpless victims. Communities have agency, and so do people. Ezra David Romero's reporting makes that clear in his coverage of the residents of

Bayview Hunters Point, who have long dealt with the realities of a nearby Superfund site. A story of reparations and justice emerges through their voices. But often, reporting on marginalized communities puts the attention on the problem rather than the solution. Instead, illustrate that people are active agents in their own stories.

Put another way: Avoid exploitation and sensationalizing stories that contribute to stereotypes or stigmatize communities. Focus on reporting that respects the community's complexity and resilience.

Understand Where Bias Lies

As a journalist and editor, I've learned to acknowledge and confront my own biases. This is ongoing and difficult work, but I have found when reporters focus on that work, their stories are deeper, more contextualized, and richer because of it. I find it inspiring to work with journalists who have done this hard work and really self-reflected, because it shows up in all aspects of their stories, from the sources they interview to the questions they ask.

Avoid Labels

Respect the terminology and language preferences of the individuals and communities you cover. This includes how people identify themselves and their community, and it extends to using pronouns and names correctly.

Protect Sources

Journalist's sources, especially in marginalized communities, might face risks in sharing their stories—threats, job loss, or worse. That's why it's important to understand a source's background before doing any interviews. Sometimes, what a reporter learns warrants anonymity to protect the source. During my time as an editor, I have had numerous conversations with reporters about the risks to sources and the protections needed. A newsroom leader will ultimately decide whether to grant anonymity. It's important to explain why anonymity was granted, to be transparent with the audience.

Diversity in the Newsroom

Just as diversity of sources matters, so does diversity in the newsroom. Bringing colleagues together from varied backgrounds helps ensure that a wide range of stories are covered, including those that might be overlooked or underreported by non-Hispanic White journalists. It can also challenge stereotypes and prevent biases from seeping into reporting. Audiences also can see their communities represented in the media, which leads to engagement and trust. Representation concerns all aspects of identity, including gender, sexual orientation, age, socioeconomic background, disability, race, and ethnicity.

Consider the award-winning reporting project "Walking While Black" by Topher Sanders, a reporter at ProPublica. As Sanders explained in a Knight Media panel, his own experience as a Black man drew him to the topic and informed his reporting. Sanders had seen police officers in Jacksonville, Florida, stop a young Black man illegally in a video that went viral. Police in the video asked the man for his identification and then attempted to give him a ticket for not having it with him.[64]

"I was offended that the officer tried to, basically, say, 'Hey, can I see your walking papers.'…That's where I start to put on my skills hat," Sanders said. "I know how to obtain the data to show that they've done that before.…As a journalist, I can ask educated questions that can lead to a story that has a profound impact on that issue."[65]

"Walking While Black" revealed that in Jacksonville, where Blacks make up 29 percent of the population, they disproportionately receive more than half of all pedestrian citations.[66]

Indeed, outrage over police discrimination and brutality pushed forward long-overdue conversations about race, including its portrayal in the media, when a Minneapolis police officer killed George Floyd in 2020, giving rise to the Black Lives Matter movement. Major news publications began to discuss how to address race in headlines and stories, as well as how newsrooms reflect their audiences. However, the road ahead remains long and rocky, as then National Association of Black Journalists president Dorothy Tucker pointed out in a 2020 Knight Media Informed & Engaged series event.[67]

"The thing that frustrates me more than anything is that many of these [news] managers come out with these statements that say, 'We support Black lives'…that they support diversity, they support inclusion," Tucker said. "Yet, when we ask them to publicize their numbers on diversity, they're silent."[68]

A Pew Research Center 2018 study found that newsrooms tended to be less diverse than the broader workforce, and significant disparities in race, ethnicity, and gender remained. The majority of newsroom employees in the United States (77 percent) were non-Hispanic Whites, whereas 65 percent of the US workforce at the time identified as non-Hispanic White. Newsrooms also continue to be male dominated, with 61 percent of newsroom employees identifying as men.[69]

The study identified a "turning tide" in diversity among younger newsroom employees. Although racial and ethnic disparities persisted across all age groups, with non-Hispanic Whites making up 74 percent of newsroom employees under age fifty, the gap narrowed slightly among the youngest workers aged eighteen to twenty-nine. Younger newsroom employees offered a glimpse of increasing diversity, particularly in gender representation, suggesting gradual shifts toward greater inclusivity in the industry.[70]

Still, journalism has difficult and essential work to do to represent society accurately. Journalist Soledad O'Brien put it this way in a *New York Times* opinion piece: "The thin ranks of people of color in American newsrooms have often meant us-and-them reporting, where everyone from architecture critics to real estate writers, from entertainment reporters to sports anchors, talk about the world as if the people listening or reading their work are exclusively White."[71]

Capital "J" journalism's diversity challenges persist in environmental journalism. In 2022, Pew Research found that 84 percent of journalists who cover energy and the environment are White. However, the two beats are fairly evenly split between men and women.[72]

Environmental journalism has a long way to go to reflect the audiences it serves, and a culture shift is under way in many newsrooms. Increasingly, digital publications, such as *Inside Climate News* and *Grist*, are leading the way on DEI.[73] For example, *Grist* started to focus on DEI and justice in 2020, publicly committing to hiring people of color for all positions and diversifying the makeup of its board. Black and Indigenous staff as of 2021 had doubled.[74]

Additionally, training and support for the next generation of journalists of color are expanding through university programs, fellowships, and news organizations. Michigan State University's Knight Center for Environmental Journalism provides tuition scholarships, paid internships at news organizations, and on-the-job training. Similarly, NPR's Reflect America fellowship supports journalists from diverse backgrounds to develop public radio experience, sometimes by completing the fellowship with NPR's climate desk. Organizations such as the Uproot Project also support DEI in environmental journalism, including partnering with the Society of Environmental Journalists to provide diversity travel fellowships to SEJ's annual conference.

Each initiative represents a step toward a shared goal that newsrooms reflect their audiences and the communities they cover. By focusing on DEI, newsrooms become more diverse, which translates to deeper and more nuanced understanding of our communities and world. That should be the goal of all reporters, not just those who want to report on issues of climate inequity and justice.

Essential Reading and Resources

Dumping in Dixie: Race, Class, and Environmental Quality, by Robert Bullard: In this book, considered a foundational text in environmental justice, Bullard examines the disproportionate placement of hazardous waste sites in African American communities.

The Color of Law: A Forgotten History of How Our Government Segregated America, by Richard Rothstein: This book explores how government policies reinforced segregation, affecting housing and social inequality.

Braiding Sweetgrass: Indigenous Wisdom, Scientific Knowledge and the Teachings of Plants, by Robin Wall Kimmerer: The author blends Indigenous wisdom and scientific knowledge, touching on the exploitation of natural resources and communities.

Sand Talk: How Indigenous Thinking Can Save the World, by Tyson Yunkaporta: The author's aboriginal traditions of storytelling and symbolic drawings are used to explore global issues. By integrating Indigenous wisdom, Yunkaporta suggests that this perspective, which values deep listening and connection to Earth, can offer solutions to the crises of our time.

CHAPTER 7

A Solutions Lens

"People are ready for something new....
The traditional idea of journalism is outdated....
People are realizing that journalists have an obligation to help
society improve."

—Karen McIntyre, journalism professor,
Virginia Commonwealth University

Cathrine Gyldensted remembers the moment when her view of journalism completely shifted. She was a television correspondent for Danish Broadcasting based in Washington, DC, when the Great Recession struck in 2008. As the economy slowed, jobs disappeared and people lost their homes. Gyldensted's assignment one day was to visit a homeless shelter in DC to talk with people about how the upheaval in the economy had affected them.

She met an African American woman in her fifties, waiting for food, who was willing to give Gyldensted an interview. The woman shared how she came to be in the food line, and Gyldensted remembers recording the conversation, thinking, "Oh, what a great interview." In her mind, Gyldensted was already editing the video, mentally noting what clips she would use in her package. That plan changed when the woman volunteered that, despite losing everything, she had learned so much—most importantly, that asking for help was okay. Gyldensted's easy, quick-turn package suddenly didn't fit the frame she'd decided on. "I remember pausing and thinking: 'that was unexpected.'"[1]

Follow-up questions revealed the woman's son had moved closer to help her, and she strengthened her faith during the mortgage crisis. She didn't see herself as a victim but as someone who persevered and changed through adversity. Gyldensted remembers sitting there, thinking: "Oh, now I have a problem."[2] Typically, she would have focused on the victim narrative: the problem. That approach didn't accurately reflect reality.

How could she write a story that acknowledged the problem but also captured the story of a resilient woman? She convinced her editor she needed to produce a TV package centered on the woman's rise from difficult times and what she had learned. The story was one of hope and resilience. Viewers responded. They wrote emails about how the story made them feel uplifted and how it inspired them. "That's where my process started," Gyldensted recalls. She began thinking about how journalists typically portray the world as "one dimensional with this victim narrative," journalism's mainstay.[3] The response to her story during one of the worst economic downturns transformed Gyldensted's journalism career. She and others in Europe and the United States would help pioneer new approaches to reporting stories that zeroed in on solutions and responses, not just problems.

Journalists know how to question, be skeptical, and root out wrongdoing through investigative reporting. That's why journalism is considered the Fourth Estate in the United States. Journalists hold the powerful to account, which makes the profession a pillar of democracy. However, traditional journalism training has created a blind spot. Reporters can see what's wrong but can miss what's good.

Suppose journalists report only on the problems brought on by a warming world, of which there are many. The collective story of human-caused climate change becomes one of existential doom—a fatalistic view that nothing can be done to stop global warming. Most climate coverage until recently has woven a predominantly apocalyptic narrative that strips possibility and agency.

Research finds such an approach alienates audiences, especially in a world where people selectively or continuously avoid news altogether. The Reuters Institute's 2024 Digital News Report found that globally, four in ten people avoid the news.[4] How stories are framed is primarily to blame. The old journalism adage "if it bleeds, it leads" has perpetuated this negative construction of stories.

In recent years, however, more journalists have recognized that the traditional problem-centric model of framing stories does not work for audiences seeking information about climate change. That realization has led journalists to think differently about how to report stories that resonate with people. It starts with understanding the audience's views on climate change.

The Yale Climate Opinion Map in 2023 found that 64 percent of Americans are worried about climate change. An even higher percentage believe global warming will harm people in the United States and developing countries, future generations, plants, and animals.[5]

Climate scientist Katharine Hayhoe describes the antidote to worry as "connecting the head with the heart."[6] Climate reporters can do that by telling stories about what climate change means for the communities they cover.

"We want to bring the issue close to hand. Not the polar bears, but my kids. Not Antarctica, but my home or my city," she told climate journalists during an on-the-record conversation with the Local Media Association's Covering Climate Collaborative.[7]

The failure to make that personal connection shows up in the Yale Climate Opinion Maps: Only 46 percent of Americans believe climate change will affect them personally. Yet climate-fueled disasters—hurricanes, wildfires, flooding, drought, and heat—directly affect people every year.[8] Weather and climate disasters in 2023, for example, broke cost records in the United States. Twenty-eight disasters resulted in a societal price tag of over $90 billion.[9] Climate change is ultimately personal, and the data highlight an opportunity for journalists to make the personal climate connection in their stories.

Research also finds people want more reporting on climate solutions. They want to know what's being done to reduce planet-warming pollution and how they can personally contribute. More than 75 percent of Americans surveyed say they are interested in stories about local actions in their communities to address climate change, as well as businesses and government responses.[10] Yet audiences say they do not see much news reporting on climate change, and they want more.[11] The same research found audiences demand a fresh approach to climate stories so they can understand the solutions and responses, the focus of this chapter.

Katharine Hayhoe's idea of connecting the heart and the hands is one way to do that. "We have to talk about what we can do," she said. People feel empowered when that connection gets made. "This is a science-based message," Hayhoe said. "Every action matters. Every bit of warming matters. Every year matters. Every choice matters. This is the IPCC saying this."[12] Hayhoe believes this approach is essential to combatting doomism—the belief that human-caused climate change is inevitable, and people won't be able to fix it.

As a climate editor, I work with reporters across the country on how to frame stories that make the climate connections fully. That includes solutions and responses. I've learned stories resonate with audiences when they help people understand what's being done to confront climate change. That doesn't mean shrinking away from the risks or impacts of climate change. The reality of climate change is stark, and emissions continue to rise.[13]

Susan Hassol, climate change communicator and a senior science writer on three National Climate Assessments, says that reality is not an easy story to tell. "We're going to struggle to stop at 1.5 (degrees Celsius). It's going to be worse. . . . It's just going to keep getting worse, until we stop doing what we're doing." The "new normal," as she defines the impacts of climate change, isn't about maintaining a status quo because as Earth's temperature climbs, the impacts become far more severe. "We're not going to solve this," she says. "Things are never going to go back to the way they were, at least not on the human timescale." But the science also offers a path forward: "Once we get to zero emissions, temperatures will stabilize quickly," notes Hassol.[14]

Scientists agree on what we must do: Reduce planet-warming pollution. "This can be a story of what we can do that's going to improve every aspect of our lives," Hassol says. Drastically cutting emissions not only slows warming but also improves the environment, the economy, the air, and health. "All of those things are going to be better as we transition to clean energy." Hassol stresses that it's inaccurate to frame climate stories as only about sacrifice and deprivation. "It's a story of improvement in our lives and flourishing in a post-fossil fuel age."[15]

However, not all proposed solutions actually work. Some promise a panacea, a silver bullet to solve human-caused climate change. This chapter examines how to distinguish a legitimate climate solution from one that is not. Proposed technologies promise to suck carbon dioxide from the air and store it underground, for example. Does that work? Or is that just greenwashing? Many suggested green technology solutions don't scale or won't be developed fast enough to address the urgency of climate change.

In the pages ahead, reporters will learn what's needed to take a solutions approach to stories and how to develop that work through rigorous reporting that recognizes the problems and incorporates real solutions. This is evidence-based reporting that acknowledges solutions' successes, limitations, and failures. It's not "puffy" or "false-hope" reporting.

In fact, nearly every climate story should contain a solution. That may seem idealistic and complicated, but it's not. Scientists know the solution to limit global warming is rapidly cutting greenhouse gas emissions. When clearly stated in stories, that context alone informs people and confronts a doomist narrative.

What Is a Climate Solution?

Climate solutions can be split into two categories: those that address the problem of climate change by reducing emissions (mitigation) and responses needed to adapt to an inevitably warming world (adaptation).[16]

Clear examples of mitigation include generating energy through renewable methods such as solar and wind and reducing deforestation. Individuals, governments, and industries can all have a hand in these efforts. Solutions at the individual level can range from making dietary changes, such as eating less beef and dairy, to voting for candidates who support climate action.

At the government level, the Inflation Reduction Act (IRA), signed into law by President Biden in 2022, is a significant example. Indeed, IRA is considered the nation's first major climate change policy because it provided billions of dollars in incentives to encourage economic sectors to transition from fossil fuels to low-carbon technologies and renewable energy. For individuals, IRA provided tax credits and rebates to make homes more energy efficient by installing a heat pump, for example, or buying an electric vehicle. That's a true climate solution.

Many of the technologies and policies needed to reduce fossil fuel emissions are already available to limit warming to below 2°C (3.6°F) above pre-industrial levels as defined by the Paris Agreement. Naomi Oreskes, a science historian at Harvard University, said in an interview with NPR that the time is now to mobilize such technologies that "already exist, that work and are cost competitive, and that essentially means renewable energy and storage."[17]

Incentivizing industries to lean into these technologies can involve putting a price on carbon, such as through taxes and cap-and-trade schemes. Washington state, for example, started a cap on industrial emissions in 2023 to address climate-warming pollution.[18] Oregon and California have broader policies to cap pollution, and at least twelve states in the East have limits on what power plants can emit. In 2023, the European Union agreed to tax products based on the emissions used to manufacture them.[19] In each case, companies now have a financial motivation to reduce their climate-warming pollution, knowing there's a price to emit.

Market pricing mechanisms are being tested at both the local and international level but can take years to implement. Future reporting will help evaluate whether these methods are effective responses to curbing emissions.

In contrast to mitigation efforts, adaptation measures do not directly address the causes of planetary warming, but they do help communities, economies, and ecosystems prepare for life on a hotter planet. Such responses can involve building infrastructures and redesigning urban landscapes that can withstand extreme weather, developing crops that require less water and can tolerate drought, or preserving biodiversity to maintain healthy ecosystems.

A. R. Siders researches climate change adaptation policies at the University of Delaware. She looks specifically at relocating people and property away from climate risks—known as managed retreat—and environmental justice. At a fundamental level, she defines adaptation as long-term shifts that make "whatever you're doing fit better with what the climate is *going to look like*, not what it looks like right now."[20]

One approach could be to build a wall to protect against storm surges or build larger storm drains. Another adaptation might be behavioral, such as tying a kayak near the front door so people can escape their homes during a flood. Institutional adaptations can also come through new laws or practices, such as developing early warning systems.

Much discussion and research are happening about what constitutes adaptation. That conversation can have real policy implications for funding priorities, such as which developing countries are able to tap into the UN Adaptation Fund. For journalists, stories about how communities are adapting or not are worth pursuing and can ultimately help audiences understand an aspect of responding to climate change.

Assess Solutions

Not all climate solutions are legitimate, as noted in the chapter on misinformation and disinformation. Greenwashing—making something seem like a climate solution when it's not—unfortunately runs rampant when it comes to solutions. However, reputable science-vetted sources exist to help journalists figure out what solutions are real and what aren't. The nonprofit Project Drawdown has a database of dozens of climate solutions that have been scientifically reviewed; it is an excellent place to start when reporting on solutions or checking out a specific approach.[21] The extensive online library captures existing solutions, the associated costs, and the impact they could have in improving the atmosphere. Examples of existing solutions include walkable cities, tropical forest restoration, smart thermostats, and methane digesters. As an example, let's examine one solution in the database: bicycle commuting.

Visitors are likely to find more bicycles than people in Amsterdam. The capital of the Netherlands has a reputation for being a bicycling mecca with extensive bike-friendly paths and traffic signals. Portland, Oregon, has also long advocated and supported bicycle commuting through protected bikeways and paths. Both cities encourage people to leave their cars at home and travel by bike instead.

Project Drawdown estimates that if cities around the globe increase bicycle commuting by 2050, between 2.73 and 4.63 gigatons of carbon dioxide equivalent emissions could be reduced. Put another way, that's roughly the annual emissions from India or those of the entire European Union. Investing in bike infrastructure to make it safe for people to ride means fewer car miles on the road, which means less road maintenance.[22] That's a legitimate climate solution, and it already exists.

Project Drawdown's site puts it this way: "Now is better than new, and society is well equipped for transformation today."

Practice Healthy Skepticism

Shiny new technologies are popping up everywhere, promising a miracle cure for reducing planet-warming emissions. Journalists must be skeptical and cautious in deciding whether to report on them. Many don't scale up or won't be ready quickly enough to help. In some cases, the science doesn't exist to support the claims.

As a national climate editor, I often see stories about "gee-whiz" technological innovations. Although one can marvel at such innovation and promise, journalists should approach such stories with rigor, grounding them in science and accountability. Climate solutions should be scalable and readily available to address the urgency of climate change, but most tech solutions miss on both accounts.

For example, a renewable energy manufacturer in Dublin, in conjunction with Arizona State University, has developed metal cylinders that promise to capture and store carbon.[23] When the wind blows, treelike cylinders pop up and capture the air. Millions of so-called MechanicalTrees would be needed to significantly lower greenhouse gas emissions. Does this technology have potential? The US Department of Energy thinks so. The agency provided $2.5 million to help develop the product.[24] Yet it remains unclear whether this technology can truly scale up quickly enough to make a difference.

In California, a new startup takes corn husks, stocks, and cobs and turns farm debris into "bio-oil."[25] The company, Charm Industrial, claims that once the product is injected into abandoned oil wells, it hardens permanently. The company has attracted millions of dollars from investors, including companies that see bio-oil as a way to offset their carbon footprint. The company claims to have locked up thousands of tons of carbon with its technology. That's actually a small amount, considering climate scientists say billions of tons of carbon dioxide must be captured and stored to slow global warming. Stories have rightly questioned whether the company can scale up. Future reporting could investigate the long-term implications of injecting bio-oil into the ground.

Both MechanicalTrees and bio-oil make for compelling storytelling because they promise a technological marvel to a planet-wide problem. Don't fall for that, though. Rigorous solutions reporting requires being transparent about a technology's limitations and effectiveness.

Time is not on our side with the climate crisis. Reporters need to evaluate how quickly a climate solution can take effect because climate-warming pollution has a head start, having built up over decades. Legitimate climate solutions must work quickly to improve the atmosphere and stop climate-harming pollution. Theorized future responses should be evaluated against known and proven solutions we already have.

Ask Hard Questions

No one solution will eliminate emissions, but together, solutions can have a significant impact in limiting global warming. The problem is time. Scientists see an acceleration under way in the effects of climate change. "We aren't doing enough to be able to deal with wildfires, heat waves, floods, hurricanes," Siders said.[26]

In the United States, for example, many levees across the country are ranked in poor condition, meaning they could fail with too much water. Increasing extreme rainfall puts pressure on already fragile systems. Consequently, many of the strategies and solutions being implemented maintain the status quo in the face of a rapidly changing climate, says Siders. "Climate change adaptation efforts are about buying time. . . . But we never say what we're buying time to do."[27]

Is the goal of adaptation to enjoy a place before it disappears, or is it to protect a place in the long term? If it's to protect a place, that will require serious investments. Siders considers such questions in her research and believes that adaptation hasn't gone well because "we haven't really grappled with the scope of the change that we are likely to encounter."[28]

Venice, Italy, has invested billions of dollars to build a flood wall to protect the historic city, for example. By 2060, that multi-billion-dollar investment won't be enough to keep rising waters at bay. Siders points to this example as one that buys time—but what's the plan for beyond 2060?

Journalists need to keep this perspective in mind when covering solutions and consider the role they have in investigating solutions and responses. How much do solutions cost? What's the long-term effect? Who benefits from the solution? Who's left behind? Is a solution about maintaining life as is, or is it about adapting to a warmer world? The list of questions below is meant to help guide reporting on climate solutions.

Does the Solution Work?

If the solution doesn't work, then why report on an idea that is not viable? The answer varies, but generally, journalists should rigorously vet solutions with experts and research. They should understand a solution's limitations, whether it can scale, and whether it's available now. Jonathan Foley, environmental scientist and executive director of Project Drawdown, asks whether the solution is effective and whether the atmosphere will notice. "Now is better than new, and time always trumps tech," said Foley.[29] That's the litmus test for all climate solutions.

Is the Solution Ready?

The concept of a MechanicalTree, for example, has been well researched and developed, with at least one cylinder operating in Tempe, Arizona.[30] However, these "trees" aren't being deployed at a scale large enough to reduce emissions. One day, that might happen, but is that a viable solution for now? Probably not.

The tech startup that turns agricultural byproducts into bio-oil has already developed the product and has injected it into the ground in at least one state. However, regulatory hurdles could stall efforts in other states. Bio-oil has the potential to be a solution, but questions remain, including the impact it could have on reducing emissions. What are the long-term impacts of bio-oil? Is it safe to do this underground? How long will this product last underground? What are the unintended consequences that could come from this technology?

What's the Cost?

Climate solutions come with a price tag. Reporters may find it difficult to follow the money. Some federally funded projects can be tracked through federal or academic databases or public records. Private companies don't have the same financial reporting requirements, however, making it hard to track the money.

Billions of federal dollars in the United States have been invested to create green jobs and industries to transition the country away from fossil fuels through the rollout of policies such as the Inflation Reduction Act and the

Bipartisan Infrastructure Law. Such investments accelerate what's possible but also increase the potential for mishandling funds. For instance, money flowing from federal coffers to states to give tax credits for, say, heat pumps and other home energy improvements may not have reliable systems to distribute the funds. That could lead to potential fraud or wasted taxpayer dollars. That's something journalists can track over time.

Does the Solution Scale?

Technological solutions can struggle to scale up fast enough to make a difference in removing greenhouse gas emissions from the atmosphere. Carbon capture and storage (CCS) is one such technology that promises to catch carbon dioxide emissions from sources such as power plants and then store it underground in geological formations, keeping planet-warming pollution out of the atmosphere.

The Intergovernmental Panel on Climate Change nodded in its latest report to the potential need for CCS to be a part of the climate solution.[31] Some major oil and gas companies have already labeled themselves as leaders on CCS, capturing carbon dioxide emissions and injecting them underground. But those claims may be overstated and amount to green-washing to save profits.[32]

Every Climate Story Is a Solutions Story

As a climate editor, I am reminded in talking with journalists across beats that knowing how to vet a climate solution isn't really taught unless a reporter actively seeks solutions journalism training or is in a newsroom that champions this approach. That's why it's crucial to know what a climate solution is and to ask critical questions about whether it's available now, the cost, and whether it can scale.

Evidence-based proof that a solution works is essential before reporting on a solution. This is why some journalists, such as freelance reporter Peter Yeung, prefer looking at solutions long under way. The reporter can then assess how well a solution has worked.

Mohammad Mohasin grows crops on floating rafts in southern Bangladesh—a traditional method. "If I grew these on a normal field, the floods would destroy them," Mohasin told Yeung for a story published by Bloomberg. "When the water levels rise here, so does my garden."[33] Mohasin is a third-generation farmer who uses floating gardens known as dhap to grow tomatoes, eggplants, potatoes, and other crops. Dhap dates back hundreds of years, and in Bangladesh, it's a solution that can withstand rising waters brought on by human-caused climate change.

Yeung's story in 2023, "How Floating Farms Are Helping Bangladesh Adapt to Climate Change," is a notable example of how journalists can frame stories in an engaging way that focuses on what can be done to address climate change.

Other narratives are more common about Bangladesh, a country among the most vulnerable to climate change. The country stands to lose a significant amount of the land that's used for agriculture because of rising sea levels. People have already had to migrate to overpopulated cities that lack jobs and economic support. Melting glaciers in the Himalayas threaten the rivers in Bangladesh and cause severe flooding in more than half the country. News headlines generally focus on the country's dire reality.

Yeung's reporting puts the scope of Bangladesh's problem into perspective. He had read about the floating gardens and had added them to a list he keeps of story ideas. When Yeung went to Bangladesh for a month to do some reporting, he checked out the gardens. "I really didn't have to look too hard to find [them]," he recalls. He traveled by motorbike to some of the places and discovered "dozens and dozens and dozens of farmers" growing crops this way.[34] Here was a long-held practice that has been working for years.

Yeung's reporting explained that floating gardens are popular with rural farmers because they are inexpensive to build. Farmers don't lose their crops during heavy rains and floods because the gardens rise and fall with the water levels. Yeung also reported the government started a pilot project a few years ago to expand floating gardens, which speaks to their scalability.

No solutions story is complete without a thorough critique of the challenges, though. "No solution, climate solution, is ever going to be the silver bullet," Yeung says. "These floating gardens can't actually just offer every kind of, I suppose, nutrition and foodstuff that Bangladeshi people need."[35] To get at that challenge, Yeung talked with an expert who questioned whether the floating gardens would help with the country's food security. Green chilies, for example, may grow well in floating beds and be economically viable, but chilis aren't a food staple and don't help shore up food security. Yeung also wrote that earlier efforts in the northern part of the country led to "mixed results."[36]

By the end of Yeung's story, the reader reconnects with farmer Mohammad Mohasin, who now teaches his children to farm using floating gardens. Such a positive anecdote brings people full circle with what a well-reported solutions story should do: learn about a climate solution, the problem it addresses, and how replicable and scalable it is while acknowledging the problems with it.

As a climate editor and news consumer, I find this approach to reporting both refreshing and satisfying. Stories about solutions don't shy away from the risks and problems, but they give people an understanding of what can be done or what is already being done to address climate change. Solutions reporting is an antidote to doom-and-gloom narratives. Ahead, we'll break down the American model of reporting solutions and consider a European concept that expands what's possible when journalists focus beyond the climate problem.

Pillars of Solutions Reporting

The Solutions Journalism Network (SJN) defines solutions reporting as journalism focused on people or communities responding to social problems, such as human-caused climate change. Solutions stories require evidence and sound reporting skills. "This isn't just positive news," explains Katherine Noble, who managed climate initiatives at SJN. "This is evidence-based," she says. "It's talking about the limitations. It's what are the insights. It's focused on the response."[37]

These foundational principles help steer solutions reporting away from simplistic "happy news" stories to provide rigor and balance to the reporting. It's what SJN calls the pillars of solutions reporting. "Those four pillars were super important, initially, for the argument that this (solutions reporting) is not fluff," Noble explains.[38]

Responses: Traditional journalism models lay out the problem or challenge. Solutions journalism identifies the social problem and then examines how people respond. Journalists can investigate the strategies communities, organizations, or policies implement to address a particular issue.[39]

Insight: Solutions journalism works when the story reveals the lessons learned from the response. SJN defines this as "insight." One way to consider this is to ask: Are there lessons to be learned that will help others implement a similar solution?[40]

Evidence: Reporting on responses is not enough. Solutions journalism requires evidence (data, qualitative results) to show whether a community response has worked. Sometimes, the answer is that it didn't, and that's a story with lessons. "Solutions stories are upfront with audiences about that evidence—what it tells us and what it doesn't," explains Noble.[41]

Limitations: When journalists write about solutions to problems, they should also acknowledge where those solutions may fall short. What works in one community may not work in another for various reasons. However, being transparent about such limitations is important, as it speaks to the complexity of responses.[42]

SJN's pillars were initially designed to establish solutions journalism as a rigorous reporting endeavor. Every story needed to meet the criteria. The solution ultimately became the hero in the story rather than the people or communities pursuing the solution. The prescriptive nature of the pillars—that every story must have these four elements to qualify as an actual solutions story—generated pushback among journalists who didn't want to be told how to report. The pillars, Noble explains, were meant to counter the narrative that solutions stories were positive, feel-good news stories.[43]

Noble says the pillars should be considered as guideposts, especially regarding reporting on climate change. They can help reporters spot greenwashing and avoid falling for pie-in-the-sky technologies that remain decades away. "You don't report something as a silver bullet," Noble says. "You don't report something that's just an idea.... That's not really solutions journalism."[44]

Peter Yeung, the international reporter who wrote about floating gardens, says most of the stories he reports are focused on solutions. He gravitated toward solutions even before he knew about solutions journalism as a reporting model. "I think I had sort of been drawn to those kinds of stories. I just found it intellectually stimulating in terms of what's actually working, what progress the world is making," Yeung says.[45]

He's interested in long time scales because data or clear evidence usually exists to show whether a solution such as floating gardens works. Scientific studies and research are one way to get at the evidence needed to meet one of the SJN pillars.

Yeung likes to talk with people on the ground and to hear the "anecdotal evidence of their testimonies" about how solutions have affected individuals. He uses these guiding questions: What is the evidence to show a solution is working? What is the scale of the impact? What could the potential scalability be? Those questions align with how to vet a climate solution. He says it's a disservice to solutions journalism and society "to be writing about things that don't work—solutions that are limited or really overselling."[46]

In 2024, Yeung was recognized by the SJN in its inaugural awards for general excellence reporting. He and Melanie Pérez Arias reported an in-depth feature about farmers in Lima, Peru, who collect water to grow crops by capturing fog using nets in their backyards.[47] It's a solution in one of the driest parts of the globe. Yeung co-reported the story with Lima-based reporter Pérez Arias to scrutinize "fog catchers." This is a well-established practice in Lima that "is looking to ramp up and potentially spread further around the world."[48]

Together, they brought voices from some of the "most disadvantaged people in the world" to light.[49] Like any excellent solutions reporters, Pérez Arias and Yeung critiqued the idea of catching fog to grow crops by exploring whether this technique could be used at a larger scale and where the limitations existed.

SJN's pillars provide a framework that's helpful for journalists when figuring out whether a response is legitimate. They also help reporters be transparent with the audience about what has worked and what hasn't. However, there are other approaches to framing climate solutions stories beyond the SJN framework. Constructive journalism methods, for example, provide a broader toolkit for responsible reporting.

The Constructive Journalism Framework

Journalists should be aware of alternative frameworks that provide more flexibility in reporting on solutions. As Katherine Noble acknowledges, the SJN traditional pillars can be restrictive. Solutions journalism, as US-based reporters are most likely to be familiar with, is considered a branch of constructive reporting, which offers journalists a valuable storytelling approach.

I first learned about constructive journalism through Cathrine Gyldensted, the reporter whose story opens this chapter. She's recognized as a pivotal figure who was among the first to bring academic rigor and practical application to the field. Gyldensted earned a master's in positive psychology at the University of Pennsylvania in 2010. She wanted to find a new way to report stories that didn't leave people filled with dread. Positive psychology doesn't ignore life's difficulties but instead equips people with tools to handle their struggles in positive ways. For Gyldensted, that was the opposite of how she was trained as a journalist. That training focused on what was wrong—the problems—or as she puts it, "the disease model of the world."[50]

Gyldensted's work led to the development of journalistic methods that focus on positive change and the media's role in contributing to a more informed and hopeful public discourse.[51] As a researcher, educator, and consultant, Gyldensted has trained journalists and news organizations worldwide on how to incorporate constructive elements into their reporting. Her contributions are often discussed alongside those of Danish journalist Ulrik Haagerup, who founded the Constructive News Institute in 2017. In Europe, this approach has caught on with major news organizations such as Swedish National Radio, the Danish Broadcasting Company, and *The Guardian*.

Take, for example, the decision by several news organizations in 2015 to change how they reported on climate change ahead of the international Paris climate talks. *The Guardian* was among them and asked its audience what they wanted reporters to cover about global warming. Readers answered, saying they wanted more positive stories. They wanted to learn about new technologies to address global warming. They wanted to know how to make renewable energy more affordable and how to invest money so they weren't supporting fossil fuel companies.

The Guardian responded publicly, saying reporters would cover the climate crisis as a story of hope. "That doesn't mean willfully ignoring the gravity of the situation we face," staff wrote in an editorial that year. *The Guardian* promised to keep reporting on the science of climate change and report on the places most affected. Reporters would also work to uncover bad corporate behavior and misinformation. "But we will also make a point of bringing positive stories to the fore."[52]

That's how *The Guardian* entered the constructive journalism space. Gyldensted recommends several entry points into this method. Unlike solutions reporting, they don't need to be practiced together.

Solution oriented: A community may be working to solve a social problem, so what are they learning, and is it working? This is similar to SJN's pillars, which require the response to a problem to be based in evidence.[53]

Depolarize the debate: Constructive journalism seeks to bridge divides rather than polarize debates.[54] This goal is to stop perpetuating a narrative that pits one perspective against another, which can lend credence to untrue claims. As we've seen, climate change reporting historically fell into this trap by creating a false equivalency between climate scientists and those who denied the science. In constructive journalism, reporters include multiple voices with diverse backgrounds and perspectives to give true balance to stories.[55]

Interview skills: Constructive journalism requires us to think differently about how reporters ask questions.[56] In this model, reporters don't just ask,

"What happened?" They ask, "What is happening? What steps are people taking to solve a societal problem? What are they learning? What are the challenges and the opportunities? What does success look like?"

Engage the community: What do our audiences want to know about climate change? What keeps them up at night? What would they like media outlets to report on? Community engagement can take time, but it can be deeply rewarding to know that your reporting reflects the audience's interests. Reporters and news leaders can co-create, which is distinctive from solutions reporting.[57] Audience feedback can then help reporters pivot as stories are published.

Future oriented: Stories that are focused on the future ask us to explore what's possible. This is an especially interesting framing for climate stories because climate change forces us to think differently and adapt. Imagine writing about utopian communities that are being created rather than the dystopias of the present day or the past. What do these communities look like? By envisioning positive futures, these distinctive stories can shape outcomes.

So what does constructive journalism look like in practice? Let's return to *The Guardian*'s decision to report on climate change constructively. In 2018, the media organization started the "Upside" series. The series' tagline? "Journalism that seeks out answers, solutions, movements and initiatives to address the biggest problems besetting the world."[58]

For example, the story "Here Comes the Sun Canoe, as Amazonians Take On Big Oil" examines solar-powered canoes as a "defiant attempt to stand up" to the oil industry in Ecuador. That industry has deforested land and caused pollution by pumping hundreds of thousands of gallons of oil daily. However, the reporter focuses on a response by the Achuar Indigenous group to bring communities together through renewable technology. The story acknowledges the challenges with the solar-powered boats, including mechanical failures, but also considers how the Achuar community is diversifying its economy to become self-sufficient.[59] Readers learn about an ecotourism project as part of the effort. The story is solution and future oriented while also examining early evidence of whether the solar canoes could work.

Solar canoes were a new idea being tested in Ecuador, so there wasn't concrete evidence to show they could work over the long term. That alone might nix it from being a solutions story under the SJN model, but the story hits on so many other pillars that it's worth mentioning to show the distinction between the two frameworks; both are valid.

Gyldensted's advice for climate journalists is to find their own way into constructive reporting. That could mean reconsidering how you ask questions, imagining a future in which emissions have dropped, or sussing out lessons learned.

"Don't think that you should do everything, embrace everything, or master everything," advises Gyldensted. "Just start on the one [idea] that has [the] most energy and you think you're most confident in."[60] By engaging this different framework, reporters will find new angles that lead to future stories. That's the power, she says, of seeing journalism through a positive lens.

What Method to Follow?

Although there are subtle distinctions between solutions journalism and constructive journalism, the goal is not to choose one method over the other but to find a balanced approach combining key elements from both. By merging the pillars of SJN with the principles of constructive journalism, we can create stronger, more engaging stories about our warming world.

"We're really all engaged in trying to add missing elements to journalism to be more accurate portrayals of the world," Gyldensted explains.[61] Noble would agree that there's a "happy medium" somewhere between the two frameworks.[62]

In 2022, SJN launched the Climate Beacon Newsroom Initiative to train newsrooms on incorporating a solutions journalism framework into climate stories. "What we are seeking to do with these newsrooms," Noble explained, "is to guide them in transforming their coverage from sort of the typical gloom and doom climate reporting to community-informed and equity-focused climate solutions reporting."[63]

Each newsroom designated a climate leader—a reporter or an editor—who went through SJN's train-the-trainer program. These leaders in turn became certified trainers who could pass on their knowledge about solutions journalism reporting—to be a "beacon for other newsrooms."[64]

The Sacramento Bee was one of the nine inaugural newsrooms to go through the initiative. Journalist and editor Emily Stigliani deployed the training to move the paper away from stories focused on the negative effects of climate change to "coverage that directly responded to community needs in Sacramento's urban core around climate equity and justice."[65] Some of that work harks back to constructive journalism by enlisting the community's input.

The newspaper spent months writing about community climate actions, such as using goats to graze overgrown parks. One of *The Bee*'s early solutions stories exemplifies what can happen when reporters focus on solutions. Reporter Ryan Lillis asked whether a historic industrial corridor known as R Street might provide an answer for imagining mixed-use neighborhoods.

"It took decades to develop, but the R Street corridor in Sacramento has not only become a flourishing transit-oriented neighborhood, it is arguably the region's most successful urban development landscape," wrote Lillis.[66] People can easily walk and access mass transit—solutions that reduce climate emissions. It's a thoroughly reported story that examines the successes of developing R Street but also its limitations. Other areas in the city could replicate this effort, making it a scalable solution.

Lillis's story caught the attention of Miami Beach, Florida, which wanted to do something similar. *The Sacramento Bee* told SJN about the impact of that story: "We had a task force committee member in Miami Beach reach out to our Sacramento reporter after reading his solutions story of a neighborhood planned to allow for residents to rely on walking, biking and mass transit."[67]

The Sacramento Bee has since deepened its emphasis on solutions by offering community grants for projects in the city's region to address climate change. The goal, Stigliani wrote in an article, is to engage communities through solutions reporting "about how we can face climate change with urgency and equity."[68] That's solutions journalism and constructive journalism at work.

Practical Tips for Solutions Reporting

This chapter has given an overview of climate solutions and how to interrogate them. It also covered two main approaches for reporting on solutions. Journalists new to solutions reporting might ask how to get started to find ideas. Climate solutions stories can be intellectually interesting and fun, but they can also be complex and nuanced. The tips below come from my experience as an editor and journalist, interviews I've done, and insights from solutions and constructive journalism.

Generate ideas: Inspiration is often not far away. One of my favorite tips comes from journalist Peter Yeung. Some of his ideas are stimulated by reading other reporters' stories that may have nothing to do with solutions. For him, "the buried leads in just a few words at the bottom of a story that mentions a project that's happening, that is a solution." That's his prompt to "dig into it."[69] It's a great way to start: Read stories and pay attention to academic papers, studies, social media threads, and climate-related forums.

Journalists can also investigate what their community is doing to address climate change. Check in with nonprofit organizations, businesses, and local governments to discover what responses they might be pursuing. Researching local initiatives, innovative technologies, sustainable practices, or policy changes can yield compelling ideas, too.

Identify the solution: Key questions include "Who is involved?" "What are they doing?" "Why are they doing it and where?" "Is it scalable?" "How much does it cost?" It's important to understand the evidence that shows the solution's effectiveness, its potential for replication or scaling, and its limitations.

Do your research: Historical documents, current studies, and conversations with sources are always key to climate stories, but particularly so with solutions stories. Journalists, I have found, need to cast a wide net to really understand a climate solution. That means reading widely and seeking out a range of experts. Reporters can also find data validating the solution or pointing out the failings or limitations. That evidence becomes part of the story. It's what makes solutions reporting rigorous.

Yeung puts it this way: "It is not the right approach to think of solutions journalism as fluffy or positive for the sake of being positive. In fact, good solutions reporting could actually be quite negative in some places."[70] That starts with research.

Seek expert insight: I have taught several reporters new to climate journalism, and often I find they will talk to a couple of sources and then want to write and be done with the story. That might pass for a daily story but rarely for a solutions story. Journalists need to develop a full view of what's at stake and what's being done. That requires talking with multiple people from different backgrounds and perspectives, from climate scientists to advocates to community members. As Yeung found in reporting on floating gardens in Bangladesh, some experts will be people using the solution, and they will help create a profoundly rich and engaging story.

Help your audience get involved: Every news organization has a different ethics policy about making a call to action in stories. But the urgency of climate change makes me question some of those policies. I don't believe journalists should promote a particular movement or march, but we do know through research that people want to know what they can do about climate change. So how can journalism help?

An easy way is to connect your audience with resources and further information to get them started. For example, a reporter might write a solutions story about federal incentives for consumers to buy electric vehicles. Why not add information about how people can tap into that incentive? Such incentives can be quite challenging to find. That's not a call to action but useful information.

Each of these strategies can help you engage audiences by giving them a glimpse of a positive future, which can help them develop a sense of agency. For instance, journalist and academic Cathrine Gyldensted's story about a woman without housing who found hope at a shelter resonated deeply with her audience, prompting many to reach out and share how the story affected them. Leaders at SJN have shared similar stories from newsrooms covering climate solutions.

Increasing audience engagement is good for both communities and journalists; opening this door helps reporters understand their audiences' interests and can guide future reporting.

Ultimately, solutions reporting is not about feel-good climate stories but about telling the whole story: describing both the problems of a warming world and the responses to those problems. Audiences are driven away by problem-only reporting. They want to know what responses to climate change are effective. Journalists should include effective responses as an essential part of their climate reporting; they should look for ways to connect the "head to the heart," as Katharine Hayhoe stresses, and they should hold any climate solution to the same high standards of journalism, interrogating solutions for effectiveness and scalability. That's the best way to tell the holistic story of our warming world.

Essential Reading and Resources

Solutions Journalism Network: SJN maintains a deep database of all types of solutions stories, including ones on climate change. It's an excellent source for story ideas and ways to do this reporting. https://www.solutionsjournalism.org/

Constructive Journalism Institute: The institute offers training tools and ideas to get started. https://constructiveinstitute.org/

From Mirrors to Movers: Five Elements of Positive Psychology in Constructive Journalism: Cathrine Gyldensted's refreshing book details how to improve journalism by drawing on the behavioral sciences, such as positive psychology.

Project Drawdown: Explore the database of hundreds of scientifically vetted solutions to draw down planet-warming pollution. https://drawdown.org/

Your Turn

Research and identify a potential story that gets at a climate solution for your class or newsroom. Do some initial reporting to find out whether the solution is scalable and available now, and look for existing data. If you're in a class, write a one-page paper detailing the solution and explaining why you should report the story. If you're in a newsroom, discuss with your editor whether you have a story to pursue.

CHAPTER 8

Climate Litigation

"It's really scary seeing what you care for disappear right in
front of your eyes."

—Sariel Sandoval, youth plaintiff, Confederated Salish
and Kootenai Tribe

Montana is known as Big Sky country for a reason: Wide open vistas give
way to endless sky. Outdoor splendor galore exists in the state, including
Glacier National Park, or what the Kootenai tribe calls Ya·qawiswit̓xuki,
"the place where there is a lot of ice." That ice has steadily retreated due to
human-caused climate change, however. About eighty glaciers existed in
1850 at the end of the Little Ice Age, memorialized in photographs and stories.
Now, only twenty-six remain.[1]

Glaciers within the park have retreated so significantly since 1900 that Montana
has the distinction of having the most glacier loss in all of the lower forty-
eight states. It is also one of the top five coal-producing states in the country. The
fate of Glacier National Park's iconic ice masses is detailed as part of the findings
in a landmark climate case brought by sixteen Montana youth, who in 2020 filed
suit against the state over its fossil fuel–based state energy system.[2] In 2011, the
state legislature passed laws to prevent state agencies from taking the impacts
of climate change into account when evaluating permits for energy projects
such as natural gas. (The Republican-led legislature updated those laws in 2023.[3])

The youth, ages two to eighteen at the time, alleged that such a system
"causes and contributes to climate change" and violates their state constitutional rights. According to Montana's constitution, every person in the state
"shall maintain and improve a clean and healthful environment in Montana
for present and future generations."[4]

Three years later, First District Court judge Kathy Seeley agreed with the
youth plaintiffs. She rejected the state's argument that Montana's overall
contributions to global warming were not significant and ruled that the
state's failure to examine greenhouse gas emissions and climate change was

179

"unconstitutional on its face." She concluded that the youth plaintiffs, now ranging in age from five to twenty-two, have a "fundamental constitutional right to a clean and healthful environment, which includes climate as part of the environmental life-support system."[5]

The case marked the first time in US history that a climate-related constitutional rights case went to trial. The decision in *Held v. State of Montana* has been seen by some in the field of climate litigation as a notable ruling that establishes a precedent for similar cases in the future.

The *Held* case is one of many types of lawsuits aimed at dealing with the consequences of climate change, from taking on specific environmental regulations to trying to hold oil and gas companies financially responsible for damages caused by their industry. To date, no court decision in the world has held fossil fuel companies or other emitters of greenhouse gases financially liable for climate change.[6]

Inside Climate News reporter Nicholas Kusnetz, who has covered climate litigation, says, "When I'm talking to people, they say it's imperfect at best. Like the lawsuits are kind of like a last-ditch effort." Oil companies that are being sued will argue the courts shouldn't be deciding these matters. Those who are suing aren't "seeking new climate policy. They're seeking money to help pay for impacts."[7]

Climate litigation is increasingly becoming a tool to address climate change, and it could have real impacts in the years to come. That's especially true if courts begin to find emitters of planet-warming pollution financially liable—akin to the decades of lawsuits against tobacco companies that eventually culminated in a multi-billion-dollar settlement with all states and territories in 1998.[8]

From Kusnetz's perspective, lawsuits that states and local jurisdictions bring against oil companies might gain momentum. "If they get any traction, it could be a huge amount of money that the oil companies would be on the hook for, and that could trigger some kind of settlement talk," he explains.[9]

Climate litigation is an ever-evolving field with many opportunities for critical reporting. Unlike the youth-led lawsuits in *Held v. State of Montana*, the stories may not always feature exceptional plaintiffs. But there are important stories to be done on challenges to environmental regulations, attempts to reduce greenhouse emissions from industry, and efforts to make fossil fuel companies pay for their contributions to climate change.

Journalists need to be familiar with how the courts work and how to read legal documents, which can have a unique language, much like climate science studies. They also need to understand past decisions that have led up to where we are today. This chapter gives an overview of a handful of landmark cases while providing basic guidance on how to read and comprehend the legal process.

Youth-Led Climate Cases

In 2015, the nonprofit public interest law firm Our Children's Trust represented twenty-one youth who filed a lawsuit against the federal government. They alleged the government violated their constitutional rights by allowing planet-warming pollution to rise. In *Juliana v. United States*, the plaintiffs argued that the federal government violated their constitutional rights to life, liberty, and property and failed to protect public trust resources.

For more than nine years, legal action went back and forth between courts, until 2023 when US District Court judge Ann Aiken ruled the youth plaintiffs could amend their complaint and have it heard in court. The case has never made it to trial, however. That hasn't slowed legal actions by Our Children's Trust, which has represented youth nationwide in several cases and rulemaking actions, including representing youth in *Held v. the State of Montana* and in a case in Hawaii.

The Missoulian, Montana Public Radio, and other local press helped readers and listeners understand the significance of the *Held* case, reporting on the passionate testimony given by the youth plaintiffs. National media covered the case, too, putting it in broader perspective by showing how *Held v. Montana* was similar to youth-led litigation in other states, including Hawaii and Utah. The significance of *Held* and future cases will continue to warrant coverage.

Julia Olson, chief legal counsel and executive director of Our Children's Trust, called Judge Seeley's ruling in Montana historic. "As fires rage in the West, fueled by fossil fuel pollution, today's ruling in Montana is a game-changer that marks a turning point in this generation's efforts to save the planet from the devastating effects of human-caused climate chaos," Olson said in a press release. "This is a huge win for Montana, for youth, for democracy, and for our climate. More rulings like this will certainly come."[10]

Climate science, the impacts of climate change from dwindling glaciers, massive wildfires, heat, and health implications, along with youth testimony, are now part of the legal record, detailed in Seeley's 103-page ruling.

Michael Gerrard, who directs the Sabin Center for Climate Change Law at Columbia University, told NPR, "I thought this was one of the strongest decisions on climate change issued by any court anywhere." The court agreed, he said, with the youth plaintiffs "that fossil fuel combustion is the main cause of climate change and [that] climate change is having all kinds of terrible health and environmental impacts which will get worse unless we stop those emissions."[11]

Indeed, during the trial, the "terrible health and environmental impacts" came to light in the courtroom, which makes for compelling context in coverage. Youth shared feelings of fear due to the loss of glaciers, anxiety over bringing future children into an unstable world, and the sense of loss they experienced by staying indoors because of wildfire smoke. One of the Indigenous plaintiffs "suffered distress due to the impacts of climate change on culturally important plants and snow for creation stories. Her cultural connection to the land increases this impact."[12]

Rikki Held, the twenty-two-year-old lead plaintiff, told NPR that having the case go to trial was "amazing" because it meant people in power had to listen to them and that long-held climate science would become part of the legal record. "This case can set a precedent for other legal cases outside of Montana's borders," Held said.[13]

That's true to an extent. The ruling could help future cases in states where similar constitutional protections exist, guaranteeing a right to a clean environment. Hawaii's constitution, for example, is similar to Montana's. Thirteen youth sued Hawaii's Department of Transportation for failing to create, operate, and maintain a transportation system. They alleged such failures violate people's right to a clean and healthy environment. In 2024, Hawaii's government settled the case just before it was scheduled for trial. The state's governor called the settlement "groundbreaking."[14] As part of it, Hawaii must develop a plan to have zero emissions from ground, air, and other transportation systems by 2045.

Once journalists become familiar with this type of litigation, they can plug into local, state, and national cases. They can provide explanatory stories about what's at stake and the motivation driving legal action. Court proceedings can be captivating, especially during a trial, which can translate to a fascinating story. Once a judge rules, journalists should follow what happens in the months and years ahead. What legal challenges arise after a particular ruling? After the *Held* decision, the state of Montana immediately appealed the decision to the state's supreme court. In December 2024 the court majority found that the state's constitutional guarantee to a "clean and healthful environment" includes a stable climate.[15]

There are other questions journalists can examine after a decision such as *Held*. How do states uphold constitutional obligations and reduce planet-warming pollution? What state agencies change practices, as in the case of Hawaii, to meet the settlement terms? What happens to the plaintiffs? There's much to explore, and reporters will probably have many opportunities to cover such cases in the coming years.

Climate Legal Cases on the Rise

The United Nations Environment Programme (UNEP) started compiling reports on climate cases every three years starting in 2017. Cases have steadily climbed since. In 2020, for example, the UNEP Litigation Report identified 1,550 cases filed in nearly forty jurisdictions globally. By the end of 2022, that number had risen to 2,180, involving sixty-five jurisdictions.[16] The number of climate cases in a five-year span has increased two and a half times.

Most cases come from the United States, but the European Union, along with Brazil, New Zealand, Mexico, and India, have also seen increases in climate litigation.

In the United States, Michael Gerrard, founder and director of the Sabin Center for Climate Change Law at Columbia University, says climate litigation is growing. Every month in the United States, he says, there are between fifteen and twenty new climate-related lawsuits. He explains the cases come from various sides. "It's brought by environmental groups that are trying to get more regulation or to stop projects they don't like," he says. "It's brought by industry to try to halt regulations that they don't like. And it's really prolific."[17]

The courts offer a way for organizations, individuals, and corporations to

Hot Take: *"It has become clear—and is now recognized by the Intergovernmental Panel on Climate Change—that inclusive approaches to climate litigation that also address the human rights of the most vulnerable groups in society can contribute in meaningful ways to compel governments and corporate actors to pursue more ambitious climate change mitigation and adaptation goals."—Global Climate Litigation Report: 2023 Status Review*

seek redress for the failure of governments and private companies to reduce climate-warming pollution.[18] These cases are driven by the fact that countries, including the United States, are behind in taking actions to reduce global warming. "Virtually no government in the world is doing enough," says Gerrard. "So people look for any other tool, and the courts are one set of obvious tools. The courts are not going to solve the problem, but they can spur action and spur progress."[19]

Climate rights litigation, like the case in Montana, represents an expanding realm of cases that have garnered public attention and media coverage. But plenty of lower-profile cases are being filed as well. "There are a large number of cases that don't get a lot of attention challenging very specific regulations," explains Gerrard.[20] Many cases involve plaintiffs claiming a federal agency failed to adequately consider how a project or action, such as a mine, could affect the climate. These cases involve the National Environmental Policy Act. Another regulatory challenge involves the Clean Air Act and what authority the Environmental Protection Agency has to regulate planet-warming pollution. Both these policies and legal challenges are covered in Chapter 3.

Cities and states have also brought lawsuits against "oil companies seeking money damages, none of which have obtained money damages." Still another area of litigation centers on holding governments accountable for failing to adapt to climate change or to prepare communities for what's to come in a warming world. Greenwashing cases against companies that have overstated their environmental activities are also gaining steam.[21] As cases move forward, new categories of litigation will probably emerge, and it benefits journalists to keep up with the trends.

Climate Rights

The youth-led climate lawsuit in Montana represents a growing number of highly visible cases that put climate rights center stage. These claims assert human or environmental rights have been violated by states or countries failing to consider climate warming pollution in a host of areas, including granting permits to oil companies and failing to reduce greenhouse gas emissions.

National constitutions and human rights laws are usually challenged in these cases. Plaintiffs argue their rights to a clean, safe, healthy environment have been violated by a government's failure to adapt to or mitigate climate change.[22]

Climate rights cases draw on quasilegal guidelines or statements that aren't legally binding, such as those of the Human Rights Council in 2021, which acknowledged people's right to a clean, healthy, and sustainable environment through a historic resolution.[23]

The council noted the negative effect climate change and environmental damage present for people, "including the rights to life, to the enjoyment of the highest attainable standard of physical and mental health, to an adequate standard of living, to adequate food, to housing, to safe drinking water and sanitation and to participation in cultural life, for present and future generations."[24]

Six Primary Categories of Climate Litigation

Climate change litigation generally falls into the six primary categories described here. Climate-related cases are on the rise globally, and legal experts predict future cases could include lawsuits from vulnerable communities and increasing legal action after extreme weather events.

- **Climate rights cases** argue that people have a constitutional or fundamental right to a clean, healthy environment.
- **Domestic enforcement** cases typically involve governments defending their commitments to climate change mitigation and adaptation efforts.
- **Fossil fuels and carbon sinks** are addressed in challenges to how a project is done or its long-term impacts on the environment.
- **Corporate liability and responsibility** cases attempt to hold the emitters of greenhouse gases or fossil fuel companies responsible for climate damages. Some cases argue companies have ignored or misused information about climate change.
- **Climate disclosure and greenwashing** litigation is brought against corporations for false claims about climate change.
- **Failure to adapt and the impacts of adaptation** are cases that seek financial compensation for adaptation efforts that have caused harm or relief for failing to adapt to the threats of climate change.

Source. Courtesy of the United Nations Environment Programme. *Global Climate Litigation Report: 2023 Status Review.* Nairobi: UNEP, 2023. https://wedocs.unep.org/bitstream/handle/20.500.11822/43008/global_climate_litigation_report_2023.pdf?sequence=3.

The UN General Assembly also passed a historic resolution similar to the council's, stating that people have a right to a clean, healthy, and sustainable environment.[25] Such resolutions can be cited in legal proceedings to reinforce climate rights claims before a court.

Dutch environmental group Urgenda Foundation filed one of the most prominent international climate rights cases when it took on the Dutch government in 2015. The foundation, which represented 900 citizens, argued the Netherlands had a legal obligation to take more critical measures to protect citizens from the impacts of human-caused climate change. At that time, the Netherlands had set a goal to reduce greenhouse gas emissions by 17 percent, which Urgenda argued was insufficient.[26]

The Hague District Court ruled in Urgenda's favor. The Dutch government was ordered to reduce its greenhouse gas emissions to 1990 levels by at least 25 percent in five years.[27] The government appealed the decision, and three years later, the Hague Court of Appeal upheld the original decision. The case eventually went to the country's Supreme Court in 2019, which affirmed the government's obligation to lower emissions.[28] With no more legal options, the Netherlands had to comply and reduce emissions.

The case marked the first time a court held a government accountable for its responsibilities to address climate change. The final ruling acknowledged the country's commitment to the United Nations Framework Convention on Climate Change and how it must meet its share of responsibility in reducing emissions to meet global goals.

Urgenda v. State of the Netherlands also serves as an example of how litigation can lead to policy. In the wake of the Supreme Court's decision, the Netherlands had to create and adopt a plan to lower greenhouse gas emissions by a quarter. The country settled on a package of emergency actions to comply with the ruling, which included reducing the country's speed limit to a maximum 62 miles per hour.[29] The government also agreed to shut down a coal-fired power plant in Amsterdam early to help reduce emissions.

Climate law expert Michael Gerrard says the Urgenda case, deservedly, received tremendous attention and that "litigation helped spur a lot of similar litigation around the world."[30] At the time of this writing, the world has been watching another case in the Netherlands. In 2019 Friends of the Earth Netherlands and others filed a lawsuit against Royal Dutch Shell.[31] The lawsuit alleged "the company needed to reduce its greenhouse gas emissions, not only in the Netherlands but globally, and not only its direct emissions, but those of its customers."[32] The Hague District Court ruled in

2021 that Shell must reduce its emissions across its entire energy portfolio "by 45 percent by 2030, relative to 2019 emission levels."[33] That was seen as a major climate victory at the time by environmental groups. In 2022, Shell appealed the decision, and in 2024 a Dutch appeals court overturned the 2021 ruling. The judge found that generally, Shell has a responsibility to reduce its CO2 emissions, but it did not set specific targets to do that.[34] Kirtana Chandrasekaran with Friends of the Earth International called the ruling a "blow to communities all over the world who are bearing the brunt of climate inaction and greenwashing by corporations." Chandrasekaran stated in a press release that despite the decision, the ruling "also gives hope—it confirms that corporations must respect human rights and that they bear responsibility for reducing emissions."[35]

If the court had ruled in favor of Friends of the Earth Netherlands, the decision would have established that a "private company violated a duty of care and human rights obligations by failing to take adequate action to curb contributions to climate change."[36]

Other cases came to light in the wake of the Urgenda decision, including *Juliana v. United States*. This case, filed in 2015, was an early legal challenge in the United States that asserted the government's responsibility to create a safe, healthy environment. It's a classic public trust doctrine case.

Twenty-one youth, including lead plaintiff Kelsey Cascadia Rose Juliana, sued the US government in the US District Court in Eugene, Oregon, arguing that the atmosphere, a natural resource, should be protected under the public trust doctrine. The government, they alleged, was violating their constitutional rights to a safe and stable environment by supporting the continued use of fossil fuels and failing to act on climate change.[37]

District Court judge Ann Aiken ruled in favor of the youth, who ranged in age from eight to nineteen, saying they did have a right to a stable climate. "Exercising my 'reasoned judgment,' I have no doubt that the right to a climate system capable of sustaining human life is fundamental to a free and ordered society," she wrote.[38]

The federal government moved to appeal the decision in 2020, and in a Ninth Circuit Court of Appeals ruling, the majority opinion found the courts were not the right place to address the complaint. The majority held that the plaintiffs' grievances were political and should be handled by Congress and the Executive Branch.[39]

Although there have been numerous legal twists and turns, *Juliana v. US* never went to trial, but the case prompted similar lawsuits in states led by youth plaintiffs. The *Held* case in Montana, for example, affirmed that a constitutional obligation exists, at least at the state level, to provide a safe, clean, and healthy environment. Hawaii settled a similar case brought by youth before going to trial. Gerrard, who watches climate litigation closely, says the Montana and Hawaii cases did well because they were based on an environmental rights provision in the state constitution. But the majority of cases brought forward by Our Children's Trust have faced significant legal hurdles and have not progressed as hoped; *Juliana* is among them.

Journalists have covered youth-led cases widely in part because the plaintiffs' stories are so compelling. "They've (youth climate cases) been a wonderful, you know, organizing tool and public outreach," Gerrard says. "But I think a lot of people put undue hope that they would actually solve the problem and lead to an enforceable court order that the US adopt good climate policies."[40] That hasn't happened yet, though.

Another noteworthy climate rights case involves Peruvian farmer Luciano Lliuya, who sued Germany's largest electric utility, RWE AG. Lliuya claimed his farm has been endangered by melting glaciers in the Andes near his town of Huaraz. A glacial lake above the town has been expanding from the melting glaciers since 1975.[41] In recent years, though, that lake has drastically expanded. Lliuya alleged that the utility is responsible for 0.47 percent of the greenhouse gases in the atmosphere and therefore should pay him 0.47 percent of his damages.[42] "Obviously, it's symbolic," explains Gerrard. The amount of money Lliuya is suing for isn't large, but the case survived an initial motion to dismiss. A panel of judges decided to go to the Andean city of Huaraz to see for themselves what was happening, and after being delayed by the COVID-19 pandemic, they visited Huaraz in 2022, "which was extraordinary."[43] As of this writing, a ruling has yet to come, but it's certainly a case to follow and could lead to similar legal attempts in the future.

Big Oil Faces Big Lawsuits

An increasing number of lawsuits brought by states and cities aim to hold oil and gas companies accountable for their role in knowingly contributing to human-caused climate change. The lengthy legal battles involving tobacco companies and their cancer-causing products may spring to mind. The storylines of Big Oil and Big Tobacco are strikingly similar. Each unleashed massive disinformation campaigns to downplay the impact of their products. Each has and will continue to deal with legal cases and consequences. A central question for journalists to track is whether such cases end up being resolved in the courts and, if so, which court makes the most sense. The following cases help put this question into perspective.

Rhode Island in 2018 became the first state in the United States to bring a climate change lawsuit against twenty-one major oil companies, including Shell Oil. The state alleged the fossil fuel giants failed to "adequately warn of the foreseeable risks posed by their products and the consequences of use" and launched a lengthy disinformation campaign about climate science.[44]

The companies are accused of not doing their "duty to prevent reasonably foreseeable harm" to people using their products; they caused sea levels to rise and messed with the public's rights to enjoy and use resources held in the public trust. The case also alleges the companies violated Rhode Island's Environmental Rights Act by "polluting, impairing, and destroying natural resources of the State."[45]

Rhode Island's lawsuit aims to hold companies liable for hiding knowledge that their products contributed to global warming, resulting in severe consequences for the state, including rising sea levels.

The case was originally filed in state court, but defendants, including ExxonMobil, Chevron, and Shell Oil, filed to remove it from state court, arguing it encroached on federal jurisdiction and should be heard in a federal court.[46] That action was denied in 2018. Since then, a flurry of legal motions and reviews have ensued, including companies arguing for the case to be dismissed. Eventually, the question of jurisdiction, whether federal or state, went to the US Supreme Court.

In fact, the high court had appeals from five oil companies, all wanting similar cases brought to federal court instead of state court. The Supreme Court in 2023 refused to hear the cases and instead pointed everyone back to state courts for consideration. Chevron attorney Theodore Boutrous told Reuters he's confident state courts will dismiss the lawsuits, saying the cases represent a matter of "national and global magnitude."[47]

The argument among oil companies is that a federal response is needed rather than piecemeal rulings from multiple state courts. "These wasteful lawsuits in state courts will do nothing to advance global climate solutions," Boutrous said to Reuters, "nothing to reduce emissions and nothing to address climate-related impacts."[48]

The Supreme Court's decision was seen as a milestone in court jurisdiction. "We filed in state court," explained Rhode Island attorney general Peter Neronha, "because that is the traditional and proper forum to hold corporations accountable for deceiving and failing to warn consumers about their products' dangerous impacts."[49]

Other legal actions have been dismissed, such as when the cities of Oakland and San Francisco took on BP, Chevron, ConocoPhillips, ExxonMobil, and Shell in 2017. The cities claimed the five major oil companies contributed significantly to global warming and didn't disclose the risks their products caused for decades. Lawyers for the cities of San Francisco and Oakland tried to use "the common law claim of 'public nuisance' to force the companies to pay for infrastructure that would combat rising sea levels."[50]

A US District Court judge dismissed the case, ruling Congress and the Executive Branch should resolve the matter, not the courts. Nearly two dozen states and cities in the United States have sued major fossil fuel companies for compensation for the damages caused by climate change.[51]

It's not just oil and gas companies sitting in the hot seat. Some international cases have taken on automakers, supermarkets, and even livestock operators over their corporate duty to reduce emissions.

French nongovernmental organizations in 2021 sued the French supermarket chain Casino. The case raises the question of whether Casino, which produces low emissions at its headquarters, is liable for outsourced pollution that comes from cattle operations it uses in Brazil and Columbia.[52]

In Germany, an environmental organization has three separate cases against Mercedes-Benz, BMW, and Volkswagen to compel the car companies to stop making fossil fuel–emitting cars by 2030. The plaintiffs are relying on the Paris Agreement and the country's climate law to argue the companies have been "violating the fundamental right to climate protection and impinging on the rights and freedoms of future generations by not adhering to a fair carbon budget."[53]

Meet the Carbon Majors

Since the early 2000s, litigation has increased that holds major oil and gas companies responsible for misleading the public and contributing to global warming. That's in part because efforts have improved to attribute a particular percentage of global CO2 emissions to some of the world's biggest oil, gas, and coal companies. Meet the Carbon Majors.

The term comes from research by Richard Heede, who founded and directs the Climate Accountability Institute.[54] He started a database in 2013 that shows the amounts of greenhouse gases companies such as Exxon, Chevron, and Shell have emitted. Heede's work also projects where emissions could go in the coming years.

The top twenty companies, according to the database, have contributed 493 billion tonnes of carbon dioxide and methane from 1965 to 2018. Collectively, these companies, with Chevron, ExxonMobil, BP, Shell, and Pemex as the top five polluters, emitted 35 percent of all greenhouse gases globally.[55]

"It is incumbent on companies that value their social license to operate to respect climate science [and] manage corporate risks accordingly," wrote Heede in a press release. He believes Carbon Majors need to commit to "reducing future production of carbon fuels" and have emissions align with the Paris Agreement trajectory to limit warming to less than 1.5°C. That means decarbonizing the world's economy and shifting "their capital investments toward renewables, carbon sequestration, and low-carbon fuels in line with science-based targets. Companies leading this transition will prosper, and laggards will perish."[56]

The Carbon Majors database sometimes shows up in climate litigation to hold companies accountable for their contributions to climate change. It is one of the few places tracking historical production data from 180 oil, gas, cement, and coal companies around the world.[57] For journalists, the database is something to be aware of and follow over time.

A Guide to Climate Law Basics

In the coming years, climate litigation will probably continue to grow as the consequences of burning fossil fuels, including extreme weather and forced migration, become ever more apparent. As international efforts to address climate change progress, the courts will increasingly be used to determine responsibility.

Reporting on court cases can be daunting. I saw this with my students in Arizona State University's Cronkite News program. Every semester, students would end up covering at least one environmental court case or legal development. At the time, legal challenges had been mounted over an international copper mining company that wanted to develop its operation on land the San Carlos Apache Tribe considers sacred.[58] The legal struggle was years in the making, and I instructed student journalists to report on the latest developments so they would learn how to cover a case. We started with the basics: who's suing whom for what, and where the lawsuit is being considered in the courts. Then I'd help students find an interesting way into the story.

In the case of the San Carlos Apache Tribe, an activist group known as Apache Stronghold occasionally held protests or long marches to the federal courthouse in Phoenix to draw attention to their cause and gain media coverage.[59] We also looked at this story through the eyes of the copper mining company and visited the area where the development would take place. My students learned how complex environmental cases can be and also the basic language used in court that journalists need to know.

Whether you are a new journalist or a veteran reporter, it's crucial to understand how the legal system works. Reporters must first figure out what court—local, state, federal, high court, international—a lawsuit was filed in. Then there's learning how to access a case and decipher what it means, akin to reading a scientific study. Cases can draw out over years, with multiple legal motions that can be difficult to track. To read and analyze climate cases, reporters should begin with the basic elements below.

Parties to the lawsuit: Plaintiffs are the people, organizations, or governments that are bringing the lawsuit. Defendants are those being sued because of an alleged wrong.

Jurisdiction: Various courts exist, which means you have to know where a lawsuit is filed. This will be noted in the case. State courts and federal courts, from district courts within the states all the way up to the Supreme Court, have their own procedures and even websites for accessing case information.

Complaint: Look at the details of the plaintiffs' complaint. What do they allege the corporation, individual, or government did or didn't do? There will be a legal rationale for their case, and you'll need to know what that is. A variety of legal motivations exist, from climate rights abuses to liability for damages caused by the burning of fossil fuels.

Request: The plaintiffs will ask the court for some sort of relief, which can become nuanced. Compensation for damages caused or compelling a company to reduce greenhouse gas emissions could be among many requests. Requested relief can be difficult to parse from the lengthy expositions of facts and legal background on a first read. One trick is to skip to the end of the complaint, where the requested relief is clearly specified.

Evidence: Every climate lawsuit will include evidence. Climate science, expert testimony, and history can all be used to make the case. Much of the evidence will not be available when a complaint is first filed but will be submitted as part of substantive pleadings filed months or even years later.

Previous cases: Past cases will be referenced in lawsuits that help support a case. This is called precedent. Understanding the legal context and possible implications can come from knowing what precedent is being relied on.

Interviews: A good practice is to talk with plaintiffs and experts to make sure you understand what's at stake and why. You should try to speak with the defendants, which can be tricky. Not all defendants will talk, especially if federal agencies are involved. Reach out, nevertheless, and be transparent in your story about why someone does or does not interview with you.

Covering Court Proceedings

Court proceedings have their own language and rhythm, from motions and hearings to trials and rulings. Below are some main points to focus on when covering a climate-related case.

Legal reasoning and interpretation: The audience will want to know not only how the court or judge ruled but why they came to this decision. When reading a court ruling, focus on the legal reasoning the court used in making its decision.

Judgment: This is the court's decision at the end of a case and can be straightforward in that one side wins their argument. Sometimes, cases can be more complex, with a court ruling in favor of one party on some issues but not on other aspects of the case.

Dissenting opinions: Appellate courts, such as circuit courts, have multiple judges. A majority opinion will be issued to represent the final ruling. Dissenting justices will also explain why they did not go with the majority opinion. Pay attention to dissenting opinions because they can give you valuable insights into alternative legal interpretations that can be drawn upon for future litigation.

Implications: The consequences of a legal decision become part of the story. Interview those involved in the case and legal experts who can provide the necessary context. Don't forget to find out how defendants view those implications too. For instance, the ruling in the Montana climate lawsuit set a legal precedent for future cases that take on state constitutional rights to a clean, safe, and healthy environment.

Court Documents

Journalists in the United States usually have the right to access case documents once a lawsuit has been filed. Courts can choose to seal documents if the information is considered sensitive. In most instances, several types of documents are available. *The Open Notebook* has pulled together an excellent breakdown of this material:[60]

Docket: Want to see what documents have been filed for a case? Start with this breakdown of all the documents and information the court has access to. Scanning the docket can also reveal whether the parties are seeking extensions in the briefing schedule to reach a settlement. That may mean the case never actually goes to trial.

Complaint: A plaintiff starts by filing this document, which begins the court proceedings. Journalists will find this helpful because it details who's being sued, why they're being sued, and what the plaintiffs want.

Motion: Parties to the lawsuit, either plaintiffs or defendants, can file a variety of motions asking the judge for a specific action. That could include dismissing a case, getting more information, or focusing the evidence before a trial happens.

Opinion: A judge issues an opinion to explain the reasoning behind a decision. In appellate courts, the majority opinion represents the decision that most judges on the panel agree upon. If some judges disagree with the majority, they may write dissenting opinions to explain their reasoning. Occasionally, a judge may issue a concurring opinion agreeing with the majority decision but based on different reasoning.

Subpoena: This is a court order that requires a person to provide relevant information or documents to a lawsuit or to appear in court to testify, usually before or during a trial.

Amicus curiae brief: Reporters might also hear this referred to as a friend of the court brief or amicus brief. Individuals or organizations not parties to a lawsuit will file these briefs to provide extra information, expertise, or perspectives to help the court decide. Amicus briefs usually advocate for a particular outcome.

Accessing Documents

Journalists will find several online resources to help access various courts and documents. Most federal court cases are available online. The media and the public can access many records through the Public Access to Court Electronic Records (PACER) service.

I can't recommend enough getting a PACER account, which allows reporters to search federal court cases. This invaluable resource takes some practice to learn.

Outside PACER and federal court litigation, courts sometimes include a section on their website for "notable" cases that are gaining a lot of attention.

Reporters can generally find some essential documents, including court orders, docket entries, and sometimes trial exhibits. Some courts also allow reporters to sign up for text or email alerts when major documents are filed for high-profile cases.

When in doubt, ask the court clerk to clarify how to access documents or what reporters can and cannot do in the courtroom. Some courts don't allow any recording devices and only a notebook, for example.

Climate-related cases have the potential to shape how laws are interpreted and influence policy, making them essential for journalists to follow and report on over time. Journalists are increasingly covering climate cases because decisions in the courts could shape the direction of future climate action. One thing journalists need to avoid is overstating a ruling's impact, something climate legal expert Michael Gerrard has seen in the media. Words such as "groundbreaking" and "landmark" can be overstated.[61] "Sometimes they are," Gerrard explains, "but not very often." For example, youth-led climate cases can be compelling because of the plaintiffs' appealing personal stories. But in the end, they might have less impact than a lower-profile case on climate regulation. The challenge with these more technical cases is to find the personal relevance that helps audiences understand their implications, big or small.

Essential Reading and Resources

The Sabin Center for Climate Change Law at Columbia University is an exceptional resource for climate litigation in the United States and abroad. Check out the climate change law databases. https://climate.law.columbia.edu/

The Sabin Center's monthly newsletter provides updates to its legal climate database. If you're interested in following climate-related cases, this is a must. https://columbia.us13.list-manage.com/subscribe?u=9906c7202590aac6a8bdbb7b9&id=a721b41b2d

The ScotusBlog is worth reading if you're interested in decisions coming from the US Supreme Court. https://www.scotusblog.com/

The UNEP report on climate litigation, published every three years, gives broad context on the areas of litigation, cases, and motivations. The latest report, *Global Climate Litigation*, was published in 2023. https://wedocs.unep.org/bitstream/handle/20.500.11822/43008/global_climate_litigation_report_2023.pdf?sequence=3

Reporters Committee for the Freedom of the Press provides an in-depth guide to accessing courts. Find information on everything from interviewing judges to accessing trial records. Although the committee doesn't focus on climate litigation, it's a portal into the legal world that's worth reviewing and referencing. https://www.rcfp.org/

A Journalist's Guide to the Federal Courts, published by the US government, is an excellent guide for journalists who are tasked with covering federal court cases. It provides information on how to access court documents, media access to court proceedings, and much more. https://www.uscourts.gov/statistics-reports/publications/journalists-guide-federal-courts

The PACER website, maintained by the US government, provides electronic access to federal court cases. pacer.gov.

CHAPTER 9

Trauma-Informed Reporting and Self-Care

"Taking care of yourself doesn't mean me first, it means me too."
—L. R. Knost

The KHOU-TV news team in Houston knew how to prepare for hurricanes. The nation's fourth-largest city is prone to hurricanes and tropical storms every year. They had plans for staffing up coverage and a backup plan should the CBS affiliate go off the air. But when the station's meteorologist warned in August 2017 about a developing hurricane that could dump 50 inches of rain over the city, they had questions.

"We're like, 'Yeah, right, 50-plus inches of rain.' Like, no way," recalls Sally Ramirez, who was executive news director at the time. "I always prepare for the worst-case scenario."[1] She had emergency contacts, a plan to move station operations to the PBS affiliate if KHOU went off the air, and a closet full of food in case anyone had to stay for a couple of days. However, as the storm intensified into a Category 4 hurricane over warm Gulf waters, Ramirez decided they needed help for what could be one of the worst hurricanes to hit Texas and the city of Houston. She knew KHOU reporters and photographers would need to be in the field reporting live, they'd be doing continuous coverage, and they'd need support. Her team would be navigating flooding and working with little sleep, getting by on adrenaline. People would be stressed. How could she help support and prepare the newsroom?

Ramirez asked the station's parent company to fly in about a dozen reporters and photographers to help with coverage. She put everyone on shifts: twelve hours on and twelve hours off. Staff practiced evacuating to the second floor in case the first-floor newsroom and studio flooded.

Ramirez recalls in vivid detail the Friday evening, August 25, when her meteorologist told her the hurricane was indeed coming, but they would face another crisis even before it made landfall.

"There's gonna be a tornado over us. Get everybody inside, make sure everything's fine," she remembers her meteorologist telling her.[2] That's when KHOU went to continuous live coverage from its first-floor studio. In the hours that followed, tornados, which can happen with the right conditions as a hurricane nears landfall, sparked fires, and the newsroom began to receive the first reports of flooding in neighborhoods across the city.

By the next night, Hurricane Harvey swept inland from the Gulf, stalled over Houston, and for three days pummeled the city with nearly 52 inches of rain.[3] Streets turned into flowing rivers. People were stranded in their homes. The station was not immune to the storm. The Buffalo Bayou across from KHOU spilled its banks. Water seeped into the studio and newsroom. Still, KHOU stayed on the air. "We're on the air continuously, and we're live on the air, and telling people, 'that's the Buffalo Bayou creeping into our newsroom.'"[4]

All around the Houston area, the water was rising. People couldn't get through to 911 for help, so they called the KHOU newsroom. "And they're like, 'I'm in my attic with my family, chopping through the roof, like trying to get on top because the water's rising,'" recalls Ramirez.[5]

She juggled between relaying information from callers to the chief of police and checking on her own team's safety and needs. "My crew at the station is melting down because these people on the calls are like, 'Don't hang up! Don't hang up! Like, you're my only help, right?'"[6]

Ramirez grabbed Post-It notes to take down information, sticking them on a board to track and follow up. She used another whiteboard for her crews in the field. Every thirty minutes, she had check-ins with teams to verify their location and safety. As KHOU staff reported on the latest developments, the station itself became part of the story. People's cars were underwater. The newsroom was no longer safe. Desks were nearly underwater.

Ramirez remembers they moved as much of the broadcasting equipment as they could up to the second floor on the elevators. Just as the last piece of gear was unloaded, the elevators stopped working. Eventually, the newsroom had to evacuate too, but they could not reach the PBS station that was in their emergency plan, because the roads were flooded. Instead, they retreated to a nearby building that was on higher ground.

During most of this chaos, KHOU managed to stay on the air. At one point, while the newsroom was being relocated, reporters passed a cell phone back and forth, using the station's Facebook Live stream to keep viewers updated.

Reporter Brandi Smith took over coverage live from the field. Pelted by rain, she explained to the audience that KHOU was evacuating but that the station would stay on the air as long as they could.[7] As she talked, her photographer spotted a nearly submerged semi with a man trapped inside. Viewers watched live as Smith waved down a rescue vehicle passing by that happened to have a boat. She alerted them that a man was trapped inside. Her photographer captured the scene as they rescued the man. An emotional Smith told viewers, "Sometimes we get flak because, yes, we are out in it. We are doing the things we're telling you not to do. We do it so that we can show you how bad the conditions are so you do not attempt them."[8]

The story of KHOU during Hurricane Harvey shows how important local journalism is to a community in crisis. It also illustrates how newsroom leaders can prepare ahead of a potential weather disaster and get staff ready for what to expect. Finally, it's a story about what happens to journalists when they, too, experience the effects of the crisis they're covering. These journalists covered the trauma and aftermath of Hurricane Harvey for months. But they also had to deal with their own losses.

"I like to say there's a before Harvey and an after Harvey of how things operated, and it's just one of those moments in time that is marked forever," Ramirez says. Some of her employees lost their homes and cars and had to navigate their own personal loss while also losing their "work home." For the next eighteen months, the KHOU team worked from the local PBS station. "We also were Harvey victims," Ramirez says.[9]

National media left after the initial crisis passed, but KHOU and other Houston media remained, committed to reporting on the aftermath of Harvey while also rebuilding their own lives. "We all came through something that we were all very proud of," Ramirez says. "[It] was the most difficult thing I've ever gone through professionally, but I wouldn't change a thing."[10]

Hurricane Harvey was extremely rare, but the rains that stayed over Houston for days were intensified by human-caused climate change. An attribution study found climate change made Harvey's record rainfall about three times more likely and 15 percent more intense. Scientists know that this is what happens with hurricanes.[11]

Increasingly, journalists will find themselves covering hurricanes, heavy rainfall, and other climate-related disasters. That can take a toll on mental well-being. Sally Ramirez gets emotional talking about Hurricane Harvey. She admits that she hasn't personally dealt fully with what happened in Houston. "It took a personal toll on me, my family, because those 18 months were unlike anything I ever experienced," Ramirez remembers. "I had to be 24/7. I was in crisis management for a long time and, you know, mentally, emotionally, physically, we're not meant for that."[12]

Not every climate disaster will be like what Ramirez and her team went through. Hurricane Harvey is an extreme example, but it illustrates the physical and emotional challenges journalists must be prepared to manage as climate change worsens. This chapter examines how journalists can keep themselves safe both physically and emotionally while reporting on a climate-fueled crisis. The chapter also offers guidance on how to sustain a career in climate journalism without succumbing to climate doomism or becoming targeted by doxing or other attacks.

The Mental Toll

Journalists increasingly find themselves on the front lines of the climate crisis. As first responders, they see trauma unfold before their eyes, from hurricanes like Harvey to a wildfire that threatens homes. Reporting on trauma, including weather and climate disasters, can lead to mental health challenges. There's growing research on those impacts.

In the months after Hurricane Harvey, one study found that one in five journalists surveyed exhibited symptoms associated with posttraumatic stress disorder (PTSD). Of every five journalists surveyed, two met the threshold for depression. More than 90 percent of news staff, including reporters, editors, meteorologists, and news anchors, reported symptoms, including nightmares and major disruptions to their lives due to what they went through during the hurricane.[13] The study revealed how the combination of length of coverage, long hours, and back-to-back days without breaks affected mental health. Retelling similar stories day after day also led to stress. Journalists also felt immense responsibility because lives were at stake. The emotional toll of covering the tragedy of others can also be immense. Hurricane Harvey also personally affected the journalists covering the disaster.

Researchers have previously documented the effects on journalists of reporting on other traumatic events, from war and mass shootings to the COVID-19 pandemic and heated presidential campaigns.[14] But talking about mental health in the newsroom has been rather taboo. Journalists, me included, have been taught to stay strong and keep going no matter the toll of long hours or what we experience. The demands have become increasingly intense over the years.

Naseem Miller is the senior editor at the Journalist's Resource at the Harvard Kennedy School's Shorenstein Center. But in 2016 she was a reporter in Orlando, Florida, when a gunman attacked a gay nightclub. Nothing, she remembers, compared to the Pulse nightclub mass shooting. "It was just a surreal moment because up to that point, we as journalists, we had seen these mass shootings happen elsewhere, and all of a sudden it was our story," Miller recalls. She remembers the "adrenaline rush" of covering the story, but it wasn't until later that she began to process the horrors of that night. "It was about a year later when I connected with another journalist who was covering a mass shooting in Texas," Miller says. They started "talking about how covering these issues has affected us in different ways." She remembers after the mass shooting she couldn't drive by the nightclub's location. If she did, "I could physically feel something changing."[15]

So Miller and Silvia Foster-Frau, who was at *The San Antonio Express-News*, decided to do something to help each other out.[16] They created a closed Facebook group to see whether "other journalists are experiencing what we are experiencing."[17] That group became a gathering place for journalists who cover traumatic events. They sent care packages and food to newsrooms covering trauma, from shootings to extreme weather. They raised money for news outlets and helped connect journalists with resources such as the Dart Center for Journalism and Trauma. The group began with about 150 members. Now it's over 1,000.

Thankfully, in recent years mental health has become less taboo to talk about. More journalists are speaking about burnout and stress brought on in recent years covering the COVID-19 pandemic but also in reporting on extreme weather and disasters. "I think a lot of credit goes to the younger journalists and Gen Z for being more comfortable talking about mental health," Miller explains. "Also expecting that people respect their mental health, and that is changing the conversation."[18]

Miller says there's been growing awareness about mental health, and the attention has been shifting to look at the "responsibilities of people who oversee us." She says she's glad to see that the conversation "has been elevated to what our organizations are doing or should do to take care of the journalists."[19]

For reporters who cover climate change, the conversation about mental health is also happening. It's okay not to feel okay. Reporters shouldn't feel guilty for feeling trauma even though the disaster or trauma didn't happen to them directly. Stress is normal. Just witnessing and interacting with people who have come through a tragic ordeal is enough to cause stress, trauma, depression, anxiety, and more.

Journalists are taught to focus on other people and not themselves. That can lead to putting oneself last. According to the Dart Center, journalists' PTSD rates range from 4 to 59 percent, depending on what they report on.[20] The center researches the psychological impacts of covering trauma and provides resources to help journalists and newsrooms navigate trauma.

Understanding Climate Change and Mental Health

Journalists work and live in a traumatized world. International conflict, school shootings, police violence, unnatural and extreme disasters—it's a lot to live through, let alone report on. Human-driven climate change amplifies trauma, causing anxiety, posttraumatic stress, and fear for the future, especially among young people.

Over the past decade, mental health effects caused by climate change have risen. Research shows that climate change affects not just physical health (e.g., through heat-related illness, allergies, and respiratory problems from wildfire smoke) but our mental health, too.[21]

A survey of people who lived through one of the deadliest wildfires in California's history—the Camp Fire in 2018—found that the rate of PTSD was on par with that of veterans who had seen war.[22] The risk for depression and anxiety also increased. The same is true for survivors of hurricanes and catastrophic floods.[23]

In the United States, even people who have not experienced a climate-related disaster report an overwhelming sense of "fear, sadness, and dread in the face of a warming planet or anxiety and worry about climate change and its effects."[24] The American Psychiatric Association has found that most Americans surveyed are "somewhat" or "extremely" anxious about how climate change is affecting the planet, and more than half share similar anxieties about how climate change affects their mental health.[25] Young adults and Latinos are more likely to experience serious levels of anxiety, depression, and psychological distress due to concerns about climate change. They are also more likely to talk about their feelings about climate change with counselors or therapists.[26] If our changing climate exerts this kind of pervasive mental strain on those who perhaps have not directly experienced the effects of climate change, imagine what it's like for reporters who regularly do.

We now have terms to explain the anxiety and trauma people feel about climate change and the effects of global warming. Eco-anxiety, sometimes called climate anxiety, is the ongoing stress and fear of environmental doom brought on by the climate crisis. Eco-grief is the overwhelming sadness and mourning people can experience with losing biodiversity and the natural world as we know it.[27] These terms can be increasingly hard to define, says Jennifer Atkinson, an associate teaching professor of environmental humanities at the University of Washington.

Emotional responses to climate change come from our lived or vicarious experiences. The emotional reaction people have to living in a warmer world hinges on multiple factors, including race, age, and geography.

Anyone working in the climate space, including scientists, activists, and journalists, is prone to feeling a range of emotions, from profound sadness over the slow global progress in addressing climate change to outrage, frustration, despair, and hopelessness over the devastation left in the wake of a warming world.

Atkinson sees the growing impacts of climate change on her students' mental health, which anyone working in the climate space can probably relate to. Many of her students come from classes where discussions concentrate on science but not necessarily on feelings. When they come to her class, "the floodgates were just opening up, like their levels of despair were, and still are, completely off the charts," Atkinson says. Students told her they planned to change majors because "environmental work was so depressing, or they felt so hopeless about the future."[28]

Her students talked about not having children. Why would they bring kids into a world that's dying? Some struggled to finish assignments because the more they learned, the more debilitated they became with anxiety. It wasn't just the despair and hopelessness she saw. Her students were deeply unhappy, which reduced their ability to think critically and imagine creative solutions—the very skills the world needs now, Atkinson says. Research finds that when people are in a state of fear or dealing with chronic anxiety, "it hijacks higher-order thinking, and that's what we're supposed to be doing in college," she says.[29] That's a significant problem for anyone whose life or work is directly affected by the climate crisis, including journalists.

Atkinson also heard her students say it was too late to do anything about climate change—that the influence of fossil fuel companies was too powerful, politicians were corrupt, and irreversible changes brought on by global warming were already happening. Why bother?

Journalists might feel that too when reporting on climate change. "The answer to that question, which I think all of us know in our hearts, is because we love the world," says Atkinson. "When you're motivated by love, you're going to push through setbacks more tenaciously than if you're simply motivated by outcomes. . . . If you care, you are hurting at some level," says Atkinson. She became more open about that with herself and her students. "It helped us kind of reconnect with the core of why we're doing this in the first place," Atkinson says.[30]

Journalists need to keep perspective on why they want to report on climate change. Halle Parker covers climate change at WWNO in New Orleans. Parker says she's always been optimistic about the state of the world. She decided to pursue journalism after learning about journalism ethics in her first high school class. She was drawn to the idea of seeking truth and minimizing harm and to the potential to change the world through informed reporting. "We're trying to change the world by providing the information that people need to make educated and positive decisions and not repeat mistakes from the past," she says.[31] But what surprised her about reporting on environmental issues, especially climate change, is how unjust and entrenched problems are.

Parker felt her worldview shift when she began reporting on oil and gas and discovered how the industry is ingrained in society. "It's like an existential crisis of this question of who we are as people and as a society," Parker says.[32] How could her reporting change the world for the better? How could it address climate change in some way?

Parker still believes in journalism's ability to influence change, but she says she's more realistic about it and where the limits are. "And maybe not putting as much pressure on myself to be the thing [the story] that changes us and makes us go, 100 percent toward renewables, at the speed that we need to be going at."[33]

Mental Preparation

Before reporters take on a potentially difficult assignment, they need a game plan for how to care for themselves during and after the assignment. Journalist and editor Naseem Miller, who has researched and written on trauma and journalism, says this is especially important for reporting on extreme weather situations. "If you have a reporter out in the field covering wildfires," she says, "keep track of on how many days they're out in the field and maybe pull them in for a few days before sending them back again."[34]

As a former public radio news director and now as a climate editor, I find myself in conversations like this with reporters, helping them prepare to cover what can be a difficult topic. What follows are strategies I've seen work before, during, and after reporting on potentially traumatic stories or events.

- What are the potential dangers physically? Emotionally?
- What part of the reporting trip might be stressful?
- What's the reporter's plan for how to handle stress?
- What ways to stay calm have worked well in the past, and what hasn't?

Just as Sally Ramirez did for her team, editors and reporters should have a plan for staying in regular communication and setting up periodic check-ins.

Feeling emotions or distress when seeing something that feels apocalyptic is normal when covering a weather or climate disaster. I encourage reporters to acknowledge their feelings and discuss them with colleagues, friends, or family. Self-care also means getting adequate rest and good nutrition. It's an excellent idea to carry food and water, because not eating enough can impair judgment. When I've been on tough assignments, I try to take breaks, even if they are brief, because that rest can rejuvenate and keep the mind sharp and focused. There is no one-size-fits-all guide for how to stay calm and grounded when under pressure. That's why each reporter needs to figure out what works best *before* reporting on a potentially traumatic event.

For some, meditation, yoga, or deep breathing will be part of their self-care plan. But those techniques don't work for everyone. Jeje Mohamed, who was a senior manager for free expression and digital safety at PEN America, said she gets stressed when someone tells her to take deep breaths. "I always love to carry a small bottle of perfume that I love," she explained. "It just brings me a sense of grounding, a sense of safety."[35] Journalists need to find what works for them and to practice those techniques so they are part of their toolkit.

Weather and climate disasters can last for days and sometimes weeks. In the aftermath, people might be searching for loved ones or returning to a destroyed home. Lives must be rebuilt and infrastructure replaced. That's a lot for any one person to witness, let alone report on.

I have found the best leaders I've worked with have coverage plans with clear roles, expectations, and deadlines to avoid confusion. For example, KHOU's news director, Sally Ramirez, had coverage and backup plans for worst-case scenarios. Everyone had a schedule: twelve hours on, twelve hours off. She knows that confusion about roles and information overload can add stress and anxiety to an already difficult situation. So she plans and gives clear guidance. Ramirez, and other newsroom leaders I've known, will also have a strategy to provide support and help in the days, weeks, and months following intense coverage. Many of these systems can be established well ahead of any disasters.

After Hurricane Harvey, Ramirez focused on helping staff with both their personal loss and the mental toll of long days covering such trauma. The station brought in counselors and motivational speakers. "I brought in puppies," she recalls. "Anything I can do to help the staff because it was a really, really difficult time."[36]

Miller, a senior editor at *The Journalist's Resource* who has researched and written about trauma and journalists, says small actions by editors can go a long way, such as checking in on reporters after they have had a hard assignment. "We're not talking about therapy sessions," she says. "Just asking your reporter, . . . 'How's it going? How are you doing?' Even those conversations could not only let the journalists know that it's okay to talk about how they're feeling, but also maybe help them process a little bit what's going on."[37]

Advocating for Self

Covering climate-related disasters can mean following the story over time, as the KHOU news team did after Hurricane Harvey. Local journalists stay with the story, and they might find it difficult to take a break. In this section, we'll look at ways to do that.

"As a profession, journalists are not taught to value themselves, period," Wudan Yan, an independent journalist who covers science and society, says.[38] Instead, journalists are encouraged to think about their impact and the greater good that can come from their work. That approach can put journalists' mental and physical well-being at risk. If basic needs aren't met, reporters can't do their best work. Feelings of burnout, disconnect, depression, sadness, and anger are emotions to pay attention to.

"We forget that everything is so interconnected," Yan says. "We can't do a good job of showing up in our work and having the impact and going forth towards the mission that we set out to if we are not taking care of ourselves."[39]

Journalists who learn to take care of themselves can ask for what they need without worrying that they might let an editor or colleague down. If they don't, those emotions only become more heightened. Environment reporter Halle Parker says she's had to learn to advocate for herself because, in the past, she had prioritized her reporting over self-care. That, she says, had led to feeling burned out.

"I just don't think that you should let it get to the point where it's really starting to affect your stress levels," Parker explains. She tries to leave her job behind when she's not at the office. "With journalism, you're always going to be thinking a little bit about work or keeping your eye on something in case there's breaking news," she says. Now Parker tries to disengage "just because my brain does need a break in order to be able to focus on the new information that I'll be taking in the next day."[40]

Reporters should not be afraid to take time off and to use all the time promised by their employer. Some newsrooms even offer sabbaticals. Fellowships are another way to recharge. In 2017, I became a Ted Scripps Fellow in Environmental Journalism at the University of Colorado Boulder. I spent nine months auditing classes and developing a reporting project. I focused primarily on public lands and environmental law classes, along with a few fun courses such as climate change fiction. Those classes and field trips gave me a needed respite and allowed me to clear my head. I realized I wanted to concentrate on public lands and climate change in some journalism capacity. That clarity led to a career pivot: teaching at Arizona State University and, eventually, becoming a climate editor at NPR. The fellowship transformed my career.

More immediate solutions are out there, too, such as picking up new hobbies for fun. For example, I'm an avid cyclist. So I ride most days to maintain energy and balance in my life. Pedaling along the road or climbing up a dirt trail in the woods helps me focus and reset my mind. I know journalists who hike, crochet, read fiction, or paint to detach from journalism life and recharge.

Newsroom culture has historically glorified self-sacrifice to get the story. That translates into many long days and sometimes nights to meet constant deadlines. This culture is slowly changing. As Dart notes, more supportive newsrooms have added access to counseling through employee assistance programs. Progressive newsroom leaders support their journalists by making it okay for people to talk honestly about what's going on. This, historically, has not been the case. As an editor, I know part of working with reporters is checking in to see how they are doing and how I can help them. I also try to recognize when reporters need a break from their regular assignments. That could be time off or doing an entirely different story that's not on their beat.

Reporters have traditionally been expected to be "human doings," but we are also human beings. We can only show up as our best selves when we don't feel overwhelmed, stressed, tired, or traumatized.

Trauma-Informed Practices for Climate Journalists

Trauma is a term with a specific meaning in the mental health field. Journalists need to understand what trauma is because their reporting assignments will probably take them to places devastated by climate-related disasters. For instance, they may talk with people living through a wildfire, flood, or a brutal heat wave. Reporters need to know what trauma is and how to recognize its effects on interviews and interactions. Journalists can also experience trauma directly when they are affected by the stories they cover, as in the case of the Houston TV news team during Hurricane Harvey.

The American Psychological Association defines trauma as any experience that brings on "significant fear, helplessness, dissociation, confusion, or other disruptive feelings intense enough to have a long-lasting negative effect on a person's attitudes, behavior, and other aspects of functioning." War, a bridge collapse, or a mass shooting are examples of traumatic situations. But so are natural disasters such as earthquakes and volcanoes. Climate disasters are also considered traumatic events. In all cases, the American Psychological Association defines trauma as challenging "an individual's view of the world as a just, safe, and predictable place."[41]

PTSD happens when someone lives through or witnesses trauma they believe is life-threatening, which generates "fear, terror, and helplessness." According to the American Psychological Association, PTSD symptoms can include "re-experiencing the trauma in painful recollections, flashbacks, or recurrent dreams or nightmares." People with PTSD may avoid certain activities or places that remind them of the traumatic event. People may also feel startled, lack concentration, or struggle to sleep. They may also feel guilty for surviving such trauma.[42]

Understanding and recognizing how people respond to trauma can help journalists assess situations calmly. It can also help them interact with someone in distress who may be so numb that they aren't thinking clearly. How can journalists develop the skill to interview people during what will probably be a highly distressing and dynamic situation? Practicing trauma-informed journalism will help immensely.

What Is Trauma-Informed Reporting?

Trauma-informed journalism recognizes the impact of upheaval and suffering on people and their communities. Reporters should always approach trauma coverage with compassion and empathy. Over the years, I have learned to slow down and not rush into interviews with people who may be traumatized, even if I feel the pressure of a looming deadline. That requires patience and showing compassion and empathy. My approach has been to show up as a genuinely caring human being first and a journalist second.

The Dart Center for Journalism and Trauma has an outstanding guide for journalists, editors, and newsroom managers on covering trauma.[43] One of the first things they recommend when reporting on a traumatic event or its aftermath is to "stop, look, and listen." This involves using all the senses to take in and understand what's happening.

Next, the Dart Center recommends that reporters collect themselves, stay calm, and be patient. That's essential to doing the job well. After all, local reporters have an important job: to gather and get information out quickly without sacrificing accuracy. This essential reporting helps people know what's happening, where they can go for assistance, and how to access resources.

Tips for Interviewing People in Distress

Interviewing survivors of climate disasters can be exceptionally difficult because trauma manifests in people in different ways. Some people will be comfortable sharing their stories right away; others may appear forgetful or shut down. That may come across as someone being evasive or suggest that they did something wrong when, in fact, they are in shock. Trauma changes a person's story about themselves. Life as they knew it is forever altered, and their story may have been taken from them unexpectedly. As long as they won't be further traumatized, people can find telling their story powerful, a way to regain control over what they have lost.

Dart recommends reporters show the utmost care, focus, and compassion when interviewing someone. A journalist may wonder how to ask a survivor about what happened without retraumatizing them. It can't always be avoided, but there are several steps reporters can take to help create a safe space for people to talk.

Here are some of the practices I've seen work best. Reporters can begin by explaining why they are doing the story and why they care about it. Jeje Mohamed, who has worked as a journalist in Egypt and the United States, asks people whether they are truly okay and whether they need anything before doing interviews. She doesn't want to interview someone if they don't feel safe or have what they need. "If there are resources in a place of disaster that you can connect them with, this is something good to do," she said during a Society of Environmental Journalists panel on trauma-informed reporting.[44]

Climate journalist Amy Westervelt says taking the time to get to know someone has helped her. She will talk with people multiple times "for long periods of time, and listen to their stories about their kids and whatever's going on to form a genuine relationship."[45]

Unlike public officials, people who go through a disaster don't have to talk with reporters. It's unethical to push someone to answer questions if they don't want to. One way reporters can avoid that is to reassure the person they're speaking with that they are in control of the interview: They can stop at any time or take breaks. A reporter can check in periodically throughout the interview to make sure the person is okay.

"Literally every couple of questions, I would ask people, do you need a break? Do you want us to talk about something else?" Jeje Mohamed explained.[46] Then she would return to asking questions. A reporter can also repeat back what a person says to ensure their story is captured accurately. Reporters are sometimes surprised to find that someone opens up and shares more because they feel safe.

Journalists also need to be prepared for emotion. I have interviewed people dealing with the aftermath of wildfires who would tear up or cry as they talked. At first, I wasn't sure what to do. But I decided to be a human first and ask whether they were okay, and I'd offer a tissue. Usually, people pause and collect themselves, and they will continue talking once the moment has passed.

Most people who live through a traumatic situation are not used to interacting with the media. Reporters should explain how the interview and pictures might be used. They should also be clear with people that their story may not end up in the article. Ideally, reporters will exchange contact information because after an interview, people will sometimes realize they have additional information to share or they want to clarify something they said. Reporters probably will have additional questions. It's also an excellent practice for journalists to let people know when the story will publish and, once it has, to follow up for feedback.

I want to leave you with one piece of advice that I've learned over my years of reporting stories about the environment and climate change: Listen to the people you interview. I mean *really* listen. The gift of listening means someone can share their story in their voice, and for some, it marks the beginning of their journey to heal. So don't feel like you need to show

how much you know by giving long preambles to questions; ask your questions and listen.

Navigating Ethical Boundaries

Journalists are trained to keep their distance from sources to avoid any perceived conflicts of interest that could compromise their integrity. Taking gifts from a source is considered taboo, and so is paying a source for an interview. That's unethical and undermines a reporter's credibility. But reporting on extreme climate-related disasters can blur these ethical lines, especially when people need help during a disaster. How does the journalist's role as a detached observer change when someone needs help, especially when they are a potential source who might share their story? And if a reporter does help, how does that affect the reporting that they're doing?

Climate journalist Amy Westervelt had to confront those questions as a stringer for *The Washington Post* while covering wildfires in northern California and southern Nevada. She remembers talking with a woman in a Walmart parking lot in northern California who had been evacuated because of a wildfire. The woman had a baby with no shoes and a heavy diaper. She told Westervelt she grabbed her child and fled her house. The woman had nothing with her—no diapers, shoes, or clothes. That's when Westervelt decided to help. She happened to have diapers and a bag of clothes that her child had outgrown sitting in her car.

"I remember being like, 'I know my editor is going to be mad that I'm doing this because it's not allowed,'" Westervelt recalls. "It wasn't like, 'I'll give you some diapers if you give me a quote.'"[47]

Westervelt gave the woman diapers and clothes. Then she talked with her editor about what happened. They reached a compromise: Westervelt could use a quote from the woman as part of the story's opening, for color, but nothing else. But Westervelt felt drained by the mental gymnastics of this ethical quandary. She says if she had just met this woman and talked with her—a human being to another human being—she would have just given the woman diapers and clothes without any hesitation. But being a journalist complicated that scenario.

Media organizations have ethics policies for good reasons. Guidelines such as the Society of Professional Journalists Code of Conduct help to maintain the integrity and credibility of journalism. But extreme weather and climate disasters put people at risk and force them from their homes or worse. That calls some of these rules into question.

"This is a rule that made sense for a world that we no longer inhabit," Westervelt says. When extreme weather events or wildfires weren't common, the rule of not giving anything to a source worked. But devastating floods, wildfires, and other events happen all the time now. "If part of your beat is regularly talking to people who have just lost their home, or have had to run from a fire, then I feel like ... it seems callous. It also seems like a bad way to cover the story."[48]

During a Society of Environmental Journalists panel on trauma-informed climate reporting, Rebecca Weston, a licensed clinical social worker and co-president of Climate Psychology Alliance North America, talked about how the climate crisis is making professions, including journalism, interrogate traditional professional boundaries. She recommends responding by being human first, as Westervelt did when asked for help. "When we teach students in the high schools about climate education and the students start crying, how do we engage with them? For me, as a clinician, do I bring up climate? Do I not bring up climate? What are the boundaries?" Weston wondered. That answer is a personal one. "We are all being called to ask what are the boundaries of our work," Weston said. "If what is most fundamental is that we actually build something large enough to save our species, that's kind of boundary crossing."[49]

Hot Take: *It's okay not to feel okay. Reporters shouldn't feel guilty for feeling trauma even though the disaster or trauma didn't happen to them directly. Stress is normal. Just witnessing and interacting with people who have come through a tragic ordeal is enough to cause stress, trauma, depression, anxiety, and more.*

Reporters who encounter ethical dilemmas can talk with their editor and be transparent about what's happened and what they'd like to do. A reporter and editor should have safety as a primary consideration and weigh any conflicts of interest from a source who's asked for something. It's one thing to give diapers and another to pay for someone's hotel room, for example. The critical question is: Would the decision to help someone fundamentally change the information the reporter is conveying to their audience? Most people a reporter speaks with during the aftermath of a climate disaster aren't whistleblowers, and chances are that giving someone diapers, for instance, is not going to influence a reporter's decision to use the information.

For Westervelt, covering the impacts of climate change means showing up as a human being. "I feel like showing empathy is also a good journalistic skill," she says.[50] Westervelt believes that by being empathetic, journalists can do better reporting because they aren't completely separating themselves from what people are going through.

The Physical Dangers of Climate Reporting

British journalist Dom Phillips believed that Indigenous communities were key to protecting the Amazon rainforest and helping address climate change. That's why, in 2022, he joined Bruno Pereira, a Brazilian Indigenous expert and activist, in the Javari Valley to see how land was protected from unwelcome visitors such as illegal loggers, poachers, and drug traffickers.[51] They took a small boat early in the morning to avoid being seen by poachers in the area. But a poacher did see the boat and recognized Pereira.[52] The poacher and another man ambushed the boat, taking Pereira and Phillips into the forest, where they were violently murdered. Their deaths are an extreme example of the risks environmental journalists face, and their fate has drawn calls for greater protections for people who dare to expose environmental crimes.

A recent international survey by UNESCO found that 300 attacks have happened to environmental journalists between 2019 and 2023, a 42 percent increase compared with the previous five-year period.[53] From 2009 to 2023, forty-four journalists who were investigating environmental issues were killed in fifteen different countries. Since 2009, more than 70 percent of journalists who report on climate disasters and environmental issues, such as deforestation in the Amazon or illegal mining in Africa, have seen an increase in intimidation, physical assault, and murder. Some journalists have reported being detained, arrested, or subjected to online harassment or legal attacks. At least 749 journalists and news media organizations faced such threats from 2009 to 2023.[54] That's the equivalent of fifty attacks every year. These are journalists who report on everything from the fossil fuel industry and the causes of climate change to extreme weather.

"We need environmental journalists more than ever, and we need to protect their freedom to cover these critical issues," Meaghan Parker, former executive director of the Society of Environmental Journalists, said at an event focused on dangers environmental reporters face and what can be done.[55]

Environmental and climate reporting can take a journalist to isolated locations. Just traveling to some of these places can be difficult, and some locations, such as the Amazon, can be so remote that reporters won't have cell service and could be miles from the nearest town. A reporting trip can quickly become unsafe, highlighting "the unique vulnerabilities associated with environmental journalism."[56]

"Without reliable scientific information about the ongoing environmental crisis, we can never hope to overcome it," notes UNESCO director-general Audrey Azoulay. "Yet the journalists we rely on to investigate this subject and ensure information is accessible face unacceptably high risks all over the world, and climate-related disinformation is running rampant on social media."[57]

This information on violence against environmental journalists isn't meant to scare reporters but rather to explain the risks so they can report as safely as possible on environmental and climate issues.

The dangers aren't limited to physical threats such as being attacked on assignment. Reporters also encounter safety concerns when covering extreme weather or climate disasters. Preparation, training, and precautions can go a long way in helping to assess and handle risks.

The Window of Tolerance

Journalists are hard-wired to run toward danger in pursuit of the story. It's easy to underestimate risks and wind up in a hazardous situation. For example, a reporter covering a wildfire has to get information quickly and make good decisions about personal safety. Sometimes these situations evolve rapidly, and a reporter may panic or feel rattled. What can a journalist do to remain calm and make safe decisions? What personal strategies can reporters use when they are surrounded by chaos? What triggers can push reporters out of their comfort zone?

Answering those questions *before* taking on a challenging reporting assignment is critical to keeping safe. Everyone has an optimal zone—a window—where they function effectively in difficult situations that allow them to adapt. Dr. Dan Siegel introduced the idea from his work on neurobiology and psychotherapy and defined this as the "window of tolerance."[58]

When someone is within their window of tolerance, they manage stress well; they can take in and process information and respond to it rationally. But if something causes them to step outside this window, they may become hyperaroused (overwhelmed, anxious, and reactive) or hypoaroused (numb, disconnected, and depressed). Outside the window of tolerance, they lose judgment, make poor choices, and take unnecessary risks.[59] Journalists should try to remain within this window of tolerance to fully take in the surroundings and assess personal safety when reporting a difficult assignment such as a hurricane or wildfire. Outside the window of tolerance, it is easier to miss threats, leading to panic or risky choices.[60]

Stay in Your Zone

In my years as an environmental reporter, news director, and climate editor, I've seen reporters face myriad emotional challenges from reporting on the environment and climate change. These experiences can take a toll on a reporter's physical and mental well-being.

Journalists who love climate reporting and hope to sustain their career over time must pay attention to their mental health. That means staying within this window of tolerance. How? A reporter must be able to recognize when they are outside their window of tolerance. A story's magnitude can push a reporter into a state of hyperarousal where they might feel emotions such as anger or panic. The reporter might feel anxious or have difficulty concentrating. These are cues.

Early in my career, I remember covering a fast-moving wildfire that became one of Arizona's most devastating fires. I was running on adrenaline, not eating much, and had hardly slept. I and another journalist were in a parking lot about to drive to a press conference when I drove the car forward and over a concrete barrier, puncturing two of the car's tires. We didn't make it to the press conference and had to figure out how to repair tires in a town that had largely been evacuated. I was out of my window of tolerance and made a trying situation even worse.

The signs of being out of one's zone can be different for individual reporters. Some may not be anxious or panicked but rather extremely tired, depressed, disengaged, and maybe feeling hopeless—a state of hypoarousal. In such situations, simple mindful practices such as meditation and deep breathing can help someone reconnect and feel grounded again. A reporter might travel with something familiar and loved that can be used to bring comfort. Perfume, a stuffed animal, a charm, a blanket—whatever works for you can become a calming aid. I have long traveled on reporting trips with a beloved wooden talisman my sister gave me because it's small and wearable. I've held it at night and breathed deeply. For me, that has worked—a tiny reminder of home, my family, and my place in the world. The point is to find a personal method that works for you.

Keeping Safe Physically

Before a trip to Kenya to report on water conflict, the fellowship program I was a part of put all the reporters through a privately run hostile environment and first aid training (HEFAT) program. We learned how to assess situations to stay safe, how to cross through checkpoints in conflict areas, and how to develop exit plans while in the field. We practiced self-defense techniques and learned to be aware of our surroundings along with learning first aid. It was practical training meant to help us stay safe.

Hostile environment training heightens a reporter's situational awareness and helps them learn how to stay calm. Historically, this training has been geared toward journalists who cover war and conflict, but it's valuable for all journalists. I consider it essential training for environment and climate journalists who find themselves reporting on disasters such as wildfires and hurricanes. Some news outlets offer HEFAT training for their reporters. A number of journalism organizations also offer HEFAT training, including the Committee to Protect Journalists and the International Women's Media Foundation. Journalists who have access to hostile environment training should take advantage of it so they are prepared, if asked to report in challenging circumstances.

Besides HEFAT training, reporters can take several other steps to help keep themselves safe and within their window of tolerance.

- **Conduct risk assessments before reporting on potentially dangerous stories.** Discuss this with an editor and identify possible threats, both physical and legal.
- **Use secure communication tools** such as Signal for sensitive discussions and data sharing. This helps ensure digital security is robust to prevent unauthorized access to your information.
- **Join journalism organizations** such as the Society of Environmental Journalists, or the Uproot Project. These nonprofits offer support, resources, and increased visibility, which can increase safety.
- **Know what legal resources are available.** Organizations such as the Committee to Protect Journalists and Reporters Without Borders can provide legal assistance and advice when facing legal threats or harassment.

Virtual Harassment on the Climate Beat

Physical risks aren't the only concern for journalists who cover the environment and climate change. Online harassment can also be a major concern, from attacks by digital trolls on a reporter's social media feed to threatening emails to doxing, the practice of maliciously exposing a reporter's personal information online. Chief meteorologist and climate expert Chris Gloninger experienced this kind of abuse after several years of incorporating climate change information in his weather forecasts.

Gloninger launched the first climate change series in the New England area when he was a meteorologist and climate reporter at NBCUniversal in Boston from 2016 to 2021. He hosted and produced a weekly social media show on climate change, and he produced documentaries that focused on climate change, social justice, and public health. He recalls that the audience's reaction was largely positive. Gloninger says his day-to-day climate change coverage elicited some comments like "You're an idiot. Stop politicizing the weather." But that wasn't unusual for TV meteorologists in the United States who brought climate change into their weathercasts. "We'll see that kind of pushback at some point, even in the most liberal cities."[61] The true harassment, he says, started in 2021 when he left to become the chief meteorologist in Des Moines, Iowa, at the CBS affiliate KCCI.

Gloninger says the harassment was almost instant when he began to bring climate change reporting into his nightly Iowa weathercasts. "There was a lot of 'You're a conspiracy theorist. You are just a liberal hack,'" he remembers. But this was what KCCI hired him to do. They wanted "somebody that would fill a void, which really no one in that market was talking about climate change, especially if the main spot is chief meteorologist."[62]

The opportunity to communicate about climate change excited Gloninger. But he also understood the state's politics. Iowa has slightly more Republicans than Democrats. The state voted for Donald Trump as president, a long-time climate denier, in the last three presidential elections. Agriculture is also a primary economic driver in Iowa, which has the third highest number of farms in the United States.[63] This was the political landscape Gloninger had to consider when doing his reporting and nightly weather forecasts. "I went into this knowing that this would not be easy, that this would be a challenge."[64]

In that first year, he received what he calls "typical nasty feedback." A more sinister tone emerged in 2022 when he received a death threat from a man upset by his climate coverage. "It wasn't even the threat that was concerning," Gloninger recalls.[65] It was the harassing emails. He says police were concerned about how deliberate it all was. The emails were distressing and alarming because they showed someone constantly obsessing about Gloninger and his reporting on climate change.

On X (formerly Twitter), on July 16, 2022, Gloninger posted a screen grab of some of the emails with certain personal information hidden in black marker: "My climate coverage has garnered negative feedback," he wrote. "But last month, I received the first threat, followed by a flow of harassing emails. Police are investigating. It's mentally exhausting, and at times, I have NOT been okay. If you're facing this and need someone to talk to, I'm here."[66]

Gloninger experienced chronic stress that left him making stumbles on air, which made him worry that people would judge him unfairly for his work. He went to therapy and focused on taking care of himself. During this time, the station hired security and asked Gloninger to pull back on his climate coverage.

"The lack of support after they hired me to talk about climate change was shocking, disappointing, disheartening, discouraging," Gloninger says. "And left me really just kind of disgusted with the whole situation." The emotional toll was so heavy that he decided to resign. "I reached that breaking point," Gloninger says.[67]

What Gloninger went through may seem extreme, but online abuse is something journalists regularly face in their coverage of the environment and climate change. It's hard enough just reporting on difficult subjects and the general trauma that comes from that. But trauma can also develop from online attacks through emails and social media, as Gloninger experienced. A steady barrage of criticism, attacks, and abuse can compound trauma a journalist is already experiencing. In fact, reporters may get so much online harassment they become desensitized to it. When that happens, a reporter's judgment can be impaired, and they may not even know when they need to ask for help.[68]

Managing Online Abuse

Anyone reporting on climate change today needs to be prepared to manage their online presence. Online abuse is the repeated or severe targeting of an individual or group online through harmful behavior, and it's meant to intimidate, which can lead to self-censorship and silence.[69] This can show up in many ways.

Doxing, for example, is a severe form of online abuse because publishing someone's home address or other highly personal information puts that reporter in danger and can be highly traumatizing.

Online abuse, in its extreme form, can involve hundreds of incoming emails every day, or subscribing a reporter to strange or graphic websites to which the reporter did not consent. A journalist might get so many of these emails and subscriptions that they lose access to their email account or other valuable information.

Another form of abuse is online impersonation, where someone creates a fake account with a reporter's photo and name, or they publish horrific things to try to discredit the reporter or get them fired. Or someone might create and publish private, intimate, or doctored imagery as a way to harm a reporter. All these kinds of online harassment can be highly stressful and traumatizing.

Unfortunately, the trauma of online abuse has too often not been taken seriously. Jeje Mohamed, who is a consultant and trainer on digital safety and free expression at PEN America, recounted working in newsrooms that "we talk about online abuse, threats of rape, threats of sexual violence, threats of killing, and like very graphic and detailed things that people receive, and it wasn't the thing that they took seriously."[70] Fortunately, these issues are now being taken more seriously as more newsrooms and journalists experience the problems of doxing and harassment.

The International Center for Journalists surveyed women journalists worldwide and found that 73 percent reported experiencing some form of online abuse. Forty-one percent of them reported being targeted in online attacks that seemed connected to an organized disinformation campaign. However, only 13 percent of respondents increased physical security as a response to threats.[71]

Protect Yourself from Online Harassment

Here are three recommendations from PEN America's *Online Harassment Field Manual* on what journalists can do to protect themselves from various forms of online abuse.[72] Any reporter should follow these essential online practices to control their digital footprint.

- **Make your passwords highly unique and complex**, and do not use personal information such as birthdates or names. Password managers can help.
- **Use two-step authentication** to help prevent your accounts from being hacked. Newsrooms often already require this to keep emails and company-wide information safe.
- **Remove potential personal information** that can be used for doxing. Online harassers count on using public records to make your

life miserable. You should assess your online presence and remove any sensitive information that could be used to locate or identify you. Services such as DeleteMe can help manage and delete personal data from the web, including data broker sites; sometimes, news outlets offer this as an employee service.

A reporter who finds themself the target of online harassment should not brush it off. Threats should be taken seriously. Whether a reporter is employed in a newsroom or as an independent journalist, find someone in leadership to discuss what's happening. Ideally, the reporter's newsroom has a culture where journalists feel supported and safe reporting and discussing online violence.[73] Newsrooms should have guidelines and policies in place to support journalists, and they may have designated people on staff to help journalists navigate online abuse.

In June 2023, Chris Gloninger announced on X that he was leaving TV after eighteen years to focus on "my health, family and combating the #climate-crisis." In his tweet, he wrote he takes "immense pride in having educated the public about the impacts of climate change during my career. Now, I will devote my full-time efforts to finding sustainable solutions and fostering positive change."[74]

Gloninger says he didn't resign because of "mean emails" or "that death threat." It was the lack of support from station leadership. "Even to this day, I still have a tough time," he says. His advice for emerging climate journalists and meteorologists is to make sure their news organizations support them, and he says that journalists must have support at whatever media outlet they work for and should pay attention to their mental health. "Quitting if your station is not supportive does not mean you're a failure," Gloninger says. "If you find yourself in a similar situation, you're not getting that support, it's okay to walk away."[75]

Reporting on climate change is, in many ways, a courageous act. Reporters on this beat risk both physical and emotional harm, whether through the experience of being a front-line reporter on a climate-fueled weather disaster or simply through the accumulated stress of covering the dire truths of human-caused climate change to audiences over time.

For too long, newsrooms perpetuated a culture that expected reporters to just tough it out. To do this important work of reporting on our warming world skillfully and sustainably, reporters must develop self-care skills to keep themselves safe both physically and emotionally.

Essential Reading and Resources

American Press Institute's Journalists and Mental Health Resource Guide: This collection of insights covers a range of topics, from dealing with trauma and anxiety to addressing burnout and online harassment. https://americanpressinstitute.org/mental-health-resources-for-journalists/

Dart Center for Journalism and Trauma: This valuable resource is a project of the Columbia University Graduate School of Journalism. It's focused on helping journalists cover conflict, violence, and tragedy. The website includes expert interviews, numerous tipsheets, and advice. https://dartcenter.org/

Journalist Trauma Support Network: JTSN trains therapists to help journalists who are affected by trauma, and it can connect journalists to therapists. https://www.jtsn.org/

Climate Psychology Alliance North America: For journalists, CPANA is a helpful resource for understanding the psychological dimensions of climate change. https://www.climatepsychology.us/

PEN America's Online Harassment Field Manual: This easy-to-use online guide gives you strategies to protect and defend yourself against online harassment and advice for newsroom leaders. https://onlineharassment-fieldmanual.pen.org/

Dart Center Style Guide for Trauma-Informed Journalism: This guide covers everything from terminology and language to the ethics of reporting on the effect of trauma on people. It's an excellent reference to have when you are on deadline. https://dartcenter.org/resources/dart-center-style-guide

Your Turn

Exercise 1: Long before you set out on an assignment, you need to know what helps you remain calm and centered. For this exercise, you'll create a self-care plan. Using the grid below from the Dart Center as a guide, write down how you currently care for yourself. Ask yourself what works for you and what doesn't. Where could you make choices to support yourself better? What goals would you like to achieve, and how could you pursue them?

Once you have answered the questions, take a photo of your answers and schedule an email with that image to arrive in your inbox a month from now. When that email arrives, take time to assess how you're doing and whether your answers have changed. This is a reliable practice to stay connected with your well-being and ensure you are taking care of yourself.

Area of well-being	Current practices	Future goals
Physical (includes exercise, healthy eating, sleeping, medical check-ups, etc.)		
Emotional (positive activities, acknowledge my accomplishments, express emotions in healthy way)		
Social (healthy relationships, time for family and friends, support from family and friends, etc.)		
Psychological (take time for yourself, unplug, journal, pursue new interests, access psychotherapy, life coaching, or counselling, etc.)		
Spiritual (self-reflection, connecting to core beliefs and community, worship, spend time in nature, etc.)		
Professional (find meaning in work, maintain work–life balance, positive relationships with co-workers, time management, etc.)		
Financial (understand how finances impact your quality of life, create a budget or financial plan, pay off debt, etc.)		

Source. https://docs.google.com/document/d/1pwlYJ4H4U9urMjcrVQU734E BaJJY5BftIBvlmoOmRy8/edit

Exercise 2: Map out your data online and take steps to either remove it or limit access to anything that's personal that you don't want online.

Acknowledgments

I have spent most of my journalism career writing for the ear. When I was a radio journalist, my stories typically ranged between 500 and 700 words, with voices from people and ambient sounds to transport the listener into an auditory landscape for the mind. So when an editor at Island Press first approached me about writing a book, I was both excited and terrified by the prospect of writing at such length and for readers instead of listeners. I'll never forget my first conversation with Emily Turner at Island Press as we explored the idea for a book to help journalists report on the environment. I was teaching at Arizona State University's Walter Cronkite School of Journalism and Mass Communication and was also board president of the Society of Environmental Journalists (SEJ). As Emily asked me questions about what I had learned from my own career and about teaching future journalists, the seeds for this book began to sprout. We had a wide-ranging conversation and talked about social media, about ethics, about writing stories that wouldn't leave readers wanting to pull the covers tightly over their heads. I shared stories from my students and how I worked with them to tell stories across TV, audio, and digital platforms. At the end of our call, Emily invited me to submit a book proposal. You have the result in your hands.

I am grateful Emily took a mighty leap of faith that a radio journalist could give life to thousands of words. I am sure early drafts may have given her pause as I adapted to long-form writing. While I was developing this book, two topic areas emerged that weren't originally in the proposal: climate litigation and self-care for journalists reporting on the extremes of climate change. I appreciate Emily's willingness to include these chapters. As a first-time author, I count myself fortunate to have had Emily's guidance, patience, and coaching to create this book.

It takes a village to bring these words to you, so I want to take this opportunity to thank so many people I am indebted to for sharing their expertise and experiences with me. I must begin with climate change communicator extraordinaire Susan Hassol. Our regular conversations about the science of climate change early on were invaluable to my writing process. Her expertise and ability to translate science jargon to nonscientists is pure magic, and I'm grateful for her support and guidance to help me get the science right.

Thanks to Joanna Pawlowska, who helped me brainstorm titles for the book when I was stuck. Her creative spirit sparked what ultimately became the title of this book. It was Joanna who first uttered the words "hot takes," and those words have lasted. I'm grateful for her kindness and support.

Hot Takes: Every Journalist's Guide to Covering Climate Change would not exist today without the generosity of time given by so many incredible people who have helped beyond measure to make this book a reality. Every conversation and every interview has affected me personally and inspired fresh ideas about how we tell the stories of our warming world. Although not everyone appears in these pages, everyone I spoke with certainly informed these words.

This book has been shaped by many journalists who shared their experiences and insights with me, each of whom taught me invaluable lessons about climate reporting. I am grateful to Michael Kodas for his friendship, support, and advice on how to approach my first book. He patiently answered questions that ranged from what type of software to use to how to develop a writing practice. His decades of environmental reporting experience and knowledge of climate journalism helped guide my overall thinking for *Hot Takes*. I am also thankful to Sammy Roth for helping me think about the role of objectivity in reporting on climate journalism and for his generous words that begin this book. Rebecca Leber's investigative work on misinformation and disinformation in the climate space spurred me to delve further into this critical issue, while Kelly Macnamara's international perspective as the global climate and environment correspondent at Agence France-Presse broadened my understanding of climate impacts worldwide and of how journalists can approach the global story of climate change.

Joan Meiners, who is a scientist turned climate journalist at *The Arizona Republic*, brought insights about what journalists need to understand about climate science. Ezra David Romero shared his journalism origin story with me and walked me through how to report on communities that have been marginalized or underreported. Halle Parker's journey to reporting on environmental and climate issues at WWNO in New Orleans helped me understand the importance of self-care while reporting on climate stories, and she offered great advice for future journalists. I am grateful to Nicholas Kusnetz at *Inside Climate News* for discussions on how to report on climate policy and litigation while making such stories come to life for readers. Thanks also to

Naveena Sadasivam at *Grist*, whose climate reporting expertise, from covering climate justice issues to the world's annual climate conference, provided such great insight. I am so thankful to Mark Schleifstein, who recently retired from *The Times-Picayune/NOLA* in New Orleans, whose tireless passion for environmental journalism infused my writing. His expertise at accessing federal agencies and information coupled with his decades of experience reporting on environmental and climate issues, including documenting Louisiana's changing coastlines and sea level rise, remains a testament to the resilience needed to cover such challenging stories.

I also owe thanks to Meera Subramanian, who reflected on her path of telling stories about our warming world and shared her wisdom on how to engage readers with complex environmental narratives. Environmental journalist and author Laura Paskus answered early questions as I developed this book. Peter Prengaman, global climate and environment news director for *The Associated Press*, offered insights into AP's expanded climate desk and how that reflects a broader move at large journalism outlets to cover climate change. Thanks to Amy Westervelt, founder of *Drilled*, who gave me confidence in how I was thinking about framing this book. Her commitment to holding the powerful to account is a testament to the pressing need for investigative reporting in the climate space. I'm grateful for her expertise and the work she's done to help climate journalists understand everything from covering misinformation and disinformation to how to take care of themselves while in the field. Nicholas Kusnetz with *Inside Climate News* shared his perspective on covering climate litigation. Wudan Yan's thoughts on the interplay between journalism and mental health underscored the importance of newsroom support in fields of difficult reporting, and Peter Yeung's work in solutions journalism illustrated the transformative power of reporting on climate solutions.

Every conversation enriched my understanding and strengthened my commitment to helping journalists, no matter where they are in their career, with reporting on climate change with clarity, integrity, and hope.

This book would not have come to life without the generosity and knowledge of so many experts who helped me navigate the core chapters of *Hot Takes*. While attending the SEJ conference in 2023, I met Rebecca Weston, co-president of Climate Psychology Alliance North America. She was speaking on a panel about trauma-informed journalism, and her perspective generated the initial inklings for adding a chapter on self-care for climate journalists and trauma-informed reporting. That's also when I connected with Jeje Mohamed, whose work on digital safety for journalists and free expression has helped inform the final chapter of this book. Jennifer Atkinson at the University of Washington shared her research on climate anxiety and the mental health impacts of climate change, particularly on young people. Her dedication to helping younger generations process eco-anxiety has had a deep influence on my work.

John Cook's groundbreaking research on climate misinformation forms a foundational piece of this book, and his work is critical to strengthening climate journalism and arming it against the forces of disinformation.

Michael Gerrard at Columbia University shared his vast expertise on climate litigation, providing invaluable insights. Gregory Jenkins at Pennsylvania State University offered his perspectives on climate justice, deeply informing my understanding of the inequities that human-caused climate change creates throughout the world. My conversation with Elina Kelsey and her research on hope significantly changed my perspective on how journalists should report on climate change. Her resilience and insights on climate positivity, communicating about climate solutions, and seeing the climate conversation as inclusive of all species has given me optimism for our future.

I am grateful also for the numerous conversations I've had with Meaghan Parker, former executive director of SEJ. Her tireless championing of women in journalism and her willingness to be a sounding board for *Hot Takes* gave me countless points of clarity and direction throughout this journey. Cathrine Gyldensted encouraged me to see journalism through a more holistic and positive lens, offering invaluable guidance on storytelling and, for me, a fresh approach to reporting climate stories. Naseem Miller, senior editor of health for *The Journalist's Resource*, shared her experience reporting on trauma and advice for journalists. Her work in supporting journalists who have had to report on everything from mass shootings to hurricanes is an inspiration. I also want to thank Katherine Noble, who used to be with the Solutions Journalism Network, who illuminated the importance of reporting on climate solutions, underscoring the need for stories that inspire as well as inform. A. R. Siders, whose research focused on climate adaptation at the University of Delaware, offered me a glimpse into the complexities of preparing for a world reshaped by climate change.

Sally Ramirez's experiences leading a television newsroom through the horrors of Hurricane Harvey provided firsthand insights into crisis reporting and how to lead with compassion. Joseph Russomanno, who's now an emeritus professor at Arizona State University's Walter Cronkite School of Journalism and Mass Communication, deepened my understanding of how people consume information and the ways social media affects modern journalism. Maxwell Boykoff, who directs the Center for Science and Technology Policy Research at the University of Colorado Boulder, helped me understand the state of climate journalism globally. Chris Gloninger, meteorologist and consultant, helped me understand the personal costs of reporting on the science of climate change and the backlash that journalists can experience in pursuit of the truth. His unique perspective on bridging the worlds of science and journalism was also insightful.

I'd also like to thank the Local Media Association's Covering Climate Collaborative for hosting several impactful on-the-record calls with climate experts, including the "father of environmental justice" Robert Bullard, climate scientist and author Katharine Hayhoe, and Anthony Leiserowitz, who directs the Yale Program on Climate Change Communication. I also want to thank David Waskow, who directs the World Resources Institute's international climate initiative. His expertise on global climate policy helped inform my thinking on international climate policy. I am deeply grateful to each of these experts for their willingness to share their knowledge and support. Their insights strengthened not only the content of this book but also my own commitment to the work.

I am profoundly grateful to SEJ for their dedication to supporting journalists reporting on environmental issues, including climate change. SEJ has been a beacon in my life since the beginning of my journalism career. It was a great honor to serve as SEJ's board president, which gave me a front row seat to the dedication and passion that drive this organization and its members. SEJ has opened many doors for me and other journalists. If you report on the environment, I highly encourage you to join SEJ.

Arizona State University's Walter Cronkite School of Journalism and Mass Communication has also played a significant role in my journey. When Christina Leonard reached out to me several years ago with an invitation to join the Cronkite School as a visiting professor of practice, I couldn't have anticipated the impact that it would have on my life and work. During my nearly five years teaching at Cronkite, I had the honor of working with a talented group of students. Their curiosity, questions, and eagerness to learn fueled my own passion for the field and provided the inspiration for much of what is in these pages. I look back on my time at Cronkite with deep fondness and gratitude for all that my students taught me.

I also want to thank NPR, especially Neela Banerjee, who leads the climate desk. She, along with Andrea Kissack, hired me and opened the door for me to follow my passion to work full time on climate journalism. That work has given me a front row seat to how this area of journalism continues to evolve. On a personal note, I want to thank Neela for making space so I could finish *Hot Takes*, as well as her ongoing support. I also want to thank NPR climate editor Rachel Waldholz, who has on several occasions provided a needed gut check or a word of encouragement.

These organizations not only supported me but also shaped the vision and purpose of this book. It is because of communities such as SEJ, institutions such as the Cronkite School, and media organizations such as NPR that journalism focused on the environment and climate continues to thrive, equipping current and future journalists to tell the critical stories of our time.

I am also incredibly grateful to my family and friends, whose support sustained me throughout my writing journey. In so many ways, this book would not exist without my mom and dad, George and Rilla Babits, who instilled in me a deep love and respect for nature and care of the Earth that carved the path of my journalism career to this day. It's because of this history and their ongoing love and support that *Hot Takes* exists.

My dear friends—including Karen Boland, Laura Jacoby, Dave Kolar and the "cycling posse"—kept me grounded with their encouragement, often asking, "Are you done yet?" I can finally say yes, and I'm thankful for their companionship and good humor along the way. I'm also thankful to Ron and Elaine Jones, my Arizona adopted family in whose kitchen several of these pages came to life, for their love and support. Life would not be the same without my dear bestie, Anne Minard, who's always just a phone call away, at the ready with impeccable advice. She also read early chapters and brought her journalistic and legal expertise to some of these pages.

I am also fortunate to have an amazing, supportive husband, Frank Mungeam, who has made countless meals and forgone many a date night so I could write. I wasn't sure I could write a book, but with his words of encouragement and love, here we are. Frank taught me the joy of building "rocket ships" in the backyard—aka big dreams—and we have certainly done that with zero emissions. Frank was also my first reader, and his wise counsel and edits helped me across the finish line. I am forever grateful for his love, generosity, and kindness.

My heartfelt gratitude to everyone who has had a part in bringing this book to life and helping this radio journalist get beyond a few hundred words. Thank you for your patience, kindness, and encouragement along the way.

Finally, I have fact-checked and tried my best to represent everyone who appears in *Hot Takes* as accurately and fairly as possible. Any mistakes are mine. I hope you find the guidance and stories imparted through these pages of benefit in your own climate reporting journey.

Notes

Chapter 1

1. Tour de France, "Yellow for Bardet in Rimini," *Tour de France 2024*, June 29, 2024, https://www.letour.fr/en/news/2024/stage-1/yellow-for-bardet-in-rimini/1317410.

2. Associated Press, "Mark Cavendish Breaks Tour de France Record with 35th Stage Win," *AP News*, July 3, 2024, https://apnews.com/article/cavendish-tour-de-france-stage-record-merckx-800f04010848e0cc81dc536f-4d5eb5b8.

3. Vanessa Friedman, "Stella McCartney Does Mushrooms in Paris," *The New York Times*, October 5, 2021, https://www.nytimes.com/2021/10/05/style/stella-mccartney-mushrooms.html.

4. Thomas Adamson, "Stella McCartney Channels Mushrooms in Trippy Paris Show," *AP News*, October 4, 2021, https://apnews.com/article/paris-fashion-week-entertainment-lifestyle-paul-mccartney-europe-7a9551d6320f-27ca66ac64ee3dad10f0.

5. Em Poncia, "Stella Mccartney's Mushrooms Are the Future," *London Runway*, August 1, 2022, https://londonrunway.co.uk/stella-mccartneys-mushrooms-are-the-future/.

6. Jody Godoy, "US Targets Surging Grocery Prices in Latest Probe," Reuters, August 1, 2024, https://www.reuters.com/markets/us/us-targets-surging-grocery-prices-latest-probe-2024-08-01/.

7. Emily Farra, "In the Rush Back to the Runways, Sustainability Slipped Out of the Headlines—Here's Who's Still Innovating," *Vogue*, October 13, 2021, https://www.vogue.com/article/sustainability-spring-2022-shows.

8. Raluca Besliu, "Oil Crisis: How Olive Farmers Are Adapting to Climate Change to Preserve a Cultural Commodity," *The Parliament Magazine*, February 15, 2024, https://www.theparliamentmagazine.eu/news/article/olive-oil-climate-change-crisis.

9.   Uriyoán Colón-Ramos, "We Need to Talk About Food Prices," *Yale Climate Connections*, March 11, 2024, https://yaleclimateconnections.org/2024/03/we-need-to-talk-about-food-prices/.

10. Michael Kodas, interview by Sadie Babits, March 3, 2023.

11. Covering Climate Now, "Q&A: Washington Post Climate Editors Talk Global Strategies for a Global Story," *Columbia Journalism Review*, February 2, 2023, https://www.cjr.org/covering_climate_now/qa-washington-post-climate-global-strategy-goldfarb-eilperin.php.

12. Adam Kommel, "New York Times Reporter Recounts His Quest for Global Sustainability," *The Bowdoin Orient*, April 28, 2006, https://bowdoinorient.com/bonus/article/1842/.

13. National Park Service, "1988 Fires," *Yellowstone National Park (U.S. National Park Service)*, February 2, 2021, https://www.nps.gov/yell/learn/nature/1988-fires.htm.

14. Marlise Simons, "Vast Amazon Fires, Man-Made, Linked to Global Warming," *The New York Times*, August 12, 1988, https://www.nytimes.com/1988/08/12/world/vast-amazon-fires-man-made-linked-to-global-warming.html.

15. John Roach, "1988 Heat Wave Had People Wondering Whether 'God Is Against Us,'" *AccuWeather*, August 8, 2019, https://www.accuweather.com/en/weather-news/heat-wave-and-drought-were-so-devastating-it-had-americans-declaring-god-is-against-us/481031.

16. *Greenhouse Effect and Global Climate Change: Hearings Before the Committee on Energy and Natural Resources, United States Senate, One Hundredth Congress, First Session*. United States: US Government Printing Office, 1988.

17. "Global Warming Has Begun, Expert Tells Senate," *The New York Times*, June 24, 1988, https://www.nytimes.com/1988/06/24/us/global-warming-has-begun-expert-tells-senate.html.

18. "History of the IPCC," IPCC, accessed September 15, 2024, https://www.ipcc.ch/about/history/.

19. Maxwell Boykoff and Jules Boykoff, "Balance as Bias: Global Warming and the US Prestige Press," *Global Environmental Change* 14, no. 2 (2004): 125–36, doi:10.1016/j.gloenvcha.2003.10.001.

20. Eric Pianin, "Group Meets on Global Warming," *The Washington Post*, December 4, 2002, https://www.washingtonpost.com/archive/politics/2002/12/04/group-meets-on-global-warming/fecd069c-3cf0-49fc-803d-21da14cc89a0/.

21. Maxwell Boykoff and Jules Boykoff, "Balance as Bias: Global Warming and the US Prestige Press," *Global Environmental Change* 14, no. 2 (2004): 125–36, doi:10.1016/j.gloenvcha.2003.10.001.

22. Intergovernmental Panel on Climate Change (IPCC), *Climate Change 2023: Synthesis Report Summary for Policymakers*. AR6 Synthesis Report, 2023. https://www.ipcc.ch/report/ar6/syr/downloads/report/IPCC_AR6_SYR_SPM.pdf.

23. Mark Barna, "Climate Change Impacts Almost Entire Global Population," *Public Health Newswire*, November 12, 2021, http://www.publichealthnewswire.org/?p=climate-update-2021.

24. World Meteorological Organization (WMO), *Provisional State of the Global Climate 2023*, 2023, https://library.wmo.int/viewer/68835/download?file=1347_Global-statement-2023_en.pdf&type=pdf&navigator=1.

25. "António Guterres (Secretary-General) on the State of the Global Climate Report Launch 2024," Video, *UN Web TV*, March 19, 2024, https://webtv.un.org/en/asset/k1a/k1aklci33h.

26. National Oceanic and Atmospheric Administration. "2024 Was the World's Warmest Year on Record," press release, January 10, 2025, https://www.noaa.gov/news/2024-was-worlds-warmest-year-on-record#:~:text=2024%20was%20the%20world's%20warmest,National%20Oceanic%20and%20Atmospheric%20Administration.

27. MeCCO, "MeCCO Monthly Summaries: Media and Climate Change Observatory," *Media and Climate Change Observatory*, 2023, https://sciencepolicy.colorado.edu/icecaps/research/media_coverage/summaries/special_issue_2023.html.

28. Ibid.

29. Max Boykoff, email message to Sadie Babits, January 12, 2025.

30. Covering Climate Now, "Q&A: Washington Post Climate Editors Talk Global Strategies for a Global Story," *Columbia Journalism Review*, February 2, 2023, https://www.cjr.org/covering_climate_now/qa-washington-post-climate-global-strategy-goldfarb-eilperin.php.

31. Peter Prengaman and Sadie Babits, February 13, 2023.

32. Covering Climate Now, "Q&A: Washington Post Climate Editors Talk Global Strategies for a Global Story," *Columbia Journalism Review*, February 2, 2023, https://www.cjr.org/covering_climate_now/qa-washington-post-climate-global-strategy-goldfarb-eilperin.php.

33. "Strategic Plan," *Inside Climate News*, December 7, 2020, https://insideclimatenews.org/strategic-plan/.

34. Michael Kodas, interview by Sadie Babits, March 3, 2023.

35. Amy Westervelt, interview by Sadie Babits, July 20, 2024.

36. Derek Harrison, Neela Banerjee, and Lisa Song, "Exxon's Own Research Confirmed Fossil Fuels' Role in Global Warming Decades Ago," *Inside Climate News*, September 16, 2015, https://insideclimatenews.org/news/02052024/from-the-archive-exxon-research-global-warming/.

37. Amy Westervelt, interview by Sadie Babits, July 20, 2024.

38. David Wallace-Wells, "When Will Climate Change Make the Earth Too Hot for Humans?," *Intelligencer*, July 10, 2017, https://nymag.com/intelligencer/2017/07/climate-change-earth-too-hot-for-humans.html.

39. Michael E. Mann, Susan Joy Hassol, and Tom Toles, "Doomsday Scenarios Are as Harmful as Climate Change Denial," *The Washington Post*, July 12, 2017, https://www.washingtonpost.com/opinions/doomsday-scenarios-are-as-harmful-as-climate-change-denial/2017/07/12/880ed002-6714-11e7-a1d7-9a32c91c6f40_story.html.

40. Halle Parker, interview by Sadie Babits, July 29, 2024.

41. Ibid.

42. Wim Thiery et al., "Intergenerational Inequities in Exposure to Climate Extremes," *Science* 374, no. 6564 (October 8, 2021): 158–60, doi:10.1126/science.abi7339.

43. "Effects," *NASA Science*, accessed September 15, 2024, https://science.nasa.gov/climate-change/effects/.

44. "Climate Change in the American Mind: Beliefs & Attitudes, Fall 2023," *Yale Program on Climate Change Communication*, January 11, 2024, https://climatecommunication.yale.edu/publications/climate-change-in-the-american-mind-beliefs-attitudes-fall-2023/toc/2/.

45. American Psychiatric Association, "APA Public Opinion Poll—Annual Meeting 2020," n.d., https://www.psychiatry.org/newsroom/apa-public-opinion-poll-2020.

46. "Climate Change in the American Mind: Beliefs & Attitudes, Fall 2023," Yale Program on Climate Change Communication, January 11, 2024, https://climatecommunication.yale.edu/publications/climate-change-in-the-american-mind-beliefs-attitudes-fall-2023/toc/2/.

47. Reuters Institute for the Study of Journalism, *Digital News Report 2024*. Oxford: Reuters Institute for the Study of Journalism, 2024. https://reutersinstitute.politics.ox.ac.uk/sites/default/files/2024-06/RISJ_DNR_2024_Digital_v10%20lr.pdf.

48. Ibid.

49. Waqas Ejaz, Mitali Mukherjee, and Richard Fletcher, "Climate Change News Audiences: Analysis of News Use and Attitudes in Eight Countries," Reuters Institute for the Study of Journalism, November 14, 2023, https://reutersinstitute.politics.ox.ac.uk/climate-change-news-audiences-analysis-news-use-and-attitudes-eight-countries.

50. "Climate Change in the American Mind: Beliefs & Attitudes, Fall 2023," Yale Program on Climate Change Communication, January 11, 2024, https://climatecommunication.yale.edu/publications/climate-change-in-the-american-mind-beliefs-attitudes-fall-2023/toc/2/.

51. Susan Hassol, interview by Sadie Babits, March 11, 2023.

52. Mark Schleifstein, interview by Sadie Babits, April 15, 2022.

53. Susan Hassol, interview by Sadie Babits, March 11, 2023.

54. Intergovernmental Panel on Climate Change, "Climate Change 2021: The Physical Science Basis," press release, August 9, 2021, https://www.ipcc.ch/2021.

55. "History of the IPCC," IPCC, accessed September 15, 2024, https://www.ipcc.ch/about/history/.

56. Intergovernmental Panel on Climate Change. "Understanding and Attributing Climate Change," *Climate Change 2007: Working Group I: The Physical Science Basis*, February 2007, https://archive.ipcc.ch/publications_and_data/ar4/wg1/en/spmsspm-understanding-and.html.

57. Intergovernmental Panel on Climate Change, "AR6 Synthesis Report: Summary for Policymakers—Headline Statements," *Sixth Assessment Report*, March 2023, https://www.ipcc.ch/report/ar6/syr/resources/spm-headline-statements/.

58. "World of Change: Global Temperatures," *NASA Earth Observatory*, January 29, 2020, https://earthobservatory.nasa.gov/world-of-change/global-temperatures.

59. Intergovernmental Panel on Climate Change, *Climate Change 2022: Mitigation of Climate Change. Summary for Policymakers. Working Group III Contribution to the Sixth Assessment Report of the Intergovernmental Panel on Climate Change*. Cambridge: Cambridge University Press, 2022. https://www.ipcc.ch/report/ar6/wg3/downloads/report/IPCC_AR6_WGIII_SPM.pdf.

60. "Evidence," *NASA Science*, accessed September 18, 2024, https://science.nasa.gov/climate-change/evidence/.

61. "Effects," *NASA Science*, accessed September 15, 2024, https://science.nasa.gov/climate-change/effects/.

62. Susan Hassol and Sadie Babits, March 11, 2023.

63. "Effects," *NASA Science*, accessed September 15, 2024, https://science.nasa.gov/climate-change/effects/.

64. NOAA National Centers for Environmental Information (NCEI), "U.S. Billion-Dollar Weather and Climate Disasters (2024)," accessed September 18, 2024, https://www.ncei.noaa.gov/access/billions/. https://doi.org/10.25921/stkw-7w73.

65. Intergovernmental Panel on Climate Change (IPCC), *Climate Change 2023: Synthesis Report Summary for Policymakers*. AR6 Synthesis Report, 2023, https://www.ipcc.ch/report/ar6/wg1/downloads/report/IPCC_AR6_WGI_Chapter09.pdf.

66. Susan Hassol, interview by Sadie Babits, March 29, 2023.

67. Intergovernmental Panel on Climate Change (IPCC), "Chapter 3: Polar Regions, Section 3.2 - The Cryosphere and Global Climate," *Special Report on the Ocean and Cryosphere in a Changing Climate (SROCC)*, accessed September 18, 2024, https://www.ipcc.ch/srocc/chapter/chapter-3-2/#:~:text=The%20resulting%20advection%20of%20warm%20air%20and,Arctic%20increased%20downward%20longwave%20radiation%2C%20delayed%20sea.

68. Ryan Kellman and Rebecca Hersher, "Why Texans Need to Know How Fast Antarctica is Melting," accessed September 18, 2024, https://apps.npr.org/arctic-ice-melting-climate-change/texas-galveston-sea-level-rise.html.

69. Susan Hassol, interview by Sadie Babits, March 11, 2023.

70. World Economic Forum, "The Climate Crisis Is Severely Impacting Animal Migration Patterns, Study Shows," October 4, 2023, accessed September 18, 2024, https://www.weforum.org/agenda/2023/10/climate-crisis-impacting-animal-migration/.

71. Susan Hassol and Sadie Babits, March 11, 2023.

72. Intergovernmental Panel on Climate Change, "AR6 Synthesis Report: Summary for Policymakers—Headline Statements," *Sixth Assessment Report*, March 2023, https://www.ipcc.ch/report/ar6/syr/resources/spm-headline-statements/.

73. Michael E. Mann, *The New Climate War: The Fight to Take Back Our Planet*. New York: PublicAffairs, 2021.

74. Abel Gustafson and Matthew Goldberg, "Even Americans Highly Concerned About Climate Change Dramatically Underestimate the Scientific Consensus," Yale Program on Climate Change Communication, October 17, 2018, https://climatecommunication.yale.edu/publications/

even-americans-highly-concerned-about-climate-change-dramatically-underestimate-the-scientific-consensus/.

75. Susan Hassol, interview by Sadie Babits, March 11, 2023.

76. Ibid.

77. Amy Westervelt, "Documents, Whistleblowers, and Public Comments Are Clear: Oil Companies Know Carbon Capture Is Not a Climate Solution," *Drilled*, July 29, 2024, https://drilled.media/news/ccs.

78. Ibid.

79. Intergovernmental Panel on Climate Change (IPCC), *Global Warming of 1.5°C: An IPCC Special Report on the Impacts of Global Warming of 1.5°C Above Pre-Industrial Levels and Related Global Greenhouse Gas Emission Pathways, in the Context of Strengthening the Global Response to the Threat of Climate Change, Sustainable Development, and Efforts to Eradicate Poverty*, edited by V. Masson-Delmotte, P. Zhai, H.-O. Pörtner, D. Roberts, et al., Chapter 2: "Mitigation Pathways Compatible with 1.5°C in the Context of Sustainable Development." Geneva: World Meteorological Organization, 2018. https://www.ipcc.ch/sr15/chapter/chapter-2/.

80. United Nations Framework Convention on Climate Change, "COP27 Reaches Breakthrough Agreement on New 'Loss and Damage' Fund for Vulnerable Countries," UNFCCC, November 20, 2022, https://unfccc.int/news/cop27-reaches-breakthrough-agreement-on-new-loss-and-damage-fund-for-vulnerable-countries.

81. Naveena Sadasivam, interview by Sadie Babits, February 2, 2024.

82. United Nations Framework Convention on Climate Change, "The Paris Agreement," UNFCCC, accessed September 18, 2024, https://unfccc.int/process-and-meetings/the-paris-agreement.

83. Ibid.

84. Naveena Sadasivam, interview by Sadie Babits, February 2, 2024.

85. *Juliana v. United States*, No. 6:15-cv-01517 (D. Or. 2015), accessed September 19, 2024. https://climatecasechart.com/case/juliana-v-united-states/.

86. "Juliana v. United States," Our Children's Trust, accessed September 19, 2024, https://www.ourchildrenstrust.org/juliana-v-us.

87. "Pending State Actions," Our Children's Trust, accessed September 19, 2024, https://www.ourchildrenstrust.org/pending-state-actions.

88. Meera Subramanian, interview by Sadie Babits, February 28, 2022.

89. Michael Kodas and Sadie Babits, March 3, 2023.

90. Ezra David Romero, interview by Sadie Babits, January 13, 2024.

Chapter 2

1. Thomas V. Orum, Nancy Ferguson, and Jeanne D. Mihail, "Saguaro (*Carnegiea gigantea*) Mortality and Population Regeneration in the Cactus Forest of Saguaro National Park: Seventy-Five Years and Counting," *PLOS One* 11, no. 8 (August 9, 2016), https://doi.org/10.1371/journal.pone.0160899.

2. Stephanie Morse, "Will Arizona's Saguaros Survive Climate Change and Drought?," *Cronkite News–Arizona PBS*, December 4, 2018, https://cronkite-news.azpbs.org/2018/12/04/arizona-saguaros-climate-and-drought/.

3. Ibid.

4. Ibid.

5. NOAA, "The Atmosphere," National Oceanic and Atmospheric Administration, July 2, 2024, https://www.noaa.gov/jetstream/atmosphere.

6. "About the Hydrosphere," *My NASA Data*, accessed September 28, 2024, https://mynasadata.larc.nasa.gov/basic-page/about-hydrosphere.

7. Water Science School, "How Much Water Is There on Earth?," U.S. Geological Survey, November 13, 2019, https://www.usgs.gov/special-topics/water-science-school/science/how-much-water-there-earth.

8. NOAA, "What Is the Carbon Cycle?," National Ocean Service, NOAA, June 16, 2024, https://oceanservice.noaa.gov/facts/carbon-cycle.html#transcript.

9. "Causes," *NASA Science*, accessed September 28, 2024, https://science.nasa.gov/climate-change/causes/.

10. NOAA, "What Is the Carbon Cycle?," National Ocean Service, NOAA, June 16, 2024, https://oceanservice.noaa.gov/facts/carbon-cycle.html#transcript.

11. Ibid.

12. Intergovernmental Panel on Climate Change, *Climate Change 2023: Synthesis Report. Summary for Policymakers. Headline Statements*. Geneva, Switzerland: IPCC, 2023. https://www.ipcc.ch/report/ar6/syr/resources/spm-headline-statements/.

13. Ibid.

14. Intergovernmental Panel on Climate Change, *Climate Change 2021: The Physical Science Basis. Summary for Policymakers. Contribution of Working Group I to the Sixth Assessment Report of the Intergovernmental Panel on Climate Change*. Geneva, Switzerland: IPCC, 2021. https://www.ipcc.ch/report/ar6/wg1/downloads/report/IPCC_AR6_WGI_SPM.pdf.

15. Intergovernmental Panel on Climate Change, *Climate Change 2023: Synthesis Report. Summary for Policymakers. Headline Statements*. Geneva, Switzerland: IPCC, 2023. https://www.ipcc.ch/report/ar6/syr/resources/spm-headline-statements/.

16. National Oceanic and Atmospheric Administration, "Arctic Report Card 2023," Arctic Program, 2023. https://arctic.noaa.gov/report-card/report-card-2023/.

17. National Aeronautics and Space Administration, "NASA Study Reveals Compounding Climate Risks at Two Degrees of Warming," NASA, last modified April 22, 2021, https://climate.nasa.gov/news/3278/nasa-study-reveals-compounding-climate-risks-at-two-degrees-of-warming/.

18. United Nations Environment Programme, *Emissions Gap Report 2022: The Closing Window—Climate Crisis Calls for Rapid Transformation of Societies*. Nairobi: UNEP, 2022, https://www.unep.org/resources/emissions-gap-report-2022.

19. National Aeronautics and Space Administration, *NASA Study Reveals Compounding Climate Risks at Two Degrees of Warming*, NASA, last modified April 22, 2021, https://climate.nasa.gov/news/3278/nasa-study-reveals-compounding-climate-risks-at-two-degrees-of-warming/.

20. National Oceanic and Atmospheric Administration, "Climate Change: Global Temperature," Climate.gov, last modified January 18, 2023. https://www.climate.gov/news-features/understanding-climate/climate-change-global-temperature.

21. Rebecca Lindsey and Luann Dahlman, "Climate Change: Global Temperature," *NOAA Climate.Gov*, January 18, 2024, https://www.climate.gov/news-features/understanding-climate/climate-change-global-temperature.

22. Intergovernmental Panel on Climate Change, *Climate Change 2023: Synthesis Report. Summary for Policymakers. Headline Statements*. Geneva, Switzerland: IPCC, 2023, https://www.ipcc.ch/report/ar6/syr/resources/spm-headline-statements/.

23. National Oceanic and Atmospheric Administration. "2024 Was the World's Warmest Year on Record," press release, January 10, 2025, https://www.noaa.gov/news/2024-was-worlds-warmest-year-on-record#:~:text=2024%20was%20the%20world's%20warmest,National%20Oceanic%20and%20Atmospheric%20Administration.

24. NOAA National Centers for Environmental Information, "2023 Was the Warmest Year in the Modern Temperature Record," *NOAA Climate.Gov*, January 17, 2024, https://www.climate.gov/news-features/featured-images/2023-was-warmest-year-modern-temperature-record.

25. Intergovernmental Panel on Climate Change, *Climate Change 2023: Synthesis Report. Summary for Policymakers. Headline Statements*. Geneva,

Switzerland: IPCC, 2023, https://www.ipcc.ch/report/ar6/syr/resources/spm-headline-statements/.

26. Intergovernmental Panel on Climate Change, *Climate Change 2023: Synthesis Report. Longer Report*. Geneva, Switzerland: IPCC, 2023, https://www.ipcc.ch/report/ar6/syr/downloads/report/IPCC_AR6_SYR_LongerReport.pdf.

27. Megan Ennes, "NNOCCI Climate Science Fundamentals," July 15, 2020, https://nnocci.org/nnocci-climate-science-fundamentals/.

28. Andrew Pershing and Frank Mungeam, "LMA Climate Collab: Climate Attribution Briefing," May 29, 2024.

29. Joan Meiners, interview by Sadie Babits, August 23, 2024.

30. Ibid.

31. Susan Hassol, interview by Sadie Babits, March 22, 2023.

32. Ibid.

33. Ibid.

34. Ibid.

35. Ibid.

36. "Nine in Ten Have Experienced Extreme Weather and Most Blame Climate Change," AP-NORC, September 25, 2023, https://apnorc.org/projects/nine-in-ten-have-experienced-extreme-weather-and-most-blame-climate-change/.

37. Dazhi Xi, Ning Lin, and Avantika Gori, "Increasing Sequential Tropical Cyclone Hazards Along the US East and Gulf Coasts," *Nature Climate Change* 13, no. 3 (February 27, 2023): 258–65, doi:10.1038/s41558-023-01595-7.

38. W. Matt Jolly et al., "Climate-Induced Variations in Global Wildfire Danger from 1979 to 2013," *Nature Communications* 6, no. 1 (July 14, 2015): 1–11, doi:10.1038/ncomms8537.

39. "Climate Shift Index," Climate Central, accessed September 2, 2024, https://www.climatecentral.org/realtime-fingerprints.

40. Frank Mungeam, "From TV Meteorologists, More Straight Talk About Climate Change," SEJ, June 2, 2023, https://www.sej.org/publications/features/tv-meteorologists-more-straight-talk-about-climate-change.

41. Yale Program on Climate Change Communication, "Politics & Global Warming, April 2022," July 7, 2022, https://climatecommunication.yale.edu/publications/politics-global-warming-april-2022/toc/11/.

42. Chris Gloninger, interview by Sadie Babits, May 20, 2024.

43. Calum X. Cunningham, Grant J. Williamson, and David M. J. S. Bowman, "Increasing Frequency and Intensity of the Most Extreme Wildfires on Earth," *Nature Ecology & Evolution* 8, no. 8 (June 24, 2024): 1420–25, doi:10.1038/s41559-024-02452-2.

44. NOAA Satellite and Research Information, "NOAA Coral Reef Watch Research," August 20, 2024, https://coralreefwatch.noaa.gov/satellite/research/coral_bleaching_report.php.

45. Max Callaghan et al., "Observed Increases in Extreme Fire Weather Driven by Atmospheric Humidity and Temperature," *Nature Climate Change* 12, no. 1 (2022): 63–70, https://doi.org/10.1038/s41558-021-01168-6.

46. World Weather Attribution, "Interplay of Climate Change-Exacerbated Rainfall, Exposure, and Vulnerability Led to Widespread Impacts in the Mediterranean Region," *World Weather Attribution*, September 19, 2023, https://www.worldweatherattribution.org/interplay-of-climate-change-ex-acerbated-rainfall-exposure-and-vulnerability-led-to-widespread-im-pacts-in-the-mediterranean-region/.

47. World Weather Attribution, "Human-Induced Climate Change Increased Drought Severity in Southern Horn of Africa," *World Weather Attribution*, April 27, 2023, https://www.worldweatherattribution.org/human-induced-climate-change-increased-drought-severity-in-southern-horn-of-africa/.

Chapter 3

1. Nicholas Kusnetz, "Why the Paris Climate Agreement Might Be Doomed to Fail," *Inside Climate News*, July 28, 2021, https://insideclimatenews.org/news/28072021/pairs-agreement-success-failure/.

2. Ibid.

3. Nicholas Kusnetz, interview by Sadie Babits, September 16, 2024.

4. "Mauna Loa," U.S. Geological Survey, accessed August 2, 2023, https://www.usgs.gov/volcanoes/mauna-loa.

5. Robert Monroe, "The Keeling Curve Hits 420 PPM," *The Keeling Curve*, May 31, 2022, https://keelingcurve.ucsd.edu/2022/05/31/2114/.

6. United Nations Office for Outer Space Affairs, "UN General Assembly Res-olution 1721 (XVI)—International Cooperation in the Peaceful Uses of Outer Space," United Nations Office for Outer Space Affairs, accessed August 2, 2023, https://www.unoosa.org/oosa/en/ourwork/spacelaw/treaties/resolu-tions/res_16_1721.html.

7. Ibid.

8. "World Weather Watch," World Meteorological Organization, October 18, 2023, https://wmo.int/world-weather-watch.

9. Thomas C. Peterson, William M. Connolley, and John Fleck, "The Myth of the 1970s Global Cooling Scientific Consensus," *Bulletin of the*

American Meteorological Society 89, no. 9 (September 2008): 1325–38, doi:10.1175/2008bams2370.1.

10. "Vegetation and Rainfall in the Sahel," January 4, 2007, https://earthobservatory.nasa.gov/images/7277/vegetation-and-rainfall-in-the-sahel.

11. United Nations, "From Stockholm to Kyoto: A Brief History of Climate Change," United Nations, accessed September 29, 2024, https://www.un.org/en/chronicle/article/stockholm-kyoto-brief-history-climate-change.

12. Thomas C. Peterson, William M. Connolley, and John Fleck, "The Myth of the 1970s Global Cooling Scientific Consensus," *Bulletin of the American Meteorological Society* 89, no. 9 (September 2008): 1325–38, doi:10.1175/2008bams2370.1.

13. "Declaration of the World Climate Conference." *Environmental Conservation* 6, no. 2 (1979): 137–38. https://doi.org/10.1017/S0376892900002630.

14. Ibid.

15. "History of the IPCC," IPCC, accessed September 29, 2024, https://www.ipcc.ch/about/history/.

16. United Nations Framework Convention on Climate Change, "The Sixth Assessment Report of the IPCC," accessed August 7, 2023, https://unfccc.int/topics/science/workstreams/cooperation-with-the-ipcc/the-sixth-assessment-report-of-the-ipcc.

17. European Commission, Joint Research Centre, "Global Greenhouse Gas Emissions 2024 Report," EDGAR, 2024, accessed September 29, 2024, https://edgar.jrc.ec.europa.eu/report_2024.

18. World Food Program USA, "The 8 Countries Most Affected by Climate Change," accessed August 7, 2023, https://www.wfpusa.org/articles/countries-most-affected-by-climate-change/.

19. Pakistan, "Pakistan Updated Nationally Determined Contribution 2021," United Nations Framework Convention on Climate Change (UNFCCC), 2021, accessed August 7, 2023, https://unfccc.int/sites/default/files/NDC/2022-06/Pakistan%20Updated%20NDC%202021.pdf.

20. "Pakistan Facing Monsoon 'on Steroids' Climate Catastrophe, Secretary-General Says, Urging Global Support of Flash Appeal for Flood Response Plan," Meetings Coverage and Press Releases, August 30, 2022, https://press.un.org/en/2022/sgsm21429.doc.htm.

21. World Food Program USA, "The 8 Countries Most Affected by Climate Change," accessed August 7, 2023, https://www.wfpusa.org/articles/countries-most-affected-by-climate-change/.

22. United Nations Climate Change, "COP27 Reaches Breakthrough Agreement on New 'Loss and Damage' Fund for Vulnerable Countries," UN Climate press release, November 20, 2022, https://unfccc.int/news/cop27-reaches-break-through-agreement-on-new-loss-and-damage-fund-for-vulnerable-coun-tries.

23. "COP29 UN Climate Conference Agrees to Triple Finance to Developing Countries, Protecting Lives and Livelihoods," *UNFCCC*, November 24, 2024, accessed January 5, 2025. https://unfccc.int/news/cop29-un-climate-confer-ence-agrees-to-triple-finance-to-developing-countries-protecting-lives-and.

24. Michael Copley, Jeff Brady, Julia Simon, Alejandra Borunda, Lauren Sommer, "With Talks Teetering, Climate Negotiators Struck a Controversial $300 Bil-lion Deal" *NPR*, November 23, 2024, accessed January 5, 2025. https://www.npr.org/2024/11/23/nx-s1-5202805/cop29-climate-change-un-azerbaijan.

25. United Nations Framework Convention on Climate Change, "UN Climate Change Timeline," accessed August 7, 2023, https://unfccc.int/timeline/.

26. United Nations, "United Nations Framework Convention on Climate Change," 1992, accessed August 4, 2023. https://treaties.un.org/doc/source/recenttexts/unfccc_eng.pdf.

27. United Nations Framework Convention on Climate Change, "About the Secretariat," accessed August 4, 2023, https://unfccc.int/about-us/about-the-secretariat.

28. Ibid.

29. Ibid.

30. Ibid.

31. United Nations Framework Convention on Climate Change, "Kyoto Protocol to the United Nations Framework Convention on Climate Change," 1997, accessed August 4, 2023. https://unfccc.int/resource/docs/convkp/kpeng.pdf.

32. United Nations, "Kyoto Protocol to the United Nations Framework Convention on Climate Change," accessed August 4, 2023. https://treaties.un.org/Pages/ViewDetails.aspx?src=TREATY&mtdsg_no=XXVII-7-a&chapter=27&clang=_en.

33. United Nations Framework Convention on Climate Change, "The Clean Development Mechanism," accessed August 7, 2023, https://unfccc.int/process-and-meetings/the-kyo-to-protocol/mechanisms-under-the-kyoto-protocol/the-clean-development-mechanism.

34. United Nations Environment Programme, "Adaptation Fund," accessed August 4, 2023, https://www.unep.org/about-un-environment-programme/ funding-and-partnerships/adaptation-fund#:~:text=The%20Adapta-tion%20Fund%20was%20established,supporting%20100%20concrete%20 adaptation%20projects.

35. United Nations Framework Convention on Climate Change, "Adaptation Fund," *UNFCCC,* accessed January 5, 2025, https://unfccc.int/ Adaptation-Fund.

36. United Nations Framework Convention on Climate Change, "The Adaptation Fund," accessed August 7, 2023, https://unfccc.int/Adaptation-Fund#:~:- text=The%20Adaptation%20Fund%20was%20established,adverse%20 effects%20of%20climate%20change.

37. "COP21: UN Chief Hails New Climate Change Agreement as 'Monumental Triumph,'" *UN News,* December 12, 2015, https://news.un.org/en/ story/2015/12/517982.

38. United Nations Framework Convention on Climate Change, "The Paris Agreement," accessed August 7, 2023, https://unfccc.int/ process-and-meetings/the-paris-agreement.

39. National Oceanic and Atmospheric Administration, "2024 Was the World's Warmest Year on Record," press release, January 10, 2025, https://www.noaa. gov/news/2024-was-worlds-warmest-year-on-record#:~:text=2024%20 was%20the%20world's%20warmest,National%20Oceanic%20and%20 Atmospheric%20Administration.

40. Ibid.

41. United Nations Framework Convention on Climate Change, "Outcome of the First Global Stocktake," accessed September 29, 2024, https:// unfccc.int/topics/global-stocktake/about-the-global-stocktake/ outcome-of-the-first-global-stocktake.

42. "COP21: UN Chief Hails New Climate Change Agreement as 'Monumental Triumph,'" *UN News,* December 12, 2015, https://news.un.org/en/ story/2015/12/517982.

43. United Nations Environment Programme, *Emissions Gap Report 2023.* Nairobi: UNEP, 2023, accessed September 29, 2024, https://wedocs.unep.org/bit-stream/handle/20.500.11822/43922/EGR2023.pdf?sequence=3&isAllowed=y.

44. United States, *Nationally Determined Contribution April 2021,* United Nations Framework Convention on Climate Change (UNFCCC), 2021, accessed August 7, 2023, https://unfccc.int/sites/default/files/NDC/2022-06/United%20 States%20NDC%20April%2021%202021%20Final.pdf.

45. The White House, "Fact Sheet: The Bipartisan Infrastructure Deal," *Briefing Room*, November 6, 2021, accessed January 5, 2025, https://www.whitehouse.gov/briefing-room/statements-releases/2021/11/06/fact-sheet-the-bipartisan-infrastructure-deal/.

46. Climate Action Tracker, "USA," accessed August 7, 2023, https://climateactiontracker.org/countries/usa/.

47. Climate Action Tracker, "Australia," accessed August 7, 2023, https://climateactiontracker.org/countries/australia/.

48. Russia, *Nationally Determined Contribution 2020*, United Nations Framework Convention on Climate Change (UNFCCC), 2020, accessed August 6, 2023, https://unfccc.int/sites/default/files/NDC/2022-06/NDC_RF_eng.pdf.

49. Climate Action Tracker, "Russian Federation," accessed August 6, 2023, https://climateactiontracker.org/countries/russian-federation/#:~:text=We%20rate%20Russia's%202030%20NDC,warming%20to%201.5%C2%B0C.

50. Climate Action Tracker, "Saudi Arabia," accessed August 6, 2023, https://climateactiontracker.org/countries/saudi-arabia/.

51. Anthony Leiserowitz et al., "Climate Change in the Indian Mind, 2022," *Yale Program on Climate Change Communication*, October 20, 2022, https://climatecommunication.yale.edu/publications/climate-change-in-the-indian-mind-2022/toc/3/.

52. European Union, *EU Submission NDC Update 2023*, United Nations Framework Convention on Climate Change (UNFCCC), 2023, accessed August 7, 2023, https://unfccc.int/sites/default/files/NDC/2023-10/ES-2023-10-17%20EU%20submission%20NDC%20update.pdf.

53. "Fit for 55: The EU's Plan for a Green Transition," *Consilium*, accessed August 7, 2023, https://www.consilium.europa.eu/en/policies/green-deal/fit-for-55/.

54. United Nations Environment Programme, *Emissions Gap Report 2024*, UNEP, 2024, accessed January 5, 2025, https://www.unep.org/resources/emissions-gap-report-2024.

55. United Nations Environment Programme, *Emissions Gap Report 2022*. Nairobi: UNEP, 2022.

56. Nicholas Kusnetz, "Why the Paris Climate Agreement Might Be Doomed to Fail," *Inside Climate News*, July 28, 2021, https://insideclimatenews.org/news/28072021/pairs-agreement-success-failure/.

57. United Nations Framework Convention on Climate Change, "The Glasgow Climate Pact—Key Outcomes from COP26," accessed August 12,

2023, https://unfccc.int/process-and-meetings/the-paris-agreement/the-glasgow-climate-pact-key-outcomes-from-cop26.

58. International Energy Agency, "The Global Energy Crisis Pushed Fossil Fuel Consumption Subsidies to an All-Time High," February 16, 2023, accessed September 29, 2024, https://www.iea.org/commentaries/the-global-energy-crisis-pushed-fossil-fuel-consumption-subsidies-to-an-all-time-high.

59. Taryn Fransen et al., "9 Things to Know About National Climate Plans (NDCs)," *World Resources Institute*, December 7, 2023, https://www.wri.org/insights/assessing-progress-ndcs.

60. James Round, "Federal Climate Policy Toolkit: Reducing Emissions," *Resources for the Future*, May 20, 2021, https://www.resources.org/archives/federal-climate-policy-toolkit-reducing-emissions/.

61. Regeringen och Regeringskansliet, "Sweden's Carbon Tax," *Regeringskansliet*, February 26, 2018, https://www.government.se/government-policy/swedens-carbon-tax/swedens-carbon-tax/.

62. Antoine Dechezleprêtre, Daniel Nachtigall, and Frank Venmans, "The Joint Impact of the European Union Emissions Trading System on Carbon Emissions and Economic Performance," *Journal of Environmental Economics and Management* 118 (March 2023): 102758, doi:10.1016/j.jeem.2022.102758.

63. "Korea Emissions Trading Scheme," *International Carbon Action Partnership*, accessed September 29, 2024, https://icapcarbonaction.com/en/ets/korea-emissions-trading-scheme.

64. Liang-Cheng Ye, João F. D. Rodrigues, and Hai Xiang Lin, "Analysis of Feed-in Tariff Policies for Solar Photovoltaic in China 2011–2016," *Applied Energy* 203 (October 2017): 496–505, doi:10.1016/j.apenergy.2017.06.037.

65. China Dialogue, "China to Set Up Special Purpose Firms to Tackle Unpaid Renewables Subsidies," *Dialogue Earth*, August 18, 2022, https://chinadialogue.net/en/digest/china-special-purpose-firms-to-tackle-unpaid-renewables-subsidies/.

66. Tom Kertscher, "US Versus China: Which Nation is Doing More to Address Climate Change," *Politifact*, March 27, 2023, https://www.politifact.com/article/2023/mar/27/us-versus-china-which-nation-doing-more-address-cl/.

67. People's Republic of China, *China's Achievements, New Goals, and New Measures for Nationally Determined Contributions*, United Nations Framework Convention on Climate Change, 2022, accessed September 29, 2024. https://unfccc.int/sites/default/files/NDC/2022-06/China%E2%80%99s%20Achievements%2C%20New%20Goals%20and%20New%20Measures%20for%20Nationally%20Determined%20Contributions.pdf.

68. Government of India, *Updated First Nationally Determined Contribution*, United Nations Framework Convention on Climate Change, 2022, accessed August 13, 2023, https://unfccc.int/sites/default/files/NDC/2022-08/India%20Updated%20First%20Nationally%20Determined%20Contrib.pdf.

69. Sarita Singh, "India Succeeds in Reducing Emissions Rate by 33% over 14 Years," Reuters, August 9, 2023, https://www.reuters.com/world/india/india-succeeds-reducing-emissions-rate-by-33-over-14-years-sources-2023-08-09/.

70. World Future Council, "The German Feed-in Tariff," *Future Policy*, accessed August 13, 2023, https://www.futurepolicy.org/climate-stability/renewable-energies/the-german-feed-in-tariff/.

71. "Indicator: Greenhouse Gas Emissions," *Umweltbundesamt*, accessed September 29, 2024, https://www.umweltbundesamt.de/en/data/environmental-indicators/indicator-greenhouse-gas-emissions#at-a-glance.

72. "Sources of Greenhouse Gas Emissions," US EPA, December 29, 2015, https://www.epa.gov/ghgemissions/sources-greenhouse-gas-emissions.

73. "Corporate Average Fuel Economy (CAFE) Standards," US Department of Transportation, August 11, 2014, https://www.transportation.gov/mission/sustainability/corporate-average-fuel-economy-cafe-standards.

74. "Passenger Vehicle Greenhouse Gas Emissions and Fuel Consumption," International Council on Clean Transportation, July 16, 2021, https://theicct.org/pv-fuel-economy/.

75. Thomas E. Lovejoy and Carlos Nobre, "Amazon Tipping Point: Last Chance for Action," *Science Advances* 5, no. 12 (2019): eaat2340, accessed September 29, 2024, https://www.science.org/doi/10.1126/sciadv.aat2340.

76. Ibid.

77. Ibid.

78. Britaldo Silveira Soares-Filho et al., "Contribution of the Amazon Protected Areas Program to Forest Conservation," *Biological Conservation* 279 (March 2023): 109928, doi:10.1016/j.biocon.2023.109928.

79. Hans Nicholas Jong, "Study: Indonesia's Forest-Clearing Moratorium Under-delivered—but So Did Donors," *Mongabay Environmental News*, March 15, 2022, https://news.mongabay.com/2022/03/study-indonesias-forest-clearing-moratorium-underdelivered-but-so-did-donors/.

80. Tabita Diela, "Indonesia's President Makes Moratorium on Forest Clearance Permanent," *World Economic Forum*, August 2019, accessed January 5, 2025, https://www.weforum.org/stories/2019/08/indonesia-president-makes-moratorium-on-forest-clearance-permanent/.

81. Ibid.

82. Ibid.

83. Ibid.

84. "Green Legacy Initiative," *Department of Economic and Social Affairs*, accessed August 14, 2023, https://sdgs.un.org/partnerships/green-legacy-initiative.

85. Ibid.

86. Judy Shin, "Explainer: What Is the 'Great Green Wall' of China?," *Earth.Org*, August 23, 2021, https://earth.org/what-is-the-great-green-wall-in-china/.

87. "State Climate Policy Maps," *Center for Climate and Energy Solutions*, January 11, 2021, https://www.c2es.org/content/state-climate-policy/.

88. Laura Klivans, "Biden Administration Approves California Plans to Ban Sale of Gas-Only Vehicles," *NPR*, December 19, 2024, accessed January 5, 2025, https://www.npr.org/2024/12/19/nx-s1-5230628/biden-administration-approves-california-plans-to-ban-sale-of-gas-only-vehicles.

89. City of Phoenix, *Climate Action Plan 2021*. Phoenix, AZ: Office of Environmental Programs, 2021, accessed September 29, 2024, https://www.phoenix.gov/oepsite/Documents/2021ClimateActionPlanEnglish.pdf.

90. David G. Victor et al., "Pledges and Progress: Steps toward Greenhouse Gas Emissions Reductions in the 100 Largest Cities across the United States," *Brookings*, October 21, 2020, https://www.brookings.edu/articles/pledges-and-progress-steps-toward-greenhouse-gas-emissions-reductions-in-the-100-largest-cities-across-the-united-states/.

91. "United Nations Treaty Collection," *C2ES*, November 2023, https://treaties.un.org/Pages/ViewDetails.aspx?src=TREATY&mtdsg_no=XXVII-7-a&chapter=27&clang=_en.

92. Lindsey Volz and Joshua Pine, "The Top 5 Ways Cities Are Addressing Climate Change," *National League of Cities*, April 22, 2022, https://www.nlc.org/article/2022/04/22/the-top-5-ways-cities-are-addressing-climate-change/.

93. Ibid.

94. Ibid.

95. Ibid.

96. Ibid.

97. National Conference of State Legislatures, "State Renewable Portfolio Standards and Goals," accessed August 20, 2023, https://www.ncsl.org/energy/state-renewable-portfolio-standards-and-goals.

98. Ibid.

99. Ibid.

100. Ibid.

101. "State of Oregon: Energy in Oregon," *Renewable Portfolio Standard*, accessed September 29, 2024, https://www.oregon.gov/energy/energy-oregon/pages/renewable-portfolio-standard.aspx.

102. Ibid.

103. Ibid.

104. "Cap-and-Trade Program," California Air Resources Board, accessed August 22, 2023, https://ww2.arb.ca.gov/our-work/programs/cap-and-trade-program/about.

105. Regional Greenhouse Gas Initiative, "RGGI 101: An Overview of the Regional Greenhouse Gas Initiative," 2021, accessed August 22, 2023, https://www.rggi.org/sites/default/files/Uploads/Fact%20Sheets/RGGI_101_Factsheet.pdf.

106. "National Environmental Policy Act (NEPA)," Center for Environmental Excellence | AASHTO, April 20, 2021, https://environment.transportation.org/state-of-the-practice/policy/nepa/.

107. Council on Environmental Quality, "National Environmental Policy Act Guidance on Consideration of Greenhouse Gas Emissions and Climate Change," *Federal Register* 88, no. 5 (January 9, 2023): 1196-207, accessed September 29, 2024, https://www.federalregister.gov/documents/2023/01/09/2023-00158/national-environmental-policy-act-guidance-on-consideration-of-greenhouse-gas-emissions-and-climate.

108. Council on Environmental Quality, "GHG Tools and Resources for NEPA Reviews," accessed August 26, 2023, https://ceq.doe.gov/guidance/ghg-tools-and-resources.html.

109. Congressional Research Service, *Judicial Review of Agency Action Under the National Environmental Policy Act (NEPA): Overview and Recent Developments*, R47205, updated August 31, 2022, accessed July 29, 2023, https://crsreports.congress.gov/product/pdf/R/R47205.

110. U.S. Environmental Protection Agency, "EPA History: Clean Air Act of 1970," accessed July 28, 2023, https://www.epa.gov/history/epa-history-clean-air-act-197019.

111. *West Virginia v. Environmental Protection Agency*, 597 U.S. (2022), accessed July 28, 2023, https://www.supremecourt.gov/opinions/21pdf/20-1530_n758.pdf.

112. Nina Totenberg, "The Supreme Court Has Narrowed the Scope of the Clean Water Act," NPR, May 25, 2023, https://www.npr.org/2023/05/25/1178150234/supreme-court-epa-clean-water-act.

113. Amy Howe, "Supreme Court Strikes Down Chevron, Curtailing Power of Federal Agencies," *SCOTUSblog*, June 2024, accessed January 5, 2025, https://www.scotusblog.com/2024/06/supreme-court-strikes-down-chevron-curtailing-power-of-federal-agencies/.

114. Nathan Rott, "What the End of Chevron Doctrine Could Mean for the Fight Against Climate Change," *NPR*, June 28, 2024, https://www.npr.org/2024/06/28/nx-s1-5023083/what-the-end-of-chevron-doctrine-could-mean-for-the-fight-against-climate-change.

115. Endangered Species Act, U.S. Fish and Wildlife Service, accessed July 28, 2023, https://www.fws.gov/law/endangered-species-act.

116. "Species and Climate Change," IUCN, accessed July 28, 2023, https://iucn.org/resources/issues-brief/species-and-climate-change.

117. Ibid.

118. "Regulatory Alert: Federal Endangered Species Protections Not Warranted for Joshua Trees," *SWCA*, March 17, 2023, https://www.swca.com/news/2023/03/regulatory-alert-federal-endangered-species-protections-not-warranted-for-joshua-trees.

119. "About: What We Manage: National," Bureau of Land Management, accessed September 30, 2024, https://www.blm.gov/about/what-we-manage/national.

120. Federal Land Policy and Management Act of 1976, U.S. Bureau of Land Management, accessed July 29, 2023, https://www.blm.gov/sites/default/files/AboutUs_LawsandRegs_FLPMA.pdf.

121. Bureau of Land Management, "Bureau of Land Management Announces Next Steps, New Analyses for Upcoming Oil and Gas Lease Sales," U.S. Department of the Interior, October 29, 2021, accessed September 30, 2024, https://www.blm.gov/press-release/bureau-land-management-announces-next-steps-new-analyses-upcoming-oil-and-gas-lease.

122. U.S. Department of the Interior, "Oil and Gas Leasing Program," Office of Congressional and Legislative Affairs, accessed September 30, 2024, https://www.doi.gov/ocl/oil-and-gas-leasing-program.

123. Scott Streater, "Biden Boosts Conservation in BLM Public Lands Rule," *E&E News by POLITICO*, April 18, 2024, https://subscriber.politicopro.com/eenews/f/eenews/?id=0000018e-f1da-dff0-a7de-fdfebaee0000.

124. Niina H. Farah, "Biden's Green Allies Promise Lawsuit over Alaska Oil Project," *E&E News by POLITICO*, March 14, 2023, https://www.eenews.net/articles/bidens-green-allies-promise-lawsuit-over-alaska-oil-project/.

125. "BOEM Governing Statutes," Bureau of Ocean Energy Management, accessed September 30, 2024, https://www.boem.gov/about-boem/regulations-guidance/boem-governing-statutes.

Chapter 4

1. Bryan Mena, "Abbott and Other Texas Republicans Blame Green Energy for Fossil Fuel Woes," *The Texas Tribune*, February 18, 2021, https://www.texastribune.org/2021/02/17/abbott-republicans-green-energy/.
2. Rebecca Leber, "Gaslit: How the Fossil Fuel Industry Convinced Americans to Love Gas Stoves," *Mother Jones*, June 17, 2021, https://www.motherjones.com/environment/2021/06/how-the-fossil-fuel-industry-convinced-americans-to-love-gas-stoves/.
3. "Carbon Capture Agreement with CF Industries," *ExxonMobil* (blog), accessed September 1, 2024, https://corporate.exxonmobil.com/what-we-do/delivering-industrial-solutions/carbon-capture-and-storage/exxonmobil-signs-carbon-capture-agreement-cf-industries-yazoo.
4. Katelyn Weisbrod, "Nine Years After Filing a Lawsuit, Climate Scientist Michael Mann Wants a Court to Affirm the Truth of His Science," *Inside Climate News*, February 7, 2021, https://insideclimatenews.org/news/07022021/michael-mann-defamation-lawsuit-competitive-enterprise-institute-national-review/.
5. Emilio Granados Franco et al., "The Global Risks Report 2022," World Economic Forum, 2022, pp. 34–49.
6. Staff SciLine, "Dr. Claire Wardle: The Science of Misinformation," SciLine, December 14, 2021, https://www.sciline.org/social-sciences/misinformation/.
7. Ibid.
8. Laura Benshoff, "Renewable Energy Is Maligned by Misinformation. It's a Distraction, Experts Say," NPR, August 24, 2022, https://www.npr.org/2022/08/24/1110850169/misinformation-renewable-energy-gop-climate.
9. Bryan Mena, "Abbott and Other Texas Republicans Blame Green Energy for Fossil Fuel Woes," *The Texas Tribune*, February 18, 2021, https://www.texastribune.org/2021/02/17/abbott-republicans-green-energy/.
10. "Global Climate Coalition," *DeSmog*, January 9, 2016, https://www.desmog.com/global-climate-coalition/.
11. Bob Burton and Sheldon Rampton, "How Big Business Is Warming Up to Global Warming," *PR Watch*, Fourth Quarter 1997, https://web.archive.org/web/20120111013854/http://www.prwatch.org/prwissues/1997Q4/warming.html.

12. Maggie Farley, "Clinton Signs Global Warming Treaty Amid Dispute," *Los Angeles Times*, December 7, 1997, https://web.archive.org/web/20160118234039/http://articles.latimes.com/1997/dec/07/news/mn-61743/2.

13. "Global Climate Coalition," *DeSmog*, January 9, 2016, https://www.desmog.com/global-climate-coalition/.

14. Riley E. Dunlap and Peter J. Jacques, "Climate Change Denial Books and Conservative Think Tanks," *American Behavioral Scientist* 57, no. 6 (2013): 699–731, https://doi.org/10.1177/0002764213477096.

15. Ibid.

16. Maxwell T. Boykoff and Jules M. Boykoff, "Balance as Bias: Global Warming and the US Prestige Press," *Global Environmental Change* 14, no. 2 (2004): 126, https://doi.org/10.1016/j.gloenvcha.2003.10.001.

17. Ibid.

18. Penelope Abernathy, "Expanding News Deserts," *The Expanding News Desert*, July 12, 2021, https://www.usnewsdeserts.com/.

19. Mason Walker and Katerina Eva Matsa, "News Consumption Across Social Media in 2021," Pew Research Center's Journalism Project, September 20, 2021, https://www.pewresearch.org/journalism/2021/09/20/news-consumption-across-social-media-in-2021/.

20. Matteo Cinelli et al., "The Echo Chamber Effect on Social Media," *Proceedings of the National Academy of Sciences* 118, no. 9 (2021), https://doi.org/10.1073/pnas.2023301118.

21. Dunlap and Jacques, "Climate Change Denial Books and Conservative Think Tanks."

22. John Cook, interview by Sadie Babits, November 12, 2022.

23. John Cook, Sander van der Linden, Edward Maibach, and Stephan Lewandowsky, *The Consensus Handbook*, 2018, https://doi.org/10.13021/G8MM6P.

24. Bud Ward, "Communicating on Climate Change: An Essential Resource for Journalists, Scientists, and Educators," edited by Sunshine Menezes, Metcalf Institute for Marine & Environmental Reporting, 21, 2008, https://www.climamed.eu/wp-content/uploads/files/Communicating-On-Climate-Change.pdf.

25. Ibid.

26. Ibid.

27. John Cook, interview by Sadie Babits, November 12, 2022.

28. Ibid.

29. John Cook, "Arguments from Global Warming Skeptics and What the Science Really Says," *Skeptical Science*, accessed September 21, 2024, https://skepticalscience.com/argument.php.

30. John Cook, "Climate Science Glossary," *Skeptical Science*, 2022, https://skepticalscience.com/Can-animals-and-plants-adapt-to-global-warming.htm.

31. Neela Banerjee, Lisa Song, and David Hasemyer, "Exxon's Own Research Confirmed Fossil Fuels' Role in Global Warming Decades Ago," *InsideClimate News*, September 16, 2015, accessed September 21, 2024, https://insideclimatenews.org/news/16092015/exxons-own-research-confirmed-fossil-fuels-role-in-global-warming/.

32. Geoffrey Supran and Naomi Oreskes, "Assessing ExxonMobil's Climate Change Communications (1977–2014)," *Environmental Research Letters* 12, no. 8 (2017): 084019, accessed September 21, 2024, https://doi.org/10.1088/1748-9326/aa815f.

33. Julia Simon, "Misinformation Is Derailing Renewable Energy Projects Across the United States," NPR, March 28, 2022, https://www.npr.org/2022/03/28/1086790531/renewable-energy-projects-wind-energy-solar-energy-climate-change-misinformation.

34. Michael Copley, Miranda Green, and Ryan Kelman, "An Activist Group Is Spreading Misinformation to Stop Solar Projects in Rural America," *Floodlight, Inc.*, February 18, 2023, https://www.npr.org/2023/02/18/1154867064/solar-power-misinformation-activists-rural-america.

35. John Cook, "A History of FLICC: The 5 Techniques of Science Denial," *Cranky Uncle*, July 15, 2022, https://crankyuncle.com/a-history-of-flicc-the-5-techniques-of-science-denial/.

36. Michael E. Mann, *The New Climate War: The Fight to Take Back Our Planet*. PublicAffairs, 2021.

37. Ibid.

38. Aya Batrawy, "What It Means for an Oil Producing Country, the UAE, to Host U.N. Climate Talks," NPR, December 9, 2023, https://www.npr.org/2023/12/09/1217970348/what-it-means-for-an-oil-producing-country-the-uae-to-host-un-climate-talks.

39. Mann, *The New Climate War*.

40. Julia Simon, "Climate Scientist Michael Mann Wins Defamation Case Against Conservative Writers," NPR, February 8, 2024, https://www.npr.org/2024/02/08/1230236546/famous-climate-scientist-michael-mann-wins-his-defamation-case.

41. Michael Mann and Kathleen Hall Jamieson, interview by Rick Weiss, April 3, 2024.

42. Ibid.

43. Rebecca Leber, "Gaslit: How the Fossil Fuel Industry Convinced Americans to Love Gas Stoves," *Mother Jones*, June 17, 2021, https://www.motherjones.com/environment/2021/06/how-the-fossil-fuel-industry-convinced-americans-to-love-gas-stoves/.

44. John Cook, interview by Sadie Babits, November 12, 2022.

45. Ibid.

46. Frank Mungeam, "The Biggest Story Newsrooms Aren't Ready to Cover," *Cronkite News Lab*, February 21, 2020, https://cronkitenewslab.com/broadcast/2020/02/21/biggest-story-newsrooms-not-ready-to-cover/.

47. Ibid.

48. Ibid.

49. Bryan Mena, "Abbott and Other Texas Republicans Blame Green Energy for Fossil Fuel Woes," *The Texas Tribune*, February 18, 2021, https://www.texastribune.org/2021/02/17/abbott-republicans-green-energy/.

50. Kevin Collier, "Fact Check: Renewable Energy Is Not to Blame for the Texas Energy Crisis," NBC News, February 17, 2021, https://www.nbcnews.com/news/us-news/fact-check-renewable-energy-not-blame-texas-energy-crisis-n1258185.

51. Camila Domonoske, "No, the Blackouts in Texas Weren't Caused by Renewables. Here's What Really Happened," NPR, February 18, 2021, https://www.npr.org/sections/live-updates-winter-storms-2021/2021/02/18/968967137/no-the-blackouts-in-texas-werent-caused-by-renewables-heres-what-really-happened.

52. Eric Bradner, "Texas Republicans Criticized for Misleading Claims That Renewable Energy Sources Caused Massive Outages," CNN, February 18, 2021, https://www.cnn.com/2021/02/18/politics/texas-power-outages-political-fallout/index.html.

53. Ryan Bort, "Millions of Texans Are Freezing and Without Power and Republicans Are Blaming . . . Windmills," *Rolling Stone*, February 18, 2021, https://www.rollingstone.com/politics/politics-news/texas-crisis-renewable-energy-1129045/.

54. Julia Waldow, "George Lakoff Says This Is How Trump Uses Words to Con the Public," *CNNMoney*, 2018, https://money.cnn.com/2018/06/15/media/reliable-sources-podcast-george-lakoff/index.html.

55. Margaret Sullivan, "Instead of Trump's Propaganda, How About a Nice 'Truth Sandwich'?," *The Washington Post*, June 17, 2018, https://www.washingtonpost.com/lifestyle/style/instead-of-trumps-propaganda-how-about-a-nice-truth-sandwich/2018/06/15/80df8c36-70af-11e8-bf86-a2351b5ece99_story.html.

56. John Cook, Stephan Lewandowsky, and Ullrich Ecker, *The Debunking Handbook 2020* (Skeptical Science, 2020), 1–18, https://skepticalscience.com/docs/DebunkingHandbook2020.pdf.

57. Noah Y. Kim, "Fact-Check: Is Texas 'Totally Reliant on Wind'?," *Austin American-Statesman*, February 18, 2021, https://www.statesman.com/story/news/politics/politifact/2021/02/18/texas-power-grid-outages-tucker-carlson-falsely-blames-green-new-deal-wind-energy/4489390001/.

58. Bryan Mena, "Abbott and Other Texas Republicans Blame Green Energy for Fossil Fuel Woes," *The Texas Tribune*, February 18, 2021, https://www.texastribune.org/2021/02/17/abbott-republicans-green-energy/.

59. Kevin Collier, "Fact Check: Renewable Energy Is Not to Blame for the Texas Energy Crisis," NBC News, February 17, 2021, https://www.nbcnews.com/news/us-news/fact-check-renewable-energy-not-blame-texas-energy-crisis-n1258185.

60. Ibid.

61. Ibid.

62. Ibid.

63. Ibid.

64. Laura Garcia, "A Guide to Pre-bunking: A Promising Way to Inoculate Against Misinformation," *First Draft*, June 29, 2021, https://firstdraftnews.org/articles/a-guide-to-pre-bunking-a-promising-way-to-inoculate-against-misinformation/.

65. Ibid.

66. Daniel Funke, "7 Ways to Avoid Election Misinformation," *Poynter*, October 6, 2020, https://www.poynter.org/fact-checking/2020/7-ways-to-avoid-misinformation-about-the-election/.

67. Ian Vandewalker, "Digital Disinformation and Vote Suppression," Brennan Center for Justice, September 2, 2020, https://www.brennancenter.org/our-work/research-reports/digital-disinformation-and-vote-suppression.

68. Micheal Copley/*NPR* and Miranda Green/*Floodlight*, "An Activist Group Is Spreading Misinformation to Stop Solar Projects in Rural America," *Floodlight*, February 18, 2023, https://floodlightnews.org/

an-activist-group-is-spreading-misinformation-to-stop-solar-proj-ects-in-rural-america/.

69. Laura Garcia, "A Guide to Pre-bunking: A Promising Way to Inoculate Against Misinformation," *First Draft*, June 29, 2021, https://firstdraftnews.org/articles/a-guide-to-pre-bunking-a-promising-way-to-inoculate-against-misinformation/.

70. Ibid.

71. Amy Westervelt, "The U.S. Anti-Wind Movement, Explained," *Drilled*, March 20, 2024, https://drilled.media/news/podcast-antiwind.

72. Ibid.

73. Frank Mungeam, "The Biggest Story Newsrooms Aren't Ready to Cover," *Cronkite News Lab*, February 21, 2020, https://cronkitenewslab.com/broadcast/2020/02/21/biggest-story-newsrooms-not-ready-to-cover/.

74. Charles H. Spurgeon, *Spurgeon's Gems: Brilliant Passages from the Discourses of the Rev. C. H. Spurgeon* (London: Passmore and Alabaster, 1859), https://www.google.com/books/edition/Spurgeon_s_gems_brilliant_passages_from/UgYDAAAAQAAJ.

75. John Cook, Stephan Lewandowsky, and Ullrich K. H. Ecker, "Neutralizing Misinformation Through Inoculation: Exposing Misleading Argumentation Techniques Reduces Their Influence," *PLoS One* 12, no. 5 (May 5, 2017): e0175799, doi:10.1371/journal.pone.0175799.

Chapter 5

1. Sammy Roth, interview by Sadie Babits, July 18, 2022.

2. Ibid.

3. Debra Kahn and Colby Bermel. "California Has First Rolling Blackouts in 19 Years—and Everyone Faces Blame," *Politico*, August 18, 2020, https://www.politico.com/states/california/story/2020/08/18/california-has-first-rolling-blackouts-in-19-years-and-everyone-faces-blame-1309757.

4. Sammy Roth, interview by Sadie Babits, July 18, 2022.

5. Ibid.

6. Ibid.

7. Sammy Roth, "As California Burns, Dealing with Climate Despair Isn't Easy," *Los Angeles Times*, August 20, 2020, https://www.latimes.com/environment/newsletter/2020-08-20/boiling-point-california-broiling-burning-boiling-point.

8. Sammy Roth, interview by Sadie Babits, July 18, 2022.

9.   "Definition of Objectivity," *Merriam-Webster*, accessed September 22, 2024, https://www.merriam-webster.com/dictionary/objectivity.

10. Martin Baron, "We Want Objective Judges and Doctors. Why Not Journalists Too?," *The Washington Post*, March 24, 2023, https://www.washingtonpost.com/opinions/2023/03/24/journalism-objectivity-trump-misinformation-marty-baron/.

11. Walter Lippmann, *Public Opinion* (New York: Harcourt, Brace and Company, 1922).

12. Walter Lippmann, "The State of Mind of the Executive," *The Atlantic*, November 1919, accessed September 22, 2024, https://cdn.theatlantic.com/media/archives/1919/11/124-5/132353920.pdf.

13. Bill Kovach and Tom Rosenstiel, *The Elements of Journalism: What News-people Should Know and the Public Should Expect*, 3rd ed. (New York: Crown Publishing Group, 2014), 50.

14. Ibid.

15. Matthew Pressman, "Journalistic Objectivity Evolved the Way It Did for a Reason," *Time*, November 5, 2018, https://time.com/5443351/journalism-objectivity-history/.

16. Daniel Hallin, interview by Sadie Babits, July 8, 2022.

17. Andrew Heyward and Leonard Downie Jr., "Beyond Objectivity," *Cronkite News Lab*, January 2023, accessed April 17, 2024, https://cronkitenewslab.com/wp-content/uploads/2023/01/Beyond-Objectivity-Report-2.pdf.

18. Hailey Reissman, "Cable News Networks Have Grown More Polarized, Study Finds," *Annenberg*, August 1, 2022, https://www.asc.upenn.edu/news-events/news/cable-news-networks-have-grown-more-polarized-study-finds.

19. Kelly McBride, "Stop Arguing About Objectivity and Start Serving Your Audience," *Poynter*, May 31, 2023, https://www.poynter.org/ethics-trust/2023/stop-arguing-about-objectivity-and-start-serving-your-audience/.

20. Bill Kovach and Tom Rosenstiel, *The Elements of Journalism: What News-people Should Know and the Public Should Expect*, 3rd ed. (New York: Crown Publishing Group, 2014), 50.

21. Christiane Amanpour (@amanpour). "Truthful, not neutral." X (formerly Twitter), October 13, 2016. https://x.com/amanpour/status/786519642416316416.

22. "CNN's Christiane Amanpour on Truth, Objectivity and the Assault on Democracy," *Poynter*, February 1, 2021, accessed September 22, 2024, https://www.poynter.org/fact-checking/2021/cnns-christiane-amanpour-on-truth-objectivity-and-the-assault-on-democracy/.

23. Ibid.

24. Al Tompkins, "It's Time for Journalism Educators to Rethink Objectivity and Teach More About Context," *Poynter*, October 12, 2020, accessed March 3, 2024, https://www.poynter.org/educators-students/2020/its-time-for-jour-nalism-educators-to-rethink-objectivity-and-teach-more-about-context/.

25. Gwen Aviles, "Journalism, Media Objectivity, and Covering the George Floyd Protests," *NBCU Academy*, June 23, 2021, accessed May 7, 2024, https://nbcuacademy.com/gwen-aviles-media-objectivity-george-floyd/.

26. Ibid.

27. Alexis Johnson (@alexisjreports), "Horrifying scenes and aftermath from selfish LOOTERS," Twitter, May 31, 2020, https://twitter.com/alexisjreports/status/1267081467731103749.

28. Al Tompkins, "It's Time for Journalism Educators to Rethink Objectivity and Teach More About Context," *Poynter*, October 12, 2020, accessed March 3, 2024, https://www.poynter.org/educators-students/2020/its-time-for-jour-nalism-educators-to-rethink-objectivity-and-teach-more-about-context/.

29. Ibid.

30. Ibid.

31. Ibid.

32. Susan Hassol, interview by Sadie Babits, March 8, 2023.

33. Damian Carrington, "Why the Guardian Is Changing the Language It Uses About the Environment," *The Guardian*, May 17, 2019, https://www.theguard-ian.com/environment/2019/may/17/why-the-guardian-is-changing-the-lan-guage-it-uses-about-the-environment.

34. Ibid.

35. "Treat Climate Change Like the Crisis It Is, Says Journalism Professor," CBC, July 5, 2019, https://www.cbc.ca/radio/sunday/the-sunday-edition-for-july-7-2019-1.5198309/treat-climate-change-like-the-crisis-it-is-says-jour-nalism-professor-1.5198311.

36. Oliver Milman, "Guardian Spurs Media Outlets to Consider Stronger Climate Language." *The Guardian*, May 24, 2019. https://www.theguardian.com/environment/2019/may/24/media-outlets-guardian-reconsider-language-climate.

37. Guardian Staff, "The Climate Emergency Is Here. The Media Needs to Act like It," *The Guardian*, April 12, 2021, https://www.theguardian.com/environment/2021/apr/12/covering-climate-now-guardian-climate-emergency.

38. Sammy Roth, interview by Sadie Babits, July 18, 2022.

39. Ibid.

40. Emily Atkin, "About," *Heated*, accessed April 30, 2024, https://heated.world/about.

41. Andrew Heyward and Leonard Downie Jr., "Beyond Objectivity," *Cronkite News Lab*, January 2023, accessed April 17, 2024, https://cronkitenewslab.com/wp-content/uploads/2023/01/Beyond-Objectivity-Report-2.pdf.

42. Sammy Roth, "As California Burns, Dealing with Climate Despair Isn't Easy," *Los Angeles Times*, August 20, 2020, https://www.latimes.com/environment/newsletter/2020-08-20/boiling-point-california-broiling-burning-boiling-point.

43. Sammy Roth, interview by Sadie Babits, July 18, 2022.

44. Andrew Heyward and Leonard Downie Jr., "Beyond Objectivity," *Cronkite News Lab*, January 2023, accessed April 17, 2024, https://cronkitenewslab.com/wp-content/uploads/2023/01/Beyond-Objectivity-Report-2.pdf.

Chapter 6

1. U.S. Environmental Protection Agency, "Cleanup Sites: Motorola, Inc. (52nd Street Plant)," accessed January 15, 2024, https://cumulis.epa.gov/supercpad/SiteProfiles/index.cfm?fuseaction=second.Cleanup&id=0902722#bkground.

2. "Why Cleaning Up Bayview-Hunters Point Is an Issue of Reparations," *KQED Newsroom*, KQED, podcast audio, August 17, 2023, accessed September 22, 2024, https://www.kqed.org/news/11920960/why-cleaning-up-bayview-hunters-point-is-an-issue-of-reparations.

3. Ibid.

4. Ezra David Romero, "For These Black Bayview-Hunters Point Residents, Reparations Include Safeguarding Against Rising Toxic Contamination," *KQED Science*, August 23, 2023, accessed January 15, 2024, https://www.kqed.org/science/1979614/for-these-black-bayview-hunters-point-residents-reparations-include-safeguarding-against-rising-toxic-contamination.

5. Ezra David Romero, interview by Sadie Babits, January 13, 2024.

6. Ibid.

7. Ibid.

8. Ibid.

9. NASA, "NASA Study Reveals Compounding Climate Risks at Two Degrees of Warming," *NASA Climate Change: Vital Signs of the Planet*, August 25, 2020, https://climate.nasa.gov/news/3278/nasa-study-reveals-compounding-climate-risks-at-two-degrees-of-warming/.

10. United Nations, "Climate Justice," *United Nations Sustainable Development*, May 3, 2019, accessed December 29, 2023, https://www.un.org/sustainabledevelopment/blog/2019/05/climate-justice.
11. Greg Jenkins, interview by Sadie Babits, January 18, 2024.
12. Ibid.
13. Ibid.
14. Robert Bullard, interview by Frank Mungeam, LMA Covering Climate Collaborative: "Connecting the Dots—Climate Change and Social Justice," July 28, 2021.
15. Ezra David Romero, "The Pajaro Flood Forced Them to Flee. California's High Rents Forced Them to Return," *KQED Science*, September 7, 2024, https://www.kqed.org/science/1994168/the-pajaro-flood-forced-them-to-flee-californias-high-rents-forced-them-to-return.
16. Ezra David Romero, interview by Sadie Babits, January 13, 2024.
17. Robert Bullard, interview by Frank Mungeam, LMA Covering Climate Collaborative: "Connecting the Dots—Climate Change and Social Justice," July 28, 2021.
18. National Integrated Heat Health Information System, "Mapping Campaigns," *Heat.gov*, accessed September 24, 2024, https://www.heat.gov/pages/mapping-campaigns.
19. American Lung Association, "Key Findings," *State of the Air 2024*, accessed September 24, 2024, https://www.lung.org/research/sota/key-findings.
20. Robert Bullard, interview by Frank Mungeam, LMA Covering Climate Collaborative: "Connecting the Dots—Climate Change and Social Justice," July 28, 2021.
21. Office of Minority Health, "Asthma and African Americans," U.S. Department of Health and Human Services, accessed December 30, 2023, https://minorityhealth.hhs.gov/asthma-and-african-americans.
22. Robert Bullard, interview by Frank Mungeam, LMA Covering Climate Collaborative: "Connecting the Dots—Climate Change and Social Justice," July 28, 2021.
23. American Society of Civil Engineers, "2021 Report Card for America's Infrastructure," *Infrastructure Report Card*, accessed December 30, 2023, https://infrastructurereportcard.org/.
24. Robert Bullard, interview by Frank Mungeam, LMA Covering Climate Collaborative: "Connecting the Dots—Climate Change and Social Justice," July 28, 2021.

25. Digital Scholarship Lab, "Mapping Inequality: Redlining in New Deal America," University of Richmond, accessed January 7, 2024, https://dsl.richmond.edu/panorama/redlining/#loc=5/36.191/-86.034.

26. Ibid.

27. Greg Jenkins, interview by Sadie Babits, January 18, 2024.

28. Ayana Elizabeth Johnson and Katharine K. Wilkinson, eds., *All We Can Save: Truth, Courage, and Solutions for the Climate Crisis* (New York: One World, 2020), 6.

29. Greg Jenkins, interview by Sadie Babits, January 18, 2024.

30. Naveena Sadasivam, interview by Sadie Babits, February 2, 2024.

31. The White House, "Justice40 Initiative," The White House, accessed November 20, 2023, https://www.whitehouse.gov/environmentaljustice/justice40/.

32. The White House, "Biden–Harris Administration Continues to Accelerate Environmental Justice in Disadvantaged Communities Through the President's Investing in America Agenda," The White House, November 29, 2023, https://www.whitehouse.gov/ceq/news-updates/2023/11/29/biden-harris-administration-continues-to-accelerate-environmental-justice-in-disadvantaged-communities-through-the-presidents-investing-in-america-agenda/.

33. Lisa Friedman, "Biden's Justice40 Promise Is at Risk of Under-Delivering, Some Say," *The New York Times*, July 20, 2023, https://www.nytimes.com/2023/07/20/climate/justice40-pollution-environmental-justice.html.

34. Ibid.

35. Naveena Sadasivam, interview by Sadie Babits, February 2, 2024.

36. Naveena Sadasivam and Clayton Aldern, "The White House Excluded Race from Its Environmental Justice Tool. We Put It Back In," *Grist*, February 24, 2022, https://grist.org/equity/climate-and-economic-justice-screening-tool-race/.

37. Robert Bullard, interview by Frank Mungeam, LMA Covering Climate Collaborative: "Connecting the Dots—Climate Change and Social Justice," July 28, 2021.

38. Jamie Smith Hopkins, "Why You Should Report on Environmental Justice—and How to Get Started," *Center for Public Integrity*, October 25, 2023, https://publicintegrity.org/environment/pollution/environmental-justice-denied/report-on-environmental-justice-title-vi-complaint/.

39. UNICEF, "Devastating Floods in Pakistan: 2022," UNICEF, accessed January 7, 2024, https://www.unicef.org/emergencies/devastating-floods-pakistan-2022.

40. World Bank, "Pakistan: Flood Damages and Economic Losses Over USD 30 Billion and Reconstruction Needs Over USD 16 Billion - New Assessment," *World Bank*, October 28, 2022, https://www.worldbank.org/en/news/press-release/2022/10/28/pakistan-flood-damages-and-economic-losses-over-usd-30-billion-and-reconstruction-needs-over-usd-16-billion-new-assessme.

41. World Meteorological Organization, "Climate Change Indicators Reached Record Levels in 2023," *World Meteorological Organization*, accessed September 24, 2024, https://wmo.int/news/media-centre/climate-change-indicators-reached-record-levels-2023-wmo.

42. Jonathan Watts and Matthew Taylor, "The Great Carbon Divide: Climate Chasm Between Rich and Poor," *The Guardian*, November 20, 2023, https://www.theguardian.com/environment/ng-interactive/2023/nov/20/the-great-carbon-divide-climate-chasm-rich-poor.

43. Jeff Tollefson, "COP26: World Leaders Agree to Historic Climate Pact," *Nature*, November 13, 2021, https://www.nature.com/articles/d41586-021-02846-3.

44. United Nations Framework Convention on Climate Change, "Step Up Climate Change Adaptation Efforts or Face Huge Disruption: UN Report," UNFCCC, November 4, 2021, https://unfccc.int/news/step-up-climate-change-adaptation-efforts-or-face-huge-disruption-un-report.

45. Michael Copley, Jeff Brady, Julia Simon, Alejandra Borunda, and Lauren Sommer, "With Talks Teetering, Climate Negotiators Struck a Controversial $300 Billion Deal," NPR, November 23, 2024, https://www.npr.org/2024/11/23/nx-s1-5202805/cop29-climate-change-un-azerbaijan.

46. Michael Copley, "Countries Push to Rework the Global Financial System and Offer Debt Relief for Climate Spending," NPR, November 28, 2023, https://www.npr.org/2023/11/28/1214428351/climate-funding-rework-financial-system-debt-relief.

47. United Nations Environment Programme, "COP27 Ends with Announcement of Historic 'Loss and Damage' Fund," UNEP, November 20, 2022, https://www.unep.org/news-and-stories/story/cop27-ends-announcement-historic-loss-and-damage-fund.

48. Kate Abnett, Maha El Dahan, and Valerie Volcovici, "COP28 Summit Opens with Hopes for Early Deal on Climate Damage Fund," Reuters, November

30, 2023, https://www.reuters.com/business/environment/cop28-summit-opens-with-hopes-early-deal-climate-damage-fund-2023-11-30/.

49. World Resources Institute, "Statement on COP28 Opening Day as Negotiators Operationalize Loss and Damage Fund," World Resources Institute, November 30, 2023, https://www.wri.org/news/statement-cop28-opening-day-negotiators-operationalize-loss-and-damage-fund.

50. Ibid.

51. United Nations Environment Programme, *Adaptation Gap Report 2023*, UNEP, 2023, https://www.unep.org/resources/adaptation-gap-report-2023.

52. Nina Lakhani, "COP28 Failing on Climate Adaptation Finance so Far, African Group Warns," *The Guardian*, December 9, 2023, https://www.theguardian.com/environment/2023/dec/09/cop28-failing-climate-adaptation-finance-so-far-african-group-warns.

53. Jake Bittle, "Inside the Marshall Islands' Life-or-Death Plan to Survive Climate Change," *Grist*, December 5, 2023, https://grist.org/extreme-weather/marshall-islands-national-adaptation-plan-sea-level-rise-cop28/.

54. United Nations Framework Convention on Climate Change, *Paris Agreement*, December 12, 2015, https://unfccc.int/sites/default/files/english_paris_agreement.pdf.

55. United Nations Development Programme, "What Is a Just Transition and Why Is It Important?," *Climate Promise*, accessed December 17, 2023, https://climatepromise.undp.org/news-and-stories/what-just-transition-and-why-it-important.

56. Lungelo Ndhlovu, "Consider These Perspectives While Reporting on a Just Transition," International Journalists' Network (IJNet), accessed December 17, 2023, https://ijnet.org/en/story/consider-these-perspectives-while-reporting-just-transition.

57. Ibid.

58. Colorado Department of Labor and Employment, "Programs for Coal Transition Communities," *Colorado Department of Labor and Employment*, accessed May 1, 2024, https://cdle.colorado.gov/offices/the-office-of-just-transition/programs-for-coal-transition-communities.

59. David Borges and Michael Goodman, *The Vanishing West: 2022 Jobs Report*, accessed September 25, 2024, https://static1.squarespace.com/static/5a2e-ae32be42d64ed467f9d1/t/63ed4fea5d36ec3e4dcef2f3/1676496874921/VW1+2022+Jobs+Report.pdf.

60. Ezra David Romero, interview by Sadie Babits, January 13, 2024.

61. Ibid.

62. Ezra David Romero, interview by Sadie Babits, January 13, 2024.

63. Julia Hotz, "How to Produce Solutions Reporting Alongside Marginalized Communities," International Journalists' Network (IJNet), February 9, 2023, accessed September 25, 2024, https://ijnet.org/en/story/how-produce-solutions-reporting-alongside-marginalized-communities.

64. Katti Gray, "The Racial Divide on News Coverage, and Why Representation Matters," Knight Foundation, September 25, 2020, https://knightfoundation.org/articles/the-racial-divide-on-news-coverage-and-why-representation-matters/.

65. Ibid.

66. Ibid.

67. Ibid.

68. Ibid.

69. Elizabeth Grieco, "Newsroom Employees Are Less Diverse Than U.S. Workers Overall," *Pew Research Center*, November 2, 2018, https://www.pewresearch.org/short-reads/2018/11/02/newsroom-employees-are-less-diverse-than-u-s-workers-overall/.

70. Ibid.

71. Clark Merrefield, "Race and the Newsroom: 7 Studies to Know," *The Journalist's Resource*, July 20, 2020, https://journalistsresource.org/race-and-gender/newsroom-diversity-7-studies/.

72. Emily Tomasik and Jeffrey Gottfried, "U.S. Journalists' Beats Vary Widely by Gender and Other Factors," Pew Research Center, April 4, 2023, https://www.pewresearch.org/short-reads/2023/04/04/us-journalists-beats-vary-widely-by-gender-and-other-factors/.

73. "Inside Climate News: Diversity, Equity, and Inclusion," *Inside Climate News*, accessed February 19, 2024, https://insideclimatenews.org/about/diversity-equity-inclusion/.

74. Grist Diversity, Equity, Inclusion, and Justice Committee, "Diversity, Equity, and Inclusion at Grist: 2021," *Grist*, May 10, 2022, https://grist.org/accountability/diversity-equity-inclusion-2021/.

Chapter 7

1. Cathrine Gyldensted, interview by Sadie Babits, June 2, 2023.

2. Ibid.

3. Ibid.

4. Nic Newman, "Overview and Key Findings of the 2024 Digital News Report," Reuters Institute for the Study of Journalism, June 7, 2024,

https://reutersinstitute.politics.ox.ac.uk/digital-news-report/2024/dnr-executive-summary.

5. "Yale Climate Opinion Maps 2023," Yale Program on Climate Change Communication, December 13, 2023, https://climatecommunication.yale.edu/visualizations-data/ycom-us/.

6. Katharine Hayhoe, interview by Frank Mungeam/Local Media Association, n.d., accessed August 23, 2024.

7. Ibid.

8. Ibid.

9. Adam Smith, "2023: A Historic Year of U.S. Billion-Dollar Weather and Climate Disasters," NOAA Climate.gov, January 8, 2024, https://www.climate.gov/news-features/blogs/beyond-data/2023-historic-year-us-billion-dollar-weather-and-climate-disasters.

10. Yale Program on Climate Change Communication, "Climate Change in the Media: 2020," accessed January 10, 2025, https://climatecommunication.yale.edu/visualizations-data/climatenews2020/.

11. "Yale Climate Opinion Maps 2023," Yale Program on Climate Change Communication, December 13, 2023, https://climatecommunication.yale.edu/visualizations-data/ycom-us/.

12. Katharine Hayhoe, interview by Frank Mungeam/Local Media Association, n.d., accessed August 23, 2024.

13. Emily Cassidy, "Emissions from Fossil Fuels Continue to Rise," NASA Earth Observatory, March 5, 2024, https://earthobservatory.nasa.gov/images/152519/emissions-from-fossil-fuels-continue-to-rise.

14. Susan Hassol, interview by Sadie Babits, March 23, 2023.

15. Ibid.

16. A. R. Siders, interview by Sadie Babits, September 16, 2023.

17. Julia Simon, "Climate Solutions Do Exist. These 6 Experts Detail What They Look Like," NPR, March 5, 2023, https://www.npr.org/2023/03/05/1160783951/6-scholars-explain-what-a-real-climate-solution-is.

18. John Ryan, "Washington State Starts Capping Climate Pollution from Its Biggest Sources," KUOW Public Radio, February 16, 2023, https://www.kuow.org/stories/washington-state-starts-capping-climate-pollution-from-its-biggest-sources.

19. Taxation and Customs Union, "Carbon Border Adjustment Mechanism Starts This Weekend in Its Transitional Phase," September 29, 2023, https://taxation-customs.ec.europa.eu/news/

carbon-border-adjustment-mechanism-starts-weekend-its-transition-al-phase-2023-09-29_en.

20. A. R. Siders, interview by Sadie Babits, September 16, 2023.

21. "Table of Solutions," Project Drawdown, accessed June 18, 2023, https://drawdown.org/solutions/table-of-solutions.

22. "Bicycle Infrastructure," Project Drawdown, accessed September 25, 2024, https://drawdown.org/solutions/bicycle-infrastructure.

23. Emma VandenEinde, "Can a MechanicalTree Remove Enough Carbon to Slow Climate Change?," Cronkite News–Arizona PBS, May 5, 2022, https://cronkitenews.azpbs.org/2022/05/05/mechanicaltree-asu-could-slow-carbon-emmissions-climate-change.

24. Jason Franz, "Carbon Collect's MechanicalTree Selected for U.S. Department of Energy Award," *ASU News*, July 2, 2021, https://news.asu.edu/20210702-carbon-collect-mechanicaltree-selected-us-department-energy-award.

25. Laura Klivans, "Could Carbon Removal Be California's Next Big Boom Industry?," KQED, March 30, 2023, https://www.kqed.org/science/1982049/could-carbon-removal-be-californias-next-big-boom-industry.

26. A. R. Siders, interview by Sadie Babits, September 16, 2023.

27. Ibid.

28. Ibid.

29. Jonathan Foley, panel discussion, "Looking Forward: Solutions," NPR, Washington DC, June 23, 2023, and email message to Sadie Babits granting permission, January 13, 2025.

30. "MechanicalTreeTM—Carbon Collect," accessed September 2, 2024, https://carboncollect.com/mechanical-tree/.

31. Intergovernmental Panel on Climate Change, *AR6 Synthesis Report: Summary for Policymakers*, 2023, https://www.ipcc.ch/report/ar6/syr/downloads/report/IPCC_AR6_SYR_SPM.pdf.

32. Amy Westervelt, "Documents, Whistleblowers, and Public Comments Are Clear: Oil Companies Know Carbon Capture Is Not a Climate Solution," *Drilled*, July 29, 2024, https://drilled.media/news/ccs.

33. Peter Yeung, "Floating Farms Offer Lessons in Hydroponic Gardening," Bloomberg, April 27, 2023, https://www.bloomberg.com/news/features/2023-04-27/floating-farms-offer-lessons-in-hydroponic-gardening?embedded-checkout=true.

34. Peter Yeung, interview by Sadie Babits, August 27, 2024.

35. Ibid.

36. Peter Yeung, "Floating Farms Offer Lessons in Hydroponic Gardening," *Bloomberg*, April 27, 2023, https://www.bloomberg.com/news/features/2023-04-27/floating-farms-offer-lessons-in-hydroponic-gardening?embedded-checkout=true.

37. Katherine Noble, interview by Sadie Babits, June 2, 2023.

38. Ibid.

39. Solutions Journalism, "Solutions Journalism: What Is It and Why Should I Care?," *The Whole Story*, June 15, 2022, https://thewholestory.solutionsjournalism.org/solutions-journalism-what-is-it-and-why-should-i-care-e5acd0ab5332.

40. Ibid.

41. Katherine Noble, interview by Sadie Babits, June 2, 2023.

42. Solutions Journalism, "Solutions Journalism: What Is It and Why Should I Care?," *The Whole Story*, June 15, 2022, https://thewholestory.solutionsjournalism.org/solutions-journalism-what-is-it-and-why-should-i-care-e5acd0ab5332.

43. Ibid.

44. Ibid.

45. Peter Yeung, interview by Sadie Babits, August 27, 2024.

46. Ibid.

47. Melanie Pérez Arias and Peter Yeung, "The Backyard Farmers Who Grow Food with Fog," *Reasons to Be Cheerful*, September 18, 2023, https://reasonstobecheerful.world/lima-fog-catchers-water-scarcity-irrigation/.

48. Solutions Journalism, "Announcing the 2023 Solutions Journalism Network Award Winners." *The Whole Story*, May 29, 2024. https://thewholestory.solutionsjournalism.org/announcing-the-2023-solutions-journalism-network-award-winners-b047acdc3a26.

49. Ibid.

50. Cathrine Gyldensted, interview by Sadie Babits, June 2, 2023.

51. Ibid.

52. James Randerson, "A Story of Hope: The Guardian Launches Phase II of Its Climate Change Campaign," *The Guardian*, October 5, 2015, https://www.theguardian.com/environment/2015/oct/05/a-story-of-hope-the-guardian-launches-phase-two-of-its-climate-change-campaign.

53. "Why Constructive Journalism? Constructive Journalism Is Important for Journalism and Society," *Constructive Institute*, December 8, 2019, https://constructiveinstitute.org/why/.

54. Ibid.

55. Cathrine Gyldensted, interview by Sadie Babits, June 2, 2023.

56. Ibid.

57. Ibid.

58. "The Upside," *The Guardian*, accessed September 25, 2024, https://www.theguardian.com/world/series/the-upside.

59. Francesc Badia i Dalmases, "Here Comes the Sun Canoe, as Amazonians Take on Big Oil," *The Guardian*, March 13, 2020, https://www.theguardian.com/world/2020/mar/13/amazon-indigenous-group-turns-to-solar-canoes-in-fight-against-rainforest-oil-extraction.

60. Cathrine Gyldensted, interview by Sadie Babits, June 2, 2023.

61. Ibid.

62. Katherine Noble, interview by Sadie Babits, June 2, 2023.

63. Ibid.

64. Ibid.

65. "Climate Beacons," *Story Tracker: Solutions Journalism Network*, accessed September 25, 2024, https://storytracker.solutionsjournalism.org/topics/climate-beacons.

66. Ryan Lillis, "Could a Historic Sacramento Corridor Hold the Key to Solving the Region's Housing Crisis?," *Sacramento Bee*, July 27, 2023, https://www.sacbee.com/news/local/sacramento-tipping-point/article276843866.html.

67. "Climate Beacons," *Story Tracker: Solutions Journalism Network*, accessed September 25, 2024, https://storytracker.solutionsjournalism.org/topics/climate-beacons.

68. Emilie Stigliani, "Climate Change Is Global, but Local Responses Can Help. What Would You Do with $5K? Pitch Us," *Sacramento Bee*, October 16, 2023, https://www.sacbee.com/news/equity-lab/article280473714.html.

69. Peter Yeung, interview by Sadie Babits, August 27, 2024.

70. Ibid.

Chapter 8

1. "Glacier's Glaciers," Glacier National Park (U.S. National Park Service), accessed September 26, 2024, https://www.nps.gov/glac/learn/nature/glaciersoverview.htm.

2. *Held v. State of Montana*, Findings of Fact, Conclusions of Law, and Order, August 14, 2023, https://static1.squarespace.com/static/571d109b-04426270152febe0/t/64da53511de19d2889830a2c/1692029780262/08%3A14%3A23+Findings+of+Fact%2C+Conclusions+of+Law+and+Order.pdf.

3. Nathan Rott and Seyma Bayram, "Montana Youth Climate Ruling Could Set Precedent for Future Climate Litigation," NPR, August 23, 2023, https://www.npr.org/2023/08/23/1194710955/montana-youth-climate-ruling-could-set-precedent-for-future-climate-litigation.

4. *Held v. State of Montana*, Findings of Fact, Conclusions of Law, and Order, August 14, 2023. https://static1.squarespace.com/static/571d109b-04426270152febe0/t/64da53511de19d2889830a2c/1692029780262/08%3A14%3A23+Findings+of+Fact%2C+Conclusions+of+Law+and+Order.pdf.

5. Ibid.

6. Michael Gerrard, interview by Sadie Babits, October 3, 2024.

7. Nicholas Kusnetz, interview by Sadie Babits, September 16, 2024.

8. National Association of Attorneys General, "The Master Settlement Agreement," NAAG, accessed October 16, 2024, https://www.naag.org/our-work/naag-center-for-tobacco-and-public-health/the-master-settlement-agreement/.

9. Nicholas Kusnetz, interview by Sadie Babits, September 16, 2024.

10. Our Children's Trust, "Montana Climate Youth Win," press release, August 14, 2023, https://static1.squarespace.com/static/571d109b04426270152febe0/t/64da6d67161d05783fbca2f9/1692036457635/08.14.2023+Montana+Climate+Youth+Win.pdf.

11. Nathan Rott and Seyma Bayram, "Montana Youth Climate Ruling Could Set Precedent for Future Climate Litigation," NPR, August 23, 2023, https://www.npr.org/2023/08/23/1194710955/montana-youth-climate-ruling-could-set-precedent-for-future-climate-litigation.

12. *Held v. State of Montana*, Findings of Fact, Conclusions of Law, and Order, August 14, 2023, https://static1.squarespace.com/static/571d109b-04426270152febe0/t/64da53511de19d2889830a2c/1692029780262/08%3A14%3A23+Findings+of+Fact%2C+Conclusions+of+Law+and+Order.pdf.

13. Nathan Rott and Seyma Bayram, "Montana Youth Climate Ruling Could Set Precedent for Future Climate Litigation," NPR, August 23, 2023, https://www.npr.org/2023/08/23/1194710955/montana-youth-climate-ruling-could-set-precedent-for-future-climate-litigation.

14. Nate Raymond, "Hawaii Agrees to 'Groundbreaking' Settlement of Youth Climate Change Case," Reuters, June 21, 2024, https://www.reuters.com/legal/hawaii-agrees-settle-youth-climate-change-lawsuit-2024-06-21/.

15. *Held v. State of Montana*, No. DA 23-0575, slip op. at 16 (Mont. Dec. 18, 2024), https://climatecasechart.com/wp-content/uploads/case-documents/2024/20241218_docket-DA-23-0575_opinion-1.pdf.

16. United Nations Environment Programme. *Global Climate Litigation Report: 2023 Status Review*, Nairobi: UNEP, 2023, https://wedocs.unep.org/bitstream/handle/20.500.11822/43008/global_climate_litigation_report_2023.pdf?sequence=3.

17. Michael Gerrard, interview by Sadie Babits, October 3, 2024.

18. Ibid.

19. Michael Gerrard, interview by Sadie Babits, October 3, 2024.

20. Ibid.

21. Ibid.

22. Ibid.

23. United Nations General Assembly, *Resolution Adopted by the General Assembly on the Human Rights to Safe Drinking Water and Sanitation*, A/RES/76/300, August 3, 2021, https://documents.un.org/doc/undoc/gen/g21/289/50/pdf/g2128950.pdf?OpenElement.

24. Ibid.

25. United Nations Environment Programme (UNEP), "In Historic Move, UN Declares Healthy Environment a Human Right," UNEP, July 28, 2022, https://www.unep.org/news-and-stories/story/historic-move-un-declares-healthy-environment-human-right.

26. Sabin Center for Climate Change Law, "Urgenda Foundation v. Kingdom of the Netherlands," *Climate Change Litigation Databases*, accessed September 9, 2023, https://climatecasechart.com/non-us-case/urgenda-foundation-v-kingdom-of-the-netherlands/#:~:text=State%20of%20the%20Netherlands,-Filing%20Date%3A%202015&text=Summary%3A,to%20prevent%20global%20climate%20change.

27. Ibid.

28. The Hague Court of Appeal, *Urgenda Foundation v. The State of the Netherlands (Ministry of Infrastructure and the Environment)*, Case No. 200.178.245/01, Judgment of January 13, 2020, https://climatecasechart.com/wp-content/uploads/non-us-case-documents/2020/20200113_2015-HA-ZA-C0900456689_judgment.pdf.

29. "Netherlands Cuts Speed Limit to Reduce Nitrogen Pollution," Reuters, November 13, 2019, https://www.reuters.com/article/us-netherlands-construction/netherlands-cuts-speed-limit-to-reduce-nitrogen-pollution-idUSKBN1XN13K.

30. Michael Gerrard, interview by Sadie Babits, October 3, 2024.

31. "Milieudefensie et al. v. Royal Dutch Shell PLC," Climate Change Litigation Databases, accessed October 16, 2024, https://climatecasechart.com/non-us-case/milieudefensie-et-al-v-royal-dutch-shell-plc/.
32. Michael Gerrard, interview by Sadie Babits, October 3, 2024.
33. "Milieudefensie et al. v. Royal Dutch Shell PLC," Climate Change Litigation Databases, accessed October 16, 2024, https://climatecasechart.com/non-us-case/milieudefensie-et-al-v-royal-dutch-shell-plc/.
34. "Milieudefensie et al. v. Royal Dutch Shell plc," *Sabin Center for Climate Change Law, Climate Case Chart*, last modified November 12, 2024, https://climatecasechart.com/non-us-case/milieudefensie-et-al-v-royal-dutch-shell-plc/#:~:text=On%20November%2012%2C%202024%2C%20the,1%2C%202%20and%203%20emissions.
35. Friends of the Earth International, "Court Approves Shell's Appeal to Dodge Emissions Cuts: Friends of the Earth to Continue Fight Against Big Polluters," press release, November 12, 2024, https://www.foei.org/court-approves-shells-appeal-to-dodge-emissions-cuts-friends-of-the-earth-to-continue-fight-against-big-polluters/.
36. Ibid.
37. *Juliana v. United States*, 947 F.3d 1159 (9th Cir. 2020), https://casetext.com/case/juliana-v-united-states-3.
38. Ibid.
39. Ibid.
40. Michael Gerrard, interview by Sadie Babits, October 3, 2024.
41. Sabin Center for Climate Change Law, "Luciano Lliuya v. RWE AG," Climate Change Litigation, accessed October 16, 2024, https://climatecasechart.com/non-us-case/lliuya-v-rwe-ag/.
42. Ibid.
43. Michael Gerrard, interview by Sadie Babits, October 3, 2024.
44. Rhode Island Attorney General, "U.S. Supreme Court Clears Way for Rhode Island's Climate Lawsuit to Proceed in State Court," *Rhode Island Attorney General's Office*, May 17, 2023, https://riag.ri.gov/press-releases/us-supreme-court-clears-way-rhode-islands-climate-lawsuit-proceed-state-court.
45. Ibid.
46. *Rhode Island v. Chevron Corp.*, No. 18-3956 (R.I. Super. Ct. filed July 2, 2018), https://climatecasechart.com/case/rhode-island-v-chevron-corp/.
47. Clark Mindock and Nate Raymond. "U.S. Supreme Court Rebuffs Exxon, Chevron Appeals in Climate Litigation," Reuters, April 24, 2023, https://www.reuters.com/business/energy/

us-supreme-court-rebuffs-exxon-chevron-appeals-climate-litigation-2023-04-24/.

48. Ibid.

49. Rhode Island Attorney General, "U.S. Supreme Court Clears Way for Rhode Island's Climate Lawsuit to Proceed in State Court," *Rhode Island Attorney General's Office*, May 17, 2023, https://riag.ri.gov/press-releases/us-supreme-court-clears-way-rhode-islands-climate-lawsuit-proceed-state-court.

50. John O'Brien, "Judge Boots Global Warming Cases of San Francisco, Oakland Against Oil Industry," *Legal Newsline*, June 26, 2018, https://legalnewsline.com/stories/511468070-judge-boots-global-warming-cases-of-san-francisco-oakland-against-oil-industry.

51. United Nations Environment Programme, *Global Climate Litigation Report: 2023 Status Review*, Nairobi: UNEP, 2023, https://wedocs.unep.org/bitstream/handle/20.500.11822/43008/global_climate_litigation_report_2023.pdf?sequence=3.

52. Ibid.

53. Ibid.

54. Climate Accountability Institute, "Press Release: The Carbon Majors Database," December 2020, https://climateaccountability.org/pdf/CAI%20Press-Release%20Dec20.pdf.

55. Ibid.

56. Ibid.

57. Climate Accountability Institute, *Carbon Majors Database*, accessed January 10, 2025. https://carbonmajors.org/.

58. Gabrielle Olivera, "45-Mile Walk Shows Solidarity against Mine Planned under Land Tribes Consider Sacred," *Cronkite News–Arizona PBS*, February 12, 2019, https://cronkitenews.azpbs.org/2019/02/12/oak-flat-solidarity-walk/.

59. Ibid.

60. Lindsay VanSomeren, "Reporting on Court Cases with a Critical Eye," *The Open Notebook*, August 23, 2022, https://www.theopennotebook.com/2022/08/23/reporting-on-court-cases-with-a-critical-eye/.

61. Michael Gerrard, interview by Sadie Babits, October 3, 2024.

Chapter 9

1. Sally Ramirez, interview by Sadie Babits, July 29, 2024.

2. Ibid.

3. National Weather Service, "Major Hurricane Harvey - August 25-29, 2017," *National Weather Service*, August 2017, https://www.weather.gov/crp/hurricane_harvey.

4. Sally Ramirez, interview by Sadie Babits, July 29, 2024.

5. Ibid.

6. Ibid.

7. "Houston Flooding: KHOU Reporter Brandi Smith Helps Save Truck Driver's Life," *CBS News*, August 28, 2017, https://www.cbsnews.com/news/houston-flooding-khou-reporter-brandi-smith-helps-rescue-truck-driver/.

8. Pete Vernon, "The Media Today: Scenes from Harvey's Destructive Path," *Columbia Journalism Review*, August 28, 2017, https://www.cjr.org/the_media_today/the-media-today-houston-harvey-coverage.php.

9. Sally Ramirez, interview by Sadie Babits, July 29, 2024.

10. Ibid.

11. World Weather Attribution, "Climate Change Fingerprints Confirmed in Hurricane Harvey's Rainfall, August 2017," August 31, 2017, https://www.worldweatherattribution.org/hurricane-harvey-august-2017/.

12. Sally Ramirez, interview by Sadie Babits, July 29, 2024.

13. Chloe Reichel, "How Journalists' Jobs Affect Their Mental Health: A Research Roundup," *The Journalist's Resource*, July 30, 2019, https://journalistsresource.org/environment/job-stress-journalists-health-research/.

14. Ibid.

15. Naseem Miller, interview by Sadie Babits, August 15, 2024.

16. Kristen Hare, "Local Journalists Created a Facebook Group with Tips and Support for Covering Mass Shootings," *Poynter*, February 28, 2018, https://www.poynter.org/reporting-editing/2018/local-journalists-created-a-facebook-group-with-tips-and-support-for-covering-mass-shootings/.

17. Naseem Miller, interview by Sadie Babits, August 15, 2024.

18. Ibid.

19. Ibid.

20. Caroline M. Pyevich, Elana Newman, and Eric Daleiden, "The Relationship Among Cognitive Schemas, Job-Related Traumatic Exposure, and Posttraumatic Stress Disorder in Journalists," *Journal of Traumatic Stress* 16, no. 4 (August 2003): 325–28, doi:10.1023/a:1024405716529.

21. Amy Novotney, "How Does Climate Change Affect Mental Health?," February 7, 2023, https://www.apa.org/topics/climate-change/mental-health-effects.

22. Sarita Silveira et al., "Chronic Mental Health Sequelae of Climate Change Extremes: A Case Study of the Deadliest Californian Wildfire," *International*

Journal of Environmental Research and Public Health 18, no. 4 (February 4, 2021): 1487, doi:10.3390/ijerph18041487.

23. Amy Novotney, "How Does Climate Change Affect Mental Health?," February 7, 2023, https://www.apa.org/topics/climate-change/mental-health-effects.

24. Ibid.

25. American Psychiatric Association, "APA Public Opinion Poll—Annual Meeting 2020," September 14-16, 2020, https://www.psychiatry.org/newsroom/apa-public-opinion-poll-2020.

26. Matthew Ballew, Teresa Myers, Sri Saahitya Uppalapati, Seth Rosenthal, John Kotcher, Eryn Campbell, Emily Goddard, Edward Maibach, and Anthony Leiserowitz, "Distress About Climate Change and Climate Action," Yale Program on Climate Change Communication, December 2022, https://climatecommunication.yale.edu/publications/distress-about-climate-change-and-climate-action/.

27. Hannah Comtesse et al., "Ecological Grief as a Response to Environmental Change: A Mental Health Risk or Functional Response?," *International Journal of Environmental Research and Public Health* 18, no. 2 (January 16, 2021): 734, doi:10.3390/ijerph18020734.

28. Jennifer Atkinson, interview by Sadie Babits, June 13, 2024.

29. Ibid.

30. Ibid.

31. Halle Parker, interview by Sadie Babits, July 29, 2024.

32. Ibid.

33. Ibid.

34. Naseem Miller, interview by Sadie Babits, August 15, 2024.

35. Jeje Mohamed, panelist in a discussion on trauma-informed climate journalism at the Society of Environmental Journalists Conference, Boise, Idaho April 21, 2023.

36. Sally Ramirez, interview by Sadie Babits, July 29, 2024.

37. Naseem Miller, interview by Sadie Babits, August 15, 2024.

38. Wudan Yan, interview by Sadie Babits, July 27, 2024.

39. Ibid.

40. Halle Parker, interview by Sadie Babits, July 29, 2024.

41. "APA Dictionary of Psychology," American Psychological Association, April 2018, https://dictionary.apa.org/trauma.

42. "APA Dictionary of Psychology," American Psychological Association, April 2018, https://dictionary.apa.org/posttraumatic-stress-disorder.

43. Mark Brayne, "Trauma and Journalism: A Guide for Journalists, Editors and Managers," Dart Center, 2007, https://dartcenter.org/sites/default/files/DCE_JournoTraumaHandbook.pdf.

44. Jeje Mohamed, panelist in a discussion on trauma-informed climate journalism at the Society of Environmental Journalists Conference, Boise, Idaho April 21, 2023.

45. Amy Westervelt, interview by Sadie Babits, July 20, 2024.

46. Jeje Mohamed, panelist in a discussion on trauma-informed climate journalism at the Society of Environmental Journalists Conference, Boise, Idaho April 21, 2023.

47. Amy Westervelt, interview by Sadie Babits, July 20, 2024.

48. Ibid.

49. Rebecca Weston, panelist in a discussion on trauma-informed climate journalism at the Society of Environmental Journalists Conference, Boise, Idaho April 21, 2023.

50. Amy Westervelt, interview by Sadie Babits, July 20, 2024.

51. Jonathan Watts, "Dom Phillips Obituary," *The Guardian*, June 24, 2022, https://www.theguardian.com/world/2022/jun/24/dom-phillips-obituary.

52. Terrence McCoy, "Dom Phillips and Bruno Pereira's Deaths Show the Amazon's Destruction." *The Washington Post*, October 12, 2022. https://www.washingtonpost.com/world/interactive/2022/amazon-brazil-bruno-dom/.

53. UNESCO, "Press and Planet in Danger: Safety of Environmental Journalists; Trends, Challenges and Recommendations," 2024, https://unesdoc.unesco.org/ark:/48223/pf0000389501?posInSet=1&queryId=N-EXPLORE-5fa8dcb3-20cd-4e45-95f8-3b3d19032f9c.

54. "UNESCO Report Reveals 70% of Environmental Journalists Have Been Attacked for Their Work," UNESCO, June 6, 2024, https://www.unesco.org/en/articles/unesco-report-reveals-70-environmental-journalists-have-been-attacked-their-work.

55. Claire Doyle, "Environmental Journalists on the Frontlines of Democracy," *New Security Beat*, June 5, 2024, https://www.newsecuritybeat.org/2024/06/environmental-journalists-on-the-frontlines-of-democracy/.

56. Patrick Greenfield, "Violent Attacks against Environmental Journalists on the Rise, Report Finds," *The Guardian*, May 2, 2024, https://www.theguardian.com/environment/article/2024/may/02/violent-attacks-against-environmental-journalists-on-the-rise-report-finds.

57. Ibid.

58. Annie Wright LMFT, "What Is the Window of Tolerance, and Why Is It So Important?," *Psychology Today*, May 23, 2022, https://www.psychologytoday.com/us/blog/making-the-whole-beautiful/202205/what-is-the-window-of-tolerance-and-why-is-it-so-important.

59. Ibid.

60. LMFT, Annie Wright. "What Is the Window of Tolerance, and Why Is It So Important?" *Psychology Today*, May 23, 2022. https://www.psychologytoday.com/us/blog/making-the-whole-beautiful/202205/what-is-the-window-tolerance-and-why-is-it-so-important.

61. Chris Gloninger, interview by Sadie Babits, May 20, 2024.

62. Ibid.

63. Casey Leins, "10 Things to Know About Iowa," *U.S. News & World Report*, October 11, 2019, https://www.usnews.com/news/best-states/articles/2019-10-11/10-things-to-know-about-iowa.

64. Chris Gloninger, interview by Sadie Babits, May 20, 2024.

65. Ibid.

66. Chris Gloninger (@ChrisGloninger), "Incredibly thankful for the hospitality and conversations today at the Iowan Latino Heritage Festival," X, July 16, 2022, 7:00 p.m., https://x.com/ChrisGloninger/status/1548382916085817344.

67. Chris Gloninger, interview by Sadie Babits, May 20, 2024.

68. Jeje Mohamed, Rebecca Weston, and Amy Westervelt, "Trauma-Informed Climate Journalism," interview by Paola Rosa-Aquino, *Society of Environmental Journalists*, April 21, 2023.

69. Online Harassment Field Manual, "Prepare for Online Harassment," May 24, 2019. https://onlineharassmentfieldmanual.pen.org/prepare-for-online-harassment/.

70. Jeje Mohamed, Rebecca Weston, and Amy Westervelt, "Trauma-Informed Climate Journalism," interview by Paola Rosa-Aquino, *Society of Environmental Journalists*, April 21, 2023.

71. International Center for Journalists, "UNESCO Online Violence Against Women Journalists: A Global Snapshot," December 2020, https://www.icfj.org/sites/default/files/2020-12/UNESCO%20Online%20Violence%20Against%20Women%20Journalists%20-%20A%20Global%20Snapshot%20Dec9pm.pdf.

72. "Prepare for Online Harassment," *Online Harassment Field Manual*, May 24, 2019. https://onlineharassmentfieldmanual.pen.org/prepare-for-online-harassment/.

73. Elisa Lees Muñoz, "How Newsrooms, Journalists, and Their Peers Can Combat Online Violence," Nieman Foundation, April 12, 2021, https://nieman.harvard.edu/articles/how-newsrooms-journalists-and-their-peers-can-combat-online-violence/.

74. Chris Gloninger (@ChrisGloninger), "I spoke with my family and we have decided to move on to the next chapter, but I will always be a meteorologist," X, June 21, 2023, 9:54 p.m., https://x.com/ChrisGloninger/status/1671534139969863680.

75. Chris Gloninger, interview by Sadie Babits, May 20, 2024.

Index

Page numbers for figures, text boxes, and photos are in italics.

in, 15. *See also* climate litigation; climate policy; greenwashing

climate justice: at Bayview Hunters Point, 133–135; climate justice movement, 141–142; defined, 57; diversity training in, 150–151; government programs addressing, 142–144; inequality in climate change effects, 135, 136; inequity in infrastructure, 140–141; interacting with and respecting community members, 151–152; social injustice and, 136; statistics on air quality for Blacks, Whites, and Latinos, 139; study on Vulnerabilities to Climate Change, *137*; and Title VI of the 1964 Civil Rights Act, 144; tracking and protecting sources in reporting, 150, 153; tree canopy locations as reflection of, 139

climate litigation: accessing court documents, 193–195; basics of climate law, 191–193; Big Oil lawsuits, 188–190; of Carbon Majors, 190–191; climate rights cases, 184–188; covering court proceedings, 193; in greenwashing cases, 184; *Held v. State of Montana*, 179–180, 181, 188; increasing in US, 183–184; involving Royal Dutch Shell, 186–187; *Juliana v. United States*, 24–25, 181, 187–188; Rhode Island lawsuit, 189; Six Primary Categories of Climate Litigation, *185*; *Urgenda v. State of the Netherlands*, 186; youth-led cases of, 181–183, 188. *See also* climate policy

climate models, 58

climate policy: in Australia, 72; under Biden administration, 71; climate action plans (CAPs) and, 80–82; examples of existing, 23; global summits, 23–24; how ESA intersects with, 89; under Obama administration, 71; pricing carbon and, 84; renewable portfolio standards (RPSs) and, 82–84; of Sweden, 75; under Trump administration, 71; using space technology to understand weather, 63. *See also* climate litigation

Climate Psychology Alliance North America, 221

climate reporting, physical dangers of, 213–216

climate science, 32–33, 39–43. *See also* carbon cycle

Climate Shift Index, 46

climate solutions: availability and scalability of, 163–164, 166; balanced approaches to reporting, 173–174; climate solutions reporting defined, 168; expense of, 165–166;

floating gardens in Bangladesh as, 166–167; overview, 160–162; pillars of climate solutions reporting, 168–170; practical tips for reporting, 174–176; reviews by Project Drawdown, 162–163; using constructive journalism framework, 170–173; workable and ready solutions, 165

coal and coal mines: caps on carbon emissions at state level, 87; and Carbon Majors, 190–191; in China, 76; coal power plants in India, 72; Glasgow Climate Compact on, 74; global warming from, 20; just transitions for workers with disappearing jobs in, 147–148; leasing of public lands to mine, 91; in Montana, 179

Collier, Kevin, 109

Color of Law, The: A Forgotten History of How Our Government Segregated America (Rothstein), 156

Colorado, 148

Columbia Journalism Review, 11, 14

Competitive Enterprise Institute, 96, 98

composting, 81

Conference of the Parties (COP). *See* COP (Conference of the Parties)

ConocoPhillips, 190

consolidated conservation, 78

Constructive Journalism Institute, 176

Cook, John, 100, 101–102, 105, 113, 226

COP (Conference of the Parties): COP21, 23, 69; COP26, 74; COP27, 23; COP28, 102–103, 146, 147; COP29, 66, 67

Copenhagen Accord, 70

Corporate Average Fuel Economy standards, 77

Council on Environmental Quality, 86

Covering Climate Now, 17, 49, 127

COVID-19 pandemic, 117, 151, 188, 200, 201

Craft of Science Writing, The: Selections from the Open Notebook (Carpenter), 59

Cranky Uncle app, 113–114

cryosphere, 32

Cushman, John, Jr., 15

CWA (Clean Water Act), 87–88

Dalai Lama, 7

Dart Center for Journalism and Trauma, 209, 221

Dart Center Style Guide for Trauma-Informed Journalism, 221

About the Author

Author photo by Eric Lee.

Sadie Babits has spent more than two decades in journalism, focused primarily on reporting on the natural world. She has been a reporter, editor, and news director at various public media outlets, as well as a journalism professor. Her work has been heard on national programs including National Public Radio shows *Morning Edition* and *All Things Considered*.

Babits is the senior supervising climate editor at NPR, where she guides coverage of climate change.

Before joining NPR, Babits was a professor of practice at the Walter Cronkite School of Journalism and Mass Communication, where she taught and mentored aspiring environmental journalists. In this role, she developed students' environmental storytelling skills, from sourcing and interviewing to field reporting and producing multimedia stories. She taught in the school's professional program *Cronkite News*, where student journalists learn by doing.

Babits' background is as diverse as her commitment to environmental journalism. She previously served as news director at Colorado Public Radio, where she helped set the strategic direction for the newsroom, including environmental coverage. She also completed the prestigious Ted Scripps Fellowship in Environmental Reporting at the University of Colorado Boulder, where she deepened her expertise in public land and environmental policy, as well as Native American law.

In addition to her work as a journalist and editor, Babits served for two years as president of the board of the Society of Environmental Journalists, the largest organization of environmental reporters in the United States. In this role, she championed diversity, equity, and inclusion and helped gain media access and transparency with federal agencies such as the Environmental Protection Agency and the US Department of the Interior.

Her work includes overseas reporting on water conflict and scarcity in Kenya, which was recognized by SEJ. She's a recipient of the national Edward R. Murrow Award for investigative journalism, and she helped edit the investigative story "Missed Treatment," done in collaboration with NPR and Colorado Public Radio, which earned a DuPont Award in 2017.

Babits lives in Oregon with her husband, Frank Mungeam. Her passion for the environment extends beyond her professional life into her personal pursuits as an avid mountain biker, hiker, cross-country skier, and birder, and her adventures often take her deep into the natural beauty of the West.